"Revoan"

Xmas 1954.

And All the Trumpets

And All the Trumpets

by

Donald Smith

London

GEOFFREY BLES

1954

Printed in Great Britain by
Wyman & Sons Ltd Fakenham
for Geoffrey Bles Ltd
52 Doughty Street London WC1

First published 1954

"So he passed over, and all the trumpets sounded for him on the other side."

PILGRIM'S PROGRESS

TO GINA

Preface

OF THE MANY BOOKS WHICH HAVE BEEN WRITTEN SINCE THE end of the Second World War, not a few have dealt with the experiences of Allied prisoners-of-war in the Far East. The nations which had stood aghast at the medieval barbarity of Belsen recoiled afresh to learn how their sons had fared during the dark years which followed the fall of Hong Kong and Singapore. It was not a pretty story. It revealed conditions of appalling human suffering—brutal treatment, long marches, savage diseases.

Yet through all those tragic pages ran unmistakably a vein of the purest gold. It was the best that is to be found in every man; it was the matchless dignity of the human soul in distress; it was its indomitable power to fight and triumph over adversity. And, in this mighty struggle, the soul of man did not stand alone.

Many men died in captivity. Many came back, grievously mauled in mind and body, to take up again as best they could the broken threads of life and happiness. Since their return other bitter wars have raged in the Far East, and there are still anxious hearts in many lands. If this book can in any way bring comfort and a new courage to those who wait, it will not have failed in its design. To those who have waited in vain it may yet provide some solace in a sea of grief.

This book does not close at the moment of release. That would mean that the story could be only half-told. It tells how a very ordinary man, with no more than ordinary courage, but with the help of God, survived the darkness of the pit, and found himself anew. With that finding came also peace and a fresh hope.

Rothesay, Bute.   *June, 1954.*

Contents

Introduction

When the u.s.s. "mount vernon" berthed at singapore Naval Base on the morning of 13th January, 1942, and the leading units of the British 18th Division began to disembark, a native pedlar, clad in brightly-coloured sarong, wheeled his bicycle a little closer to the dock-yard gates. He was a seller of choice fruits, and as the first of the young British soldiers passed him by on their way towards a long line of waiting transport-lorries, he propped his machine against a wall, laid his basket down on the sun-baked ground, and commenced to proclaim in strident tones the excellence of his wares.

The men from Britain seemed strangely unwilling to buy, however. A few curious glances were cast at the unfamiliar fruits, but that was all. The pedlar lapsed into sulky silence.

"Here, Wrigley, this is right up your alley, isn't it?" A small group of men had gathered round the basket. The native became alert. The man called Wrigley picked up a durian and sniffed it cautiously. There was a burst of laughter. "Go on, Wrig," came a voice, "have a bite. Let's know if it's poisonous!" A thick-set, fair-haired officer joined the group. "Everybody here, Sergeant-Major?" Wright saluted smartly and turned to face the section, now drawn up in two ranks before him. The durian had gone back to its place in the basket. The native spat contemptuously.

"Nunn, O'Shea, Boyd, Livesley, Dorfman, Harris, Taylor, Ullman, Wrigley, Gibberd, Shaw, Smith, Bussey—all here, sir." Sergeant-Major Wright saluted again. The officer pointed with his cane. "Get the men aboard the last of those lorries, and tell the driver to take you to the medical camp, near Bukit Timah. He'll know the place. We'll have our usual conference tomorrow morning at ten o'clock." The group moved off. The seller of fruits picked up his basket and set it firmly on the carrier of his bicycle. Then he pedalled slowly away.

In the pages which follow, those men have their exits and their entrances. At the eleventh hour five of them succeeded in making their escape from Singapore. Of the ten who became prisoners-of-war, five died in captivity.

And the seller of fruits? No further mention is made of him. He can safely be forgotten. He did not perish in the ruins of Singapore. Remarkably enough, he was not actually a seller of fruits at all. He was a seasoned Japanese Intelligence Officer.

I

I Enter the Cage

OF COURSE IT HAD BEEN A MISTAKE FROM THE VERY BEGINNING. We should never have gone to Singapore at all. That I came to be with the 18th Division in the first place was due solely to my having broken one of the Army's elementary rules for the self-preservation of young soldiers. "Never volunteer for anything," they had said, "Never stick your neck out." Yet I had volunteered for the Intelligence Corps. I had come to the 18th Division just in time to discover, to my infinite dismay, that it was under immediate orders to move out to the Middle East. Even when we reached the Cape early in December, 1941, our final destination was still Basra. We were desert-trained, desert-equipped, desert-minded.

Then *Prince of Wales* and *Repulse* went down, and the Japanese swept into Northern Malaya. In the twinkling of an eye our floating Division was moved, like a mere pawn on an immense chess-board. We received fresh routing orders. We were to proceed with all speed to Singapore to add our fresh young strength to the stealthy jungle war. Our kinsmen of the Commonwealth had sent out the Fiery Cross.

Thus it was that the 15th Field Security Section came to find itself on 13th January, 1942, in a Field Ambulance base-camp near the little Singapore village of Bukit Timah. I had certainly stuck my neck out.

I was the only Scotsman in the little company, and had always been called Mac. They were a rare group of men. I had taken to them instinctively from the day of our first meeting. Our Commanding Officer, Captain Lemin, a man of great personal charm and sympathy, had travelled widely before the war, and was an actor of more than average ability. Sergeant-Major

3

Wright had served in the Brigade of Guards, and maintained, in the face of the dourest challenge, an unswerving faith in the justice of our cause. Denis O'Shea, a gently-spoken Irishman, had temporarily exchanged his priesthood training for that of the battlefield. Andrew Boyd, young, but mature in outlook, had mastered several foreign languages. Louis Dorfman, on the other hand, had barely mastered the elements of English, having escaped from his native France with the retiring British forces in 1940. He was a Jew, as was also John Ullman. The two generally conversed together in fluent Parisian argot, to the considerable astonishment of any casual strangers in our midst.

Stewart Livesley, quick-tempered on occasion, but always supremely generous, had been a teacher of Spanish in a Sussex town. Percy Wrigley, often called Spearmint, was of Lancashire stock. John Taylor, a benign giant from Leeds, was as gentle in nature as he was powerful in physique. John Harris, bluff and bi-lingual, had been with the Imperial War Graves Commission in France. Stanley Bussey, Lemin's personal servant and driver, was every inch a Londoner.

I had three special friends, Gibberd, Shaw and Nunn. Howard Gibberd was one of those unfortunate beings who become the constant target of the leg-puller, and practical joker. At all times he accepted such treatment with an irrepressible cheerfulness which endeared him to his many friends. He was a small man with a big heart. In striking contrast stood Bill Shaw, whose middle name was Evelyn—after a seventeenth-century diarist, he used to say—but of course we never really believed him. Bill was a quiet Bradford lad, with a slow friendly smile and a dogged Yorkshire grit. Although naturally reserved, he was never bashful, but would stand his ground steadfastly in every situation. He never changed, even when the end came.

Jack Nunn, of unflinching personal courage, was a philosopher, accepting his varying fortunes with a cool nonchalance which he preserved to his dying hour. He had come from London to serve the cause in which he so earnestly believed, and he would not relinquish it till he saw it triumph. It was not his will that

4

he sheathed his sword a short hour before the dawning of his ideal. That was his Captain's command.

I stood alone on the summit of Bukit Timah, gazing northwards over an undulating plain of dark green forest. It was two days since our arrival on Singapore Island, and already the surrounding landscape was becoming familiar. Down in the valley below the Bukit Timah road cut across the island like a great white ribbon, joining the town of Singapore with the Causeway and the mainland of Malaya. The distant waters of the Straits shimmered in the bright afternoon sunshine. I strained my ears in an effort to catch the sounds of battle from the north, but all was peace, save for the dry rustle of the waving lalang * around me.

There was something unreal about this silence. It was almost as if the whole island waited, with bated breath, for the next act of an intense drama to be presented. I wished that I could part the green curtain, even for a brief moment, to see what lay beyond.

From our conference that morning with Captain Lemin, it was evident that the tide of war still flowed against us. We had heard, with rising anxiety, that there had been a severe engagement on the banks of the Muar River, only 150 miles north in Malacca, that the Japanese had, for the first time since the beginning of the campaign, brought their crack Imperial Guards Division into action, and that our 45th Indian Brigade, assailed from front and flank, had been decimated. The Australians were apparently falling back too, to fresh positions a little farther south. They had been in constant action for weeks past, and were being sorely pressed. It was rumoured that the Norfolks, who had travelled out with us on the *Mount Vernon*, were now at Batu Pahat, awaiting hourly the grim onslaught of the enemy. I thought of those young, eager boys whom I had come to like so well, and of those fierce Imperial Guardsmen, the much-vaunted spearhead of the Japanese attack, and felt strangely sick at heart.

Even the most optimistic members of our Section had begun to realise, after only two short days on the island, that our task

* Tall tropical grass.

as Field Security personnel was one of enormous difficulty. Although we had pored for hours over maps of the area, and had consulted numerous police dossiers on persons suspected of Fifth Column activities, our almost complete ignorance of native tongues and dialects was a stumbling-block which both disheartened and infuriated us. I had picked up sufficient Malay to enable me to order a native to halt, but so far I appeared to have halted only loyal and law-abiding citizens. My success with the Chinese tongue had been even more deplorable, for I had learned only one word—"tinki". This apparently signified "identity card" for the masses of grinning orientals whom I encountered daily in the course of my duties. They scampered joyfully into their shops and houses, returning with neatly-tied paper packages which contained the identity cards of the entire family. As this family might, with adherents and other friends, number as many as thirty or forty, valuable time was being constantly frittered away with the most galling and generally fruitless checking and counter-checking of passes. It never seemed to occur to these individuals that the normal place to carry an identity card was on their persons.

Of the existence of an efficient Fifth Column force, working for the enemy by day and night, we had ample proof. Our every movement of troops and materials was watched and reported. We rushed impotently on motor-cycles the length and breadth of the island, investigating the activities of unseen enemy agents. They played a grim game of hide-and-seek with us most effectively. Piles of rice appeared mysteriously in the middle of the island's paths and highways as a mute signal to any roving enemy aircraft; white laundry stretched out on the hot, red earth to bleach, suddenly assumed the form of a gigantic arrow or cross; lights flashed out at night from the lalang like devilish will-o'-the-wisps. We invariably arrived on the scene too late. The strewers of rice and flashers of lights had moved to some other part of the island.

The apparent apathy, with which the bulk of the native population regarded the approach of the Japanese armies, filled us with increasing anxiety. Refugees from the battle-front had already begun to swell the teeming community in Singapore.

Their gaunt faces and fear-stricken eyes told their own tale of horror. They had hurriedly gathered up their meagre belongings and fled before the rising tide of barbarism which swept ever southwards. They bore with them tales of arson, looting and rape; of mass executions and savage decapitations; of tortured prisoners and bayoneted children. Yet the native population accepted them all with an unconcerned shrug of the shoulders, which seemed to betoken complete and abject resignation to their fate. To make matters worse, many of the white residents appeared to be even still blissfully unaware that the enemy was hammering at their very gates. On our arrival, we expected to find the whole island a scene of busy, purposeful preparation, as prickly with defences as a porcupine with quills. Instead, we discovered to our ever-increasing disquietude that Singapore was a truly naked island, a hollow and broken shell of defence only. This was no lofty citadel which could withstand long siege or sudden attack. Its bulwarked ramparts faced the empty sea forlornly; its postern gates lay open to the mainland. The realisation of our fearful vulnerability shocked us all. We reckoned that there was, however, still time to press-gang thousands of those indolent natives into throwing up a massive earthen wall around our undefended shores. With the vegetation cleared to the very edge of the Straits, searchlights and trip-wires placed in position and gun-emplacements dug in the wall, we could at least give a reasonable account of ourselves, and not be butchered like babes in a cradle. But the wall was not built, and the crowds of fear-crazed refugees continued to throng back daily from Johore. Despite our most determined efforts to keep the roads clear, they impeded our vital north-bound convoys in a most unforeseen and tragic manner. We longed to be permitted to cast aside, once and for all, our apparently ineffective security duties on the island, and to go forward like men to join our kinsmen in the fight. But our orders were to stay where we were.

The island had yet another gaping rift in its armour. Its three reservoirs—the Seletar, Pearce, and MacRitchie—normally held sufficient water for the needs of the community, but they had to be replenished through a pipe-line which led across the

Straits from the mainland of Malaya. Should the Japanese finally press forward as far as this vital link and sever it, all of us on Singapore must assuredly perish of thirst. I had read before of death by thirst. The unhappy victim died slowly and in considerable agony.

Fate was setting the stage inexorably for the last act of this heart-breaking tragedy.

It was the morning of 20th January. In Bukit Timah camp the alert had just sounded, and a Malay medical orderly was beating violently upon an iron drum to give warning of an approaching enemy air-raid. We hurried to our deep slit trenches in the green undergrowth and awaited further developments. As I crouched in the narrow trench like some hunted beast, I could hear the distant drone of approaching aircraft. Through the bushy lattice-work above my head I counted the bombers as they flew over. Fifty Navy-O's in neat formation, heading towards Singapore town. I prayed that some at least of that miserable community had had the sense to take cover. Eagerly I scanned the skies for some sign of an Allied fighter, but none could I see. During the Battle of Britain I had watched our Hurricanes and Spitfires roaring into the attack far above the quiet Kentish hop-fields, wreaking havoc and destruction amongst the serried Nazi squadrons. I had cheered myself hoarse more than once to see how those squadrons broke and turned for home, or spiralled earthwards in a mighty column of smoke and flame. Then I had stood in marvelling admiration for the exploits of those dauntless Few; now I knelt in a slit trench in bitter agony of spirit, watching this enemy armada go by unmolested.

As they passed I crawled from my hole to a point of vantage nearby. The skies above Singapore were studded with fleecy shell-bursts. Our anti-aircraft, at least, had not been caught unawares. Even as I gazed, one of the enemy bombers was struck and disintegrated in mid-air. One less, I reflected grimly. Another was winged and had dropped out of the formation with smoke belching from its fuselage. This was better.

The first bombs had begun to fall. I could hear the distant

thud of their landing, and shivered to think of the hideous destruction which must now be taking place amongst those packed houses and streets. Thud followed thud, and a great column of smoke and flame eddied up slowly from the distant town. An oil-dump had been hit. The sounds of distant gunfire became more intense. A veritable wall of bursting shells seemed to stand over the town, and, as I gazed, the enemy wheeled and made off northwards, still maintaining a semblance of battle order. It had been a lightning raid, pressed vigorously home. Where in Heaven's name were our fighters? A solitary Buffalo droned over my head in tragic irony. It was not even flying in the right direction. Even as I stood with a terrible anxiety in my heart, another wave of fresh enemy aircraft roared overhead and I bolted for my trench. Once again the tortured town was struck and left maimed and bleeding. The poor old Buffalo had, by some mischance, headed straight into the oncoming enemy formation, and now appeared from the ground to be actually flying through it. Its fate was certain. Shattered by machine-gun fire, it reeled crazily earthwards, flame pouring from its crumpled wings. The second raid did not last as long as the first, for the Japanese seemed to have merely dropped their entire bomb-load at random and made off swiftly. A huge ever-spreading pall of black smoke now hung over the distant town.

Less than ten minutes after the last enemy plane had departed, I could hear the sound of a high-powered car racing along the Bukit Timah road towards our camp. It came from the direction of Singapore. The car swept into the camp and halted with a screech of brakes in the middle of our dusty parade-ground. Even as I ran towards it, I could see that its chassis was dented and its windscreen shattered. Its sole occupant was a Corporal of Military Police, one of the members of a section stationed temporarily in the area. His light tropical shirt was in ribbons; his face a mass of grime and blood. We helped him out of the car gently, for he seemed on the point of collapse. He gasped out his message hysterically. "A house was hit—in the Bras Besar Road—Veal and I were taking cover there—I got out, but he's underneath the ruins—get him out quick." The man's strength was spent, and he sank back on the ground, coughing and spluttering. Leaving him to the care of an orderly, we gathered every available pick and shovel and piled hurriedly into our two remaining cars. I was in the first car, sitting on top of Shaw in the front seat. Sergeant Nunn was at the wheel. I was glad, for Nunn was a fast and skilful driver, who could be relied upon to take us to the Bras Besar Road in the shortest possible time. We roared down the Bukit Timah road as if all the devils pursued us.

Long before we reached our destination we saw in the shattered buildings and devasted streets ample proof of the severity of this lightning enemy attack. The soft, white, chalky houses had collapsed on every side, and the pavements were piled high with splintered woodwork and dusty rubble. Telegraph wires lay across the streets and light standards swayed drunkenly. We had to slacken speed to avoid panic-stricken masses of inhabitants, rushing to and fro in search of lost relatives and friends. At a street-corner I had just time to see a blood-bespattered wall, and the horribly mangled remains of what had been a group of human beings.

As we went forward cautiously, I could not help thinking about Veal, lying buried under a mass of rubble. I had not known him very well, as we did not come greatly into contact with the Military Police. I had chatted with him over a glass of beer, once or maybe twice, and had admired his broad shoulders and massive physical strength. He was a quietly-spoken, friendly sort of chap. I thought of him now, lying writhing in agony under some giant coping-stone, and prayed most earnestly that we might yet arrive in time to get him out alive.

We swept into the Bras Besar Road and pulled up sharply near the mountainous ruins of what had once been a Chinese jeweller's shop. Two Malay policemen kept back with difficulty a large crowd of natives, who surged to and fro, jabbering together excitedly in many tongues. From one of the policemen we learned that this was the place we sought. Armed with our picks and shovels, we hurriedly left the car and fought our way by sheer brute force through the jostling press of onlookers. They fell back before us, and we began digging grimly as we had never dug before in our lives.

It was a truly superhuman task. At every stroke of the shovel, piles of choking white dust would rise, and eventually we had to work with handkerchiefs over our mouths and nostrils. The sun beat down on us mercilessly from out of a blue sky, and we were bathed in perspiration. After an hour's gruelling toil, we seemed to have made little impression on the shifting mass of torn wood and shattered masonry around us. I never realised until then the enormous difficulty of locating exactly the position of a buried person. From one of the Malay policemen we learned that at least ten people, including a little girl, were under the shop when it collapsed. A light crane arrived from some other part of the town, and commenced to remove some of the larger beams and pieces of stonework. This enabled us to tunnel more deeply into the pile.

It was two whole hours before we reached the first body. It was that of a Malay, and as I gazed at the crushed limbs and hideously disfigured countenance of what had once been a young man in the prime of life, my heart was filled with a cold black fury, not so much against the actual men who had dropped the bombs, as against the shocking inhumanity and senselessness of war. That morning this youngster had risen from his bed as I also had done, filled with the eagerness and joy of youth: now he lay in the dust, his hands unsullied with the blood of any man, a victim of the cruellest fate, a maimed sacrifice to the gods of darkness and evil.

It was Shaw who first located Veal's body. I was digging down from above and had just removed a massive iron grille, when Shaw pounced into the debris and clasped Veal's out-stretched arm, which still bore the C.M.P. armlet. It was above his head in a last frantic attempt to ward off the mass of fallen masonry. It seemed almost as if he had been trying desperately to shield someone or something from impending doom. Tenderly we lifted the rubble away from around the dead man. After what seemed an eternity we had him out on the stretcher and carried him into the open roadway. Then we found what he had been shielding from harm. A little Malay girl lay in the dust as peacefully as if she were but asleep. Her features were unscarred by war, her limbs unbroken. At the last moment Veal had thrown himself on top of her to protect her frail body from harm. I went back to the roadway and stood gazing on the countenance of this very gallant gentleman. A kind Malay woman had gently wiped his face clear of dust, and he lay unmarked, with the faintest of smiles on his lips. I knelt beside him for a brief moment and offered up a silent prayer of thankfulness for a valiant soul.

The hour-glass of Fate was slowly running out. On the night of 31st January, the great withdrawal of our forces began from the mainland of Malaya across the narrow Causeway to Singapore Island. The whole gigantic movement was carried out successfully. I stood with Nunn in Bukit Panjang village, and silently watched the long lines of covered lorries and gun-carriages roll by. It was a heart-rending sight. The lorries moved slowly on their way, packed to overflowing with British, Australian and Indian troops. Their drawn faces and drooping limbs told their own tale of mental agony and physical exhaustion. Many had bandages wrapped round their heads and arms; some of the Punjabis whimpered like frightened children; others muttered strangely to themselves, having seen terrible things; there was no singing. I spoke for a moment with an Australian officer. He could hardly keep his eyes open for sheer weariness. He told me of long nights without sleep, of constant enemy ambushes, of apparently ever-fresh hordes of Japanese troops. In our present sorry state, he doubted whether we could hold Singapore for more than two days. Fearfully I inquired whether our men still held the pipe-line. "I haven't the foggiest idea," he replied. "Nobody seems to know what's happening. The Jocks are still over there, though," he added, with a movement of his head towards the mainland, "I hope to God they can manage to get out in time, for they're a great bunch of jokers."

They came back in good order, with their piper at their head, skirling a last defiance to the skies. The Causeway was blown up behind them, and we awaited hourly the coming of the first enemy units. For reasons unknown, however, they hung back in Johore, suspecting a trick. Their aircraft flew over us incessantly, probing our positions with bombs. Singapore was raided many times. The Japanese commanded the skies. They dropped leaflets too, advising us to surrender. I found one of those in the lalang one day. It bore the crude drawing of a ferocious dragon, and underneath were scrawled the words "Burn the white devils in the sacred flame of victory." I wondered idly how the red flame of barbarism, now sweeping through Johore, could ever be termed sacred. Perhaps the Shinto gods demanded such hideous sacrifices.

During the first week in February, conditions on the island grew steadily worse. There was an ever-increasing lack of cohesion about our defences, which was not improved by thousands of homeless refugees. For the Fifth Columnist and saboteur, it was paradise. Despite these setbacks, however, we succeeded in maintaining some semblance of preparedness, although we realised that we were fighting 'blind' without adequate recce support. It was actually a deadly game of blind man's buff. Rumours of Japanese forces, massing in the plantations across the Straits, drove our patrols eastwards and westwards alternately, from Nee Soon village to Ama Keng. It was reported that the enemy, with supreme impertinence, had actually radioed our headquarters, informing all and sundry that he would land on the western shore of the island on 8th February. We grimly strengthened our eastern defences, suspecting bluff.

The leading enemy units landed during the evening of Sunday, 8th February, in the mangrove swamps on the western shore. They fell suddenly on the 22nd Australian Brigade. By the following day they were near Ama Keng village, two miles into the island. At the same time strong Japanese forces set foot on the northern shore, near Kranji. As we had feared from the beginning, they had entered the citadel by its wide-open postern gates. They were now within our walls.

On 5th February, three days before the Japanese landing, our section had moved its quarters back to the outskirts of Singapore. We inhabited an evacuated house on the road to Paya Lebar village. There was, at that time, no thought of surrender in our minds, for we looked confidently to our Navy to lend us support at this eleventh hour. We had practically given up all hope of ever seeing our Air Force again. By day the skies were black with aircraft—but they were Japanese.

Owing to the very enclosed area in which we could operate after the first enemy landing, we found that our security duties were greatly curtailed. I travelled backwards and forwards by motor-cycle, trying to preserve some sort of liaison between our scattered units; I helped to collect drums of high octane petrol in mighty piles in the undergrowth for possible future demolition; I assisted in the laying of booby-traps on roads; I mounted guard at road-blocks.

I had often wondered how I should react under enemy shell-fire, and now I had ample opportunity to find out. The Japanese had brought up long-range artillery and shelled us regularly. They also commenced a depressingly accurate mortar-fire. I reacted to this incessant barrage in a most unsoldierlike fashion, for I was scared to death. Every time I heard that ominous snarling scream of an approaching shell, I gave an excellent imitation of an ostrich, burying my head in the nearest hole. Sometimes I sought shelter in some friendly monsoon drain, while the whole world swayed and rocked around me, and shell-splinters pinged past my head. I simply could not understand how any human being could summon up sufficient courage to face this deadly blast.

I was soon obliged to abandon my motor-cycle, for the noise of its engine drowned the sound of an approaching bomb or shell. I left it sorrowfully on 11th February on the road to Tanglin. I had tried to get through with a message to the 44th Indian Brigade, now hard-pressed on the Jurong river, but was halted by Military Police, who told me that part of the road had been mined. As I turned back towards Singapore, moving fairly slowly, I saw a friendly Chinese man signal excitedly to me from the roadside. Turning half-round in my saddle, and looking in the direction of his upward-stretched arm, I had just time to see a Japanese aeroplane roaring down on top of me. As I flung myself off my cycle, head-first into the bushy undergrowth, I could hear the angry chatter of a machine-gun above the noise of the plane's engines. From the sound, I guessed that the aircraft was circling the trees, searching for me. I burrowed deeper and deeper into the dusty bushes, for my airborne friend was now probing at me with bombs. I heard one explode not far away, and a branch cracked above me. I covered my head and lay motionless, afraid even to open my eyes. After what seemed an eternity, the aircraft droned away and I cautiously raised my head and looked around. The little wood seemed to be full of drifting smoke. As this slowly cleared away, I found that I was lying with my body wedged against a wall of ammunition boxes. Mills bombs and unexploded Bofors shells lay nearby. I had stumbled on one of our ammunition piles. A cold sweat broke out on my forehead. I was quivering with fear as I crawled back to the roadway. My motor-cycle lay in the ditch, upended, its petrol tank leaking, its mudguards and wheel-spokes twisted and crumpled. With shaking hands I tried to lift it back on the roadway, but it was firmly wedged in the concrete ditch and would not budge. I looked round for my Chinese friend, intending to summon his assistance. He was nowhere to be seen, so I moved cautiously across the road and glanced into the ditch at the other side. There he lay on his back, amidst a little pile of dry leaves and gravel, with a great pool of blood spreading out like a lake from the back of his head. I scrambled into the ditch beside him and lifted him gently by the shoulders. His sightless eyes stared heavenwards; the back of his head had been shot entirely away. That first machine-gun burst must have got him just as he dived for shelter. I was violently and painfully sick.

Late in the evening of 11th February the Japanese barrage became so intense that we were driven from our quarters in Paya Lebar. Cautiously, under cover of darkness, we moved to Thomson Road police station, on the northern outskirts of the city. On every side was the hideous destruction of war. Grisly piles of unburied dead lay at every street-corner, their torn limbs suppurating and decomposing horribly. We heard that 10,000 of the civilian population alone had been killed on that day. The terrible stench of death made us all feel ill.

Our stay at Thomson Road was short, but not sweet. The police station stood at the junction of four roads, and came under the most devastating cross-fire from enemy artillery. Those gunners had the range to an inch. Just as we sat down to a hurried and uneasy breakfast on the morning of the 12th, a shell smashed into the upper part of the building, and the ceiling came down on top of us in a choking cloud of plaster. Another salvo carried away two small outhouses and shattered the garden wall. Then the enemy mortars had a turn. Down they came with a screech and a crash around us. We did not wait for the next salvo, but pelted out of the building into a nearby wood. We were just in time. Even as I flung myself earthwards, a shell scored a direct hit on the room which we had just left. As the smoke and dust cleared, I saw the outside walls were riven asunder.

I lay in that wood, behind the bole of a rubber tree, wondering how far away the Japanese might be. Our field artillery, set up behind us in gardens and other open spaces, continued to roar defiance at unseen foes, but I had the unpleasant feeling that the enemy mortar-teams had come in under our barrage, and were close at hand. Our units were now so scattered that no accurate details of the battle could be gathered. The sun poured down on us and the red earth was warm to the touch. I felt terribly thirsty, but dared not drink from my water-bottle, in case my precious ration gave out before nightfall. I had no great stomach for that water, somehow, as we had heard the previous day that the island's reservoirs were choked with Allied and Japanese dead. I feared a widespread typhus epidemic almost as much as those vicious mortar-shells.

We were not alone in the wood. Men from many different units lay around me, sheltering from the deadly hail. There were remnants of the 18th Division, men from the Service and Ordnance Corps. Beside me lay a gigantic Sikh, with black beard and flashing eyes. He muttered constantly to himself in the strange, high-pitched language of his people. He gripped my arm excitedly, pointing to a clump of palms which grew just across the roadway, to the left. I strained my eyes but could see nothing unusual about the trees. My Indian comrade had probably been badly shell-shocked. Suddenly he flung forward his rifle, and shouted something which was drowned in the roar of the discharge. I gazed again at the distant palms, and was just in time to see a man fall from the top of one of the trees. The body lay inert on the ground. The sniper had fired his last shot. The Sikh laughed delightedly as he quickly ejected the spent shell from his rifle.

After an hour on that shell-pocked hillside, we moved to fresh quarters in Newton Road. Our new place of refuge was a large, white dwelling-house, set in its own grounds. The house was raised several feet off the ground on concrete stilts, and the space underneath gave us good cover. It was nearly noon, and the enemy shelling had abated somewhat. The house was empty, so we removed all the mattresses we could find inside and wedged them around our fox-hole for protection. Then, with a couple of shovels which Bussey picked up in the garden, we dug ourselves in securely and allowed ourselves to relax a little. It had been a trying morning.

Our peace was short-lived. Having completed a leisurely lunch, the Japanese gunners turned again to business with increased enthusiasm. To their motley armament they had now apparently added a new weapon of frightfulness. This was a quick-firing gun, which hurled a small calibre, high-velocity shell at us approximately every three seconds. The missile did little material damage, but it had a most demoralising effect on us all. It burst in our ears like a near pistol-shot, and we called it the 'whizz-bang special'. Nunn was trying to explain to us exactly what this shell looked like, but none of us was very interested. We knew what it did to our nervous system.

That night I slept sprawled on a mattress on the dug-out floor. I slept peacefully, like a child, for twelve solid hours, and not one of the section had the heart to wake me. Before falling off to sleep, I said my prayers as I had been taught to do, and now, in this wild place the words seemed to mean so much more than they had done in peace-time. "Father, guide us through the perils that lie ahead; strengthen our minds and our bodies; bless our loved ones and grant us rest." I awoke from a dreamless sleep on the morning of 13th February, much refreshed in mind and body. I must have been utterly exhausted, for I discovered, on looking out of the dug-out, that a shell had exploded not more than six feet away from my head. I had heard nothing.

It was in the gathering dusk of that February evening that Captain Lemin was hurriedly summoned to an emergency meeting at Divisional Headquarters. In his absence the sergeant-major took over command of the section, and I was posted on guard at the gateway of the house, about thirty yards distant from the building. As I judged that only the most reckless man would stand openly on guard on that exposed roadway, with whizz-bangs and mortar-shells bursting all around, I dropped down into the four-foot deep monsoon drain which bordered the road. Not far away, also in the drain, lay a dead Punjabi, his cold fingers still clutching his rifle.

The enemy barrage had moved round to another quarter of the town, and only an occasional mortar-shell burst nearby. In the far distance I could hear the tumpa-tumpa of a Bofors gun, which had now apparently come unexpectedly into service as a field-piece. From a little clump of palms to my right came the chatter of a machine-gun. I glanced round at the shell-torn trees and bushes, wondering if, even now, the crafty enemy might be crawling silently forward to the attack. I tried to take my mind off the war.

But where had Lemin gone? What sort of meeting was taking place at Headquarters? Would we see him again? Was the battle for Singapore already lost? I tortured my mind to find a likely answer to these questions, but could find none.

A dim figure suddenly loomed out of the darkness and hurried towards our dug-out before I had even time to shout. A watchful sentry I, I reflected bitterly. I should have to be faster than this if I were to stop a Japanese. What had the sergeant-major said? "Don't bother asking questions. Shoot him first!" The figure had stopped outside our dug-out and I slowly raised my rifle. I hurriedly lowered it again as I heard Lemin's resonant voice. He spoke agitatedly, quite unlike his usual self.

"Sergeant-Major," I heard him say, "get the men together at once." There followed a short conversation between Lemin and

Wright, which I could not catch, though I was straining my ears. I saw the other members of the section file silently out of the dug-out, and stand in line before Lemin. I wondered whether I should join them, but remembered that I had been put on guard, and dared not leave my post. Lemin was checking over the names. "Where's Smith?" I heard him say. "On guard, sir," replied Wright. I cautiously crawled from my ditch, nearer the group of men. The enemy shelling had now almost ceased, and I could hear Lemin plainly. "It breaks my heart to have to say this," he said, "but I have received orders to leave you, together with four men from the section. I understand that we are leaving on a special mission, but I have no idea where we are going. I have had to draw lots for the four places on my party, but I didn't count you in, Sergeant-Major, for you must take over command after I have gone." O'Shea, Boyd, Taylor and Gibberd had been the selected four. Against all orders, I abandoned my post and hurried up the path to the dug-out. I had time only to shake the hands of my four comrades, before they moved off with Lemin in the direction of the town. I sat down beside Shaw, feeling sad and lonely. Bill was smiling that broad, friendly Yorkshire smile of his, which made any man feel good. "I was never such a devout Christian as you, Mac," he said, laying a hand on my shoulder, "but I think I'll try a bit of a prayer tonight. Do you mind if I join you in it?" I gripped his hand and said nothing, for I could not trust myself to speak. "Cheer up, son," he went on kindly, "I think maybe that you and I are fated to be thrown together. Lemin told us that the battle wasn't going too badly, so, by tomorrow we'll maybe be advancing again. We'll miss Gibbie most, but we have each other, and that's a good thing." "Thank God for that, Bill," I muttered. "Aye," said Shaw, "thank God." It was a bitter moment. In my heart of hearts I doubted whether Lemin spoke the truth when he had said the battle wasn't going too badly. I inclined to think that it was going exceptionally well for the Japanese. By morning they would have over-run our positions.

The 14th February we called Black Saturday. From early

morning till late evening the Japanese kept up an almost continual bombardment of our positions, both from the ground and from the air. Enemy fighters, flying at little over tree-top height, raked us with a pitiless machine-gun fire. Their mortars had a field day. Owing to severe shortage of ammunition, our guns could only fire intermittently. Water was growing hourly scarcer. Nunn made a short recce of the neighbourhood in the early afternoon, returning with the news that the town was a shambles. From one of the Military Police he had heard that Lemin and his four men had been seen on the Docks early that morning. We prayed that they had managed to get away before this hell-fire began. On his way back to the dug-out, Nunn had been sniped at constantly from surrounding houses. On one occasion he had had a brief glimpse of his assailant, but had been unable to get his rifle up in time. The man was almost naked, Nunn said, and looked like a Malay. The enemy Fifth Column had apparently come more boldly into the open. It did not appear that we were winning this battle. Nunn thought it more likely that the Japanese would attack any time.

In the section, however, our morale was fairly high, for we had fared better than many other men. Through a tap in the back garden a trickle of muddy water still flowed, and we were not entirely parched with thirst. We had a meagre supply of food and cigarettes. Above all, we had, thanks to our mattresses and shovelwork, constructed what seemed to be a really secure dug-out. The upper storey of the building had been hit repeatedly with shells, and parts of the masonry had fallen thickly round us, strengthening our defences against blast and splinter. We could now reach the outside only by crawling on our stomachs through a narrow tunnel in the debris. We took turns at guarding the tunnel entrance. As an experiment, Bussey stuck out his rifle beyond the edge of the house, with his helmet perched on the muzzle. In a matter of seconds it was severely dented by a shot fired from somewhere behind us. A sniper had apparently taken an interest in us. We cautiously tried to spot his position, but failed. It would have been sheer lunacy to venture out in that storm of shrapnel.

During the long night of 14th February, I dozed only for a few

moments at a time. Again and again I awoke with a start, thinking the Japanese were upon us. I clutched my rifle tightly,
peering out into the darkness, but nothing stirred. The night
was quiet, save for an occasional distant burst of machine-gun
fire. Far in the east dawn was breaking, and I wondered whether
I should be alive to see another morning. Back at home, my
folks might still be sitting up, listening to a late news summary.
Before the Japanese landed on the island, I had managed to send
off a cable to them, telling them of my whereabouts. By now
they would be desperately anxious, knowing that I was in Singapore. In many ways I wished that I had not sent that wire. Yet
it was surely better that they knew the truth. They would be
bound to find out when the casualty lists appeared, and then it
would come as an even greater shock. Before the war I had
feared death instinctively, for I was young and unacquainted
with its ways. Here, in this tragic city, I had walked hand in
hand with death for weeks past, and was becoming familiar with
its grim visage. The Bras Besar Road rose again before my eyes,
and I remembered the quiet peace which I had seen on the faces
of Veal and of that little Malay girl. Surely it could not be so
terrible to die after all, if those had passed through the dark
valley so easily and securely.

I shook myself free from such thoughts. A new day was
beginning, and while there was life, there was also surely hope.
Perhaps this Sunday would bring a change in our fortunes.
Perhaps, even now, fresh forces were hurrying to our aid, ready
to throw back the Japanese, and begin a steady advance against
them. It was unworthy not to be ready to support them when
they arrived. Perhaps even now our fighters and bombers were
preparing to take off from some airstrip in Sumatra or Java,
ready to turn the tide of war and blast the enemy concentrations.
I longed to see those yellow devils getting a taste of their own
bloody medicine. They would rush back screaming to the
Straits, but might not find them so easy to cross a second time,
if our Navy were waiting for them there. I must be ready for
our advance. I carefully checked my rifle and ammunition, and
then, with the aid of a small pocket-mirror and a cupful of
muddy water from the garden supply, managed a quick shave.

I was dragging a comb through my tousled hair when Livesley crawled from the dug-out and told me not to be such a vain ass. He scowled at me for a moment and said I had better turn in for a rest. The atmosphere inside the dug-out was foul with men's breath and cigarette smoke, but I wormed my way between Shaw and Nunn, and was asleep immediately.

I awoke with a start just after noon, and found myself alone in the dug-out, except for Wrigley, who still snored in a corner. After all my careful preparations, I had missed the advance! This was terrible. Nudging Wrigley awake with my elbow, I grasped my rifle and bandolier of ammunition, and went through the narrow tunnel like an eel. In my haste, I almost knocked Shaw down at the outside entrance. "Whoa, there!" cried Bill, "where do you think you're off to?" "I thought you'd gone forward and left me," I cried. "We're not going no place," said Bill, shortly. "We're waiting for the sergeant-major to come back." "Where's he gone, then?" I asked. "Over to the C.M.P. Headquarters to see Major Trench. There's something in the wind, and we're all waiting for news." I glanced about me. The section were sitting round, waiting expectantly, like dogs for their dinner. I burst out laughing suddenly at their mournful countenances. "I don't know what you've got to be so happy about," growled Harris. "Well, Mac's had a shave and we haven't," said Nunn, with a smile, "I think I'll have one too."

As I sat, cross-legged on the hot earth, gazing out into the sunlit garden, I suddenly saw a man, rifle in hand, double across the open space and disappear in the direction of the town. Another followed, glancing round carefully to see if he were observed. I called out to Shaw and he wriggled across to join me. A third man broke cover, and raced off after the others. I turned to Bill questioningly. The enemy barrage had practically ceased. Bill was smiling, but his eyes were sad and troubled. "These are our boys," he said slowly. "Yes, I know," I replied, "but what are they doing?" "Well, Mac, if you want my opinion, they're running away." "Running away?" I repeated stupidly, "but where?" "At a rough guess, I should say they are making for the docks," said Bill. I raised my rifle and took careful aim at the last man who was still just visible on the distant roadway. I was quite composed as I took first pressure on the trigger. I should drill this deserter straight between the shoulder-blades. With a sudden movement of his wrist Bill pushed up the barrel of my gun. "Let him go, Mac," he said firmly, "don't have the blood of one of our own boys on your hands. It isn't worthy." I laid aside my rifle, feeling strangely glad that I had not fired. We all waited impatiently for the sergeant-major to return.

In a short time he came back hurriedly, accompanied by Major Trench. The major was a regular officer, short in stature and soldierly in bearing. He crept into our hide-out with the sergeant-major, and glanced round at us all keenly. We waited in silence for him to speak. "I'm truly sorry to have to tell you," he said, "that, as far as we are concerned, the war is nearly over. We are surrendering Singapore to the Japanese at four o'clock this afternoon." A great gasp of dismay burst from us all. I stared at the man as if unable to believe my ears. "There is only a few more hours' supply of water left," continued Trench in level tones, "our artillery ammunition is practically gone, and it would be sheer suicide to fight on any longer. The Japs are in complete control of the whole island, of the air and of the sea. The G.O.C. wants to thank you all for the very gallant defence which you have put up these past few days." I glanced vacantly at my wrist-watch. Two o'clock. In two more hours we should lay down our arms, and await our fate. I still could hardly grasp the news. There was to be no glorious advance after all, no bombers, no ships. I smiled grimly to myself as I remembered how optimistically Lemin had spoken before he left of the progress of the battle. Still, perhaps he had had his orders to cheer us up as best he could. I could not blame him. I only hoped that he and the others were well away by four o'clock. They, at least, should live to fight on with the free peoples. Our future was dark and menacing. What had the pamphlet said again? "Burn the white devils in the sacred flame of victory." That did not give much promise of a long and happy life for any of us. I hoped the end would come quickly. I recoiled in horror from the thought of being tortured slowly to death, or of being used as a living bayonet target. We had heard many times already that the Japanese took no prisoners.

Major Trench was speaking in a matter-of-fact sort of way. "If any of you want to try to make a break for it now, you may go, and good luck to you. But I warn you that there are no boats to be had anywhere in the harbour. A few got away last night, I understand, and one or two more early this morning, but now there is little chance of escape. The docks have taken a tremendous hammering." The sergeant-major looked round at us inquiringly, but we all shook our heads. "I don't think any of them are keen to go, sir," he said. "Well, in that case," said Trench, "I think it would be best for me to take you under my wing. You can all come over the road with me and join up with my police. At the very end, when the Japs come in, there might be some small safety in numbers." Taking our equipment with us, and still holding on to our weapons, we left our dug-out and moved across the road to join up with the Military Police. It was exactly two-thirty. The news of the impending capitulation seemed to have spread like wildfire, and already I could see whole groups of men moving hurriedly through the undergrowth in the direction of the docks. "Shall we join them, Bill?" I asked Shaw. "No, Mac," he replied, "I don't really think it will make any difference in the end. Besides," he added, with a smile, "you can't swim, and we might have to dive for a boat."

The Japanese gunners were apparently still unaware that they had won the day, for they continued to shell our positions. Our guns still fired back, but it was their swan song. They had played their part magnificently, giving back salvo for salvo with a doggedness and grit which were in the finest traditions of the British Army. We had all fallen victims to the most cruel and tragic misfortune, but we were no dishonoured garrison. Our forces had battled dourly and steadfastly against a foe vastly superior in both numbers and fire-power. For days and nights on end they had faced the most appalling land and aerial bombardment which they had ever known. And all this in the sorest straits of thirst and exhaustion. The free peoples of the world, now united in a common cause, would have no call to be ashamed of their sons in Singapore. Some day our armies would return, although we might not be alive to see them, and our spirits would arise, spectre-like, and go joyfully with them on the path which led to victory. The hot sun would smite us no more; no more would we face the dangers of shot and shell. The trumpets would sound, the lips of the dead would be opened, and there would be much singing.

At four o'clock that Sunday afternoon an uneasy peace fell on our small sector of the line. Our artillery was silent. Ten minutes later the Japanese guns were silent also, although sporadic bursts of machine-gun fire could still be heard in the distance. We waited tensely, watching for a sudden rush of armed men, but nothing stirred in the dusty undergrowth. An enemy recce aircraft droned lazily over our heads, flying so low that we could easily make out the figure of the pilot at the controls. We watched the plane circle the tree-tops like some giant vulture. Suddenly a single shot rang out from one of our nearby gun-positions. We ducked instinctively. The plane broke in two, as if cloven by a giant axe, and hurtled earthwards. A distant cheer went up from our sharp-shooting gunners. We froze in our positions, expecting immediate reprisals. But the enemy guns were still silent. Apparently the incident had passed unobserved. I breathed a sigh of relief, for, though sympathising fully with the men who had fired this lucky shot, I realised only too well what another such incident might do at this delicate stage in the proceedings. Hostilities would be reopened all along the line, and the Japanese would swarm in on us, like angry bees.

Major Trench was a wise officer. Feeling certain that the enemy would be more unlikely to massacre out of hand a large group of men than a small party of stragglers, he marched us down the main road to Singapore until we found a large mansion-house, in which many more members of the Military Police were gathered together. We still carried, besides our normal equipment, our rifles and ammunition, for distant gun-fire could still be heard. We had absolutely no guarantee that the Japanese would keep their word. If, at the last moment, under cover of approaching night, they treacherously broke faith and over-ran us, they would find to their cost that the defeated British Army had still soldiers who could load quickly and fire straight. There would be no sudden slaughter of the innocents.

About eight-thirty all firing ceased in the city, and we made ourselves comfortable for the night. Loaded rifles lay conveniently near to every man's hand. We all stretched ourselves out on the dusty floor of the ruined house, busy with our thoughts. Before turning in for the night, I stood gazing from a shell-splintered window upon the stricken city. Distant buildings were ablaze, and the flames cast a red, angry glow on the far horizon, against which were silhouetted, in stark and tragic relief, the charred skeletons of trees and houses. The Lion City of Singapore, this once proud outpost of empire, lay dying at my feet. Only four short months before, we had departed, as free men, on this high adventure; now we were captives of a fierce, oriental foe whose ways were not our ways, whose hands were red with the blood of our comrades, whose god was not our God. As I fell into a troubled sleep, I seemed to see before me the face of Christ Himself, and His eyes were filled with tears.

As dawn broke the following day, a messenger arrived with orders from Headquarters that we were to pile our arms and ammunition in front of the house immediately, as the Japanese vanguard had now entered the city. We obeyed the order at once. The rising sun gave promise of another scorching day. We scanned the distant roadway keenly, wondering from what direction the triumphal procession of our enemies would arrive. As time passed and the street remained deserted, save for a passing Malay or Chinese, we allowed ourselves to relax, some sitting on a low wall that bordered the building, others sprawling out full-length on what had once been a well-tended front lawn. Major Trench strolled down to the gate, and gazed along the quiet street, A tall Malay came past, and, seeing us all gathered silently in the garden, shouted something at us which none of us could catch. I thought I could just make out the word 'Nippon'. Then the native brought from the breast of his dirty white shirt a small flag which he waved insolently at us from afar. It was the Rising Sun of Japan. Livesley, with an oath, seized his revolver, but the Malay had gone, convulsed with laughter. They might not laugh so loudly under Japanese domination, these useless guttersnipes of Singapore. I could not think that all the native population would behave towards us so badly.

Suddenly I saw Major Trench draw himself up to attention, and give us a quick, urgent signal with his hand. We struggled to our feet.

The Major saluted smartly. Round the corner of the massive gatepost came the first Japanese soldier whom any of us had ever seen. I almost burst out laughing, but caught Shaw's warning glance. This was the triumphal procession, this the victorious army of Imperial Japan! The newcomer was the most slovenly, shuffling apology for a soldier that I had ever seen. He stood not much over five feet in height, with sloping shoulders and slightly bowed legs. As Trench saluted him again, he looked up, almost timidly, brought his heels together and bowed. Then, with Trench at his side, he turned up the path towards us. No two men could have presented a greater contrast. On one side the British officer, erect in bearing and steady of step, on the other, the minute Japanese, shambling along like some obedient orang-outang, carrying his rifle over his shoulder like a fishing-rod. Was this the makeshift semblance of a man that had driven our armies back at Batu Pahat and Bukit Timah? I stared at the newcomer curiously as he approached.

He was a young man—not more than 22 I judged. He was clad in a ragged, ill-fitting uniform, not unlike our own tropical attire in colour. Above the left-hand breast-pocket of his open-necked shirt, he carried two small metal stars, which presumably denoted his rank or his particular unit. He wore long trousers, loosely wrapped around with puttees, and brown leather boots. Round his waist he carried a brown leather ammunition belt, secured with a brass buckle, and on his head was tightly jammed a sort of rough forage-cap, from which hung down strips of dirty green and brown canvas, probably for use as camouflage. On the peak of the cap a five-pointed star was fixed. His sole weapons seemed to consist of a rather old-fashioned, long-barrelled rifle and a short bayonet, in a sheath by his side.

27

For a moment I studied the countenance of my enemy, trying to gain some insight into his possible character. Here I drew a complete blank. His face was quite impassive and inscrutable. His skin was brown, not yellow, and he wore a short beard. His cheek-bones were high and his eyes two thin slits, as he surveyed us with apparent disinterest. Then, with a slight, lazy movement of his hand, he indicated that we were to arrange ourselves in two ranks. We fell in unquestioningly before him. Without even glancing at our piled-up arms and ammunition, he began to count us, softly under his breath in a strange tongue. We stood stiffly to attention. Having come to the end of the file, he began again from the beginning. Something was wrong. Our small friend could not apparently get his figures right. With Major Trench, we numbered thirty-four, but, as the officer had stood out from the ranks while the count was taking place, there was a blank file. This was evidently a phenomenon with which the Japanese was unfamiliar. He began again, and this time Trench stepped forward quickly to explain. Then we had the first glimpse of the sudden tempestuous fury of this oriental race. Like lightning the Japanese had his rifle round, with the muzzle not more than an inch from our officer's throat. Bursting into an unintelligible torrent of words, he shouted at Trench till the veins showed up like cords on his neck. His finger trembled on the rifle-trigger. I closed my eyes for a moment, expecting to hear the roar of the discharge. Trench was no coward. He stood his ground, watching the raging little demon calmly, until his fury had spent itself. Then, coolly turning on his heel, he quietly fell in the blank file, and faced his front with the rest of us. The Japanese counted us again, and was satisfied with the result.

With the Japanese shambling along beside us, we marched across the city to a great open space near Newton Circus. On our way we passed other little groups of our men, marching in the same direction. We carried our packs, haversacks, kitbags and water-bottles. The sun was stiflingly hot. No attempt had apparently been made to bury the piles of dead which lay along the dusty streets. It was a city of dead men, and dead animals. I saw an ox lying on its side near the roadway. It was bloated like a giant balloon, and looked as if it might burst at any moment. Its head was black with flies which rose in a droning whirl as we passed. Then they settled again. The air had the nauseating stench of decomposing human flesh. We did not speak, but stared straight ahead, striving to ignore such horrid sights.

At the Newton Circus camp, thousands of men and scores of lorries were assembled. The lorries were arranged wheel to wheel in a gigantic circle, and in the circle, on the hot grass, sat Indians, Australians and British in a great, unhappy mass. Every moment fresh additions were swelling the throng. A mighty cheer went up as the Northumberland Fusiliers marched in. They had fought most gallantly, and the Japanese had suffered heavy casualties under their deadly machine-gun fire. Now they swung along the Bukit Timah road as light-heartedly as if they were off on a picnic. And as they marched, they sang the old familiar song "Blaydon Races". We all joined in spontaneously, whether we knew the words or not, and a great chorus greeted those smiling lads from Northumberland. Their spirit was indomitable.

Round the edge of the circle, at some small distance from us, squatted Japanese infantrymen and machine-gunners, their weapons ready to hand. It was a circle of steel, and I wondered whether this was to be the place of our execution. It seemed incredible that thousands of men could be murdered in cold blood. Yet, if those machine-guns opened up on us, it would not take long to blow great gaps in our massed ranks. I had heard a tale that the Japanese had once massacred twelve thousand prisoners in an earlier war. From the enemy's point of view, we must be a useless impediment in their advancing path, a fearful liability which could be wiped off quickly if the necessary order were given. I scrutinised the face of the nearest Japanese as he sat cross-legged, his loaded rifle across his knees, and could find no trace of compassion there. Rather I seemed to see a faintly contemptuous sneer. I desperately tried to take my mind off our unhappy plight.

The Japanese had, apparently, no intention of feeding us, for we received nothing to eat or drink. By early afternoon the position had become almost intolerable. The hot sun beat down on us, and we were parched with thirst. If this starvation policy were to be continued, the enemy would have no need to expend a single round of ammunition on us. Perhaps that was the idea. If such were the case, then we were indeed in a more miserable position than I had at first thought. To die in a hail of machine-gun bullets would be infinitely preferable to lingering on in agony, perhaps for days.

Then Major Trench hit on a brilliant idea. The Military Police all possessed lettered armbands for general use when on duty. Could we not put on these armbands, and bluff the Japanese into thinking that we belonged to some particularly elite group with powers far beyond those of the ordinary soldier? The C.M.P. armlet might yet be our Open Sesame. It was a simple plan, and likely, therefore, to be successful. The Japanese were carrying buckets of water from somewhere for their own use. Why could we not bring some also for our parched comrades? There were at least twenty armlets available. We could divide ourselves into twos, and try our fortune anyway. There was, of course, no guarantee that the Japanese would not shoot us out of hand, but even that fate was better than sitting still till our tongues clave to our mouths. We could ask them to lend us their buckets. As I tied on the armlet, and went off with Nunn, I wondered whether this was to be our last adventure.

As we neared the entry gate, after ploughing our way through a jostling, whimpering throng of Indian troops, my heart fell, for the way out was barred by two most villainous-looking Japanese. They were giants of their race, both standing over six feet in height. Both were armed to the teeth with a forbidding array of weapons attached to their persons. One carried no fewer than three looted British revolvers in his belt, in addition to rifle and bayonet. "Let's have a word with Buffalo Bill," murmured Nunn in my ear, indicating this moving arsenal of a man. I could not help smiling and my spirits rose again slightly. Nunn's grim sense of humour had sustained me several times in the past. It was refreshing to be with such a brave man.

As we halted four feet from him and saluted, Buffalo Bill snarled at us like an infuriated beast, and leapt forward with rifle-butt raised. His ugly companion snarled in sympathy, but did not move. We stood our ground although my knees were shaking badly. Nunn faced the raging brute unflinchingly. "We C.M.P." he said, in his best pidgin English, "we big men. We want water." Buffalo Bill eyed him viciously, and the rifle-butt trembled in mid-air. "Curra, Englando!" screamed Buffalo Bill, lapsing into a flood of the most bestial-sounding Japanese. His companion joined in, assisting his comrade when his breath gave out. But I saw that the menacing rifle-butt had been lowered, and the man, though still shouting and gesticulating, was beginning to calm down slightly. Then, suddenly, while Nunn and I stood waiting for the storm of oaths to abate, our guardian angel appeared in the shape of a short, bespectacled Japanese officer. He carried a gigantic sword, almost as big as himself, in a brown leather scabbard. On his arrival, Buffalo Bill and his companion froze to attention, and bowed quickly. There followed a rapid conversation in Japanese between the officer and the men. Buffalo Bill waxed eloquent. He glared at us, and again raised his rifle to demonstrate how nearly he had clubbed us to death. The officer listened attentively, nodding his head and muttering "Hai" over and over again. I took this to mean 'yes'. At last he turned towards us, and, in very halting tones, began to address us in English. He was a young man, and his eyes, though solemn, did not hold that cold animal ferocity which we had seen in Buffalo Bill's. We saluted together, and the officer bowed slightly. "You try escape?" he inquired mildly, "my soldiers shoot quickly. You foolish men." Nunn was the spokesman. "No sir," he replied, "we not escape. We policemen. All men very hungry and thirsty. We bring water." The Japanese looked at Nunn searchingly. "You policemen?" he inquired, "you kempi?" "Hai," said Nunn, learning fast. I determined that I should remember this magic word 'kempi' for long days to come. It was apparently a useful term, and it was not until afterwards that I discovered that the Japanese kempi, or military police, were the most feared members of the Imperial Nipponese Army. The officer turned to his two waiting henchman, and we were then privileged to witness for the first time one of those curious exhibitions of authority and discipline, which were so much part and parcel of the Japanese military system. The officer carefully laid his sword down on the grass, and then, drawing himself up to a position of attention, began to speak to his two men softly, almost tenderly, I thought. Suddenly the quiet voice began to rise, and I saw Buffalo Bill's legs tremble with fear. The officer was transformed from a quiet, studious-looking young man into a raging demon. His eyes flashed, his face was suffused with blood, and his words cracked on our ears like a whiplash. Then, divesting himself of a stout binocular-case, which he carried over his shoulder by a long leather strap, he grasped it firmly in his right hand, and smashed it mercilessly into the middle of Buffalo Bill's terror-stricken countenance. The unhappy wretch staggered, but regained his position immediately. Then his comrade was similarly attacked. He fell to the grass, for the blow was a severe one. His fall seemed to drive the fiery officer utterly beserk with rage. Leaping forward, he delivered a full-blooded kick at the fallen man with the toe of his brown riding-boot, and the soldier caught the blow squarely on the mouth. A thin trickle of blood began to flow from the wound. This was a type of corrective discipline which I had never before witnessed, and I was thankful that I was not a member of this barbarous army. The officer quietened down as quickly as he had flared up, and carefully restored his binocular-case to its position. Then he picked up his great sword, and after a few softly-spoken instructions to his two battered soldiers, calmly turned on his heel and walked off.

The two Japanese were now as ready to assist us as they had previously been desirous of obstructing us. One of them rushed off to the nearest lorry, and returned laden with four large buckets, which he proceeded to thrust into our hands. Buffalo Bill pointed down the road, indicating the position of the nearest water supply. As we passed them, they both drew themselves up stiffly to attention. We had won our case. We found the tap easily, and the water looked fresh and clean. Japanese engineers had apparently repaired the water-mains and pipes. On our return to the camp, we were joined by other police and by the rest of the section, and a water-carrying party was formed. Eventually, the Japanese themselves placed a water-cart at our disposal, and gradually the prime needs of the multitude were satisfied. I felt much happier when I saw that water-cart, for it did not now look as though our captors intended to butcher us after all.

We all slept fitfully that night, for the encircling Japanese were too close to us for real comfort. At regular intervals throughout the night I awoke with a start as the enemy sentries were changed. But we were not disturbed by them until early morning, when they came round prodding us awake with their fixed bayonets. Another day had begun. As so often in the past few days, I wondered how many of us would be alive to see the night.

With the permission of the Japanese, we lit fires and break-fasted on tea and our emergency rations. After breakfast, Nunn and I decided to try our fortunes again. At the main gate of the camp, the sentries had been changed. Buffalo Bill and his companion were probably in bed with broken jaws. Marching boldly up to the first Japanese we encountered, we stuck out our armlets and shouted "kempi". We both saluted smartly. There was a click of heels and a bow from the sentry, and we were out on the open roadway, marching towards the centre of the town as temporarily free men. It was a delicious sensation.

As we strolled along as unconcernedly as we dared, groups of Japanese soldiers passed us by, some even getting out of our way on the pavement. Nobody stopped us, nobody questioned us. It was fantastic that we could walk around the town so freely in the very midst of our enemies. Open lorries, manned by Japan-ese teams, were now slowly moving along the streets, gathering in the piles of unburied dead. It was a grisly and unwholesome task, and I did not envy them. Bodies were thrown on the lorries in much the same way as I had seen turnips loaded on farm-carts in pre-war days. Sometimes limbs were separated from bodies, but the grim work continued without respite. Everywhere there were flies—myriads of great, black, droning blue-bottles—swarming over dead flesh. The Japanese worked with masks over their mouths and nostrils.

As we moved on, we began to realise the extent of the damage which bombing and shelling had done to the city. Roads were cracked and pitted with holes; drains were blocked with debris; telephone cables lay twisted like giant serpents; walls of buildings were riven from top to bottom, and blackened with smoke and flame; trees were bereft of foliage, their branches torn and splintered. It was indeed a grim and unhappy city.

At every turn Japanese flags were fluttering. There seemed to be thousands of them, some large, some small. Even the children whom we passed waved their flags innocently. Poor kids, they were living in a city of death and destruction, and could not see the reason for it all. Their parents gone, their homes gone, they wandered unhappily to and fro, waifs of the storm, infants of a new and terrible régime. Their minds were numbed with the hideous events of the past few days, and their eyes were hollow and empty. I pitied them intensely. They might grow up to learn the ways of peace again, but this horror would never be quite wiped from their memory.

On our way back to the camp, we came upon a British lorry, lying on its side, near a small copse of trees. It was, or had been a residential area, and large houses faced the quiet street. Each stood in its own grounds. There was no one near, and, as we passed, we glanced into the lorry. It contained crates of tinned fruit—apricots, peaches and pears. One of the crates was open, and, in a matter of seconds, Nunn and I had acquired a large tin of peaches each. I had just opened the tins with my clasp-knife, when Nunn suggested that they would go down better with a cup of tea. I glanced quickly up and down the street, but it was empty. The nearest house was only a stone's throw away. I could ask the residents to make us a cup of tea, and then, if the Japanese appeared, we could always stroll on, as if on duty. Nunn promised to whistle if he saw anyone coming.

As I expected, the front door of the house was locked, but I moved round to the back. The kitchen door lay ajar, and I knocked. Nothing stirred inside. The house was as quiet as the grave. I moved into the neat, clean kitchen and found some tea in a canister on a shelf. A small electric cooker stood near one wall, but I did not understand its workings. Near the cooker, however, was a large spirit stove with kettle. I filled the kettle with water from the tap, lit the stove, and set the kettle upon it to boil. This would take some little time, so, fearing that I had intruded too far on the hospitality of this quiet house, I called out "Is anybody there?" There was still no reply. I ran quickly outside. Nunn stood at the gate, unconcernedly. All was well. I returned to the kitchen.

There was, I admit, no call for me to explore that empty house, but, as the kettle boiled, I moved from room to room, gazing round curiously at the modern furniture, and the rich rugs on the floors. The house had practically escaped damage, only certain of the windows being splintered. It made me feel almost civilised again to look round at this beautiful home. A broad, carpeted staircase led up to the upper half of the building, and I climbed quickly. Several closed doors gave on a broad landing, and I tried them in turn. They opened on trim, comfortable bedrooms, rich in tapestry and hangings. In each the Venetian blinds were up and the rooms looked bright and cheerful. I pitied the residents of this lovely place having to leave it, hurriedly perhaps by night.

I tried the last door and stepped into a dark room. The blinds were down, and, for a moment, I could see nothing, until my eyes became more accustomed to the gloom. But once more, in this quiet room, that terrible smell of death hung heavy in the air. I hurried fearfully across the floor to pull up the blinds and shed some light upon what I felt sure must be another ghastly tragedy. I tugged at the window-cord and immediately the whole room was flooded with sunshine.

I felt sick and horrified by what I saw. Unlike the other neat bedrooms which I had entered, this one was in a state of utter confusion. A great double-door wardrobe stood open, its contents strewn across the floor. A small chest-of-drawers lay wrecked in the centre of the room. A large porcelain vase lay in splinters at my feet. But it was not upon these things that my eyes were riveted. Half-hanging out of the great, double bed, her head resting on the carpet, and her arms frenziedly outstretched towards me, lay a young and beautiful Eurasian woman with her throat cut. The bed-clothes were twisted and wrapped around her slim body, and the white sheets were soaked with blood. Though I had walked hand-in-hand with death for days past, I stood utterly petrified at this most foul murder. I could not take my gaze off the poor creature's staring eyes. She had been dead for several days, so the fatal blow could not have been struck by a Japanese. Some faithless native servant perhaps, some Malay armed with a murderous kris, bent on loot or rape. As I stood shaking in every limb, I heard Nunn's urgent warning whistle from the roadway. With an effort I moved towards the door, and fairly pelted down the staircase. In the kitchen, the kettle was boiling, but now I did not in the least feel like tea. As I turned to leave that house of death, a shadow fell across the kitchen doorway. I looked up quickly. A Japanese stood, gazing at me suspiciously. Suddenly his hand flew to a revolver at his belt, and I stood stock-still. "Chay" I stammered, using the native word. I pointed to the canister. The Japanese examined it, so I took the opportunity to shout 'kempi' once more. Immediately he turned and bowed. I saluted smartly. "O.K." he growled, "chay O.K." My hand shook as I poured the boiling water into a teapot. The Japanese turned and went off to explore the rest of the building, just as I had done a short time before. I heard him thumping up the stairs. There was a pause as he reached that room where the dead woman lay. I wondered whether he too stood gazing at that awful sight, moved to the depths of his oriental soul by such vile wickedness. Then I heard him coming back. Although I did not want that tea, I judged it best for my own sake and for Nunn's, to carry on unconcernedly. The Japanese stepped into the kitchen. I stood to attention. No sign of emotion showed on his mask-like face. Suddenly he laughed—a hideous cackle of a laugh—and jerked his thumb in the direction of the upstairs bedroom. "Womanka," he growled, "womanka mató." * He drew his finger across his throat significantly. Then he leered at me, a horribly bestial leer, which made me shudder. "No goodterna," he said, and strode out into the sunshine.

We arrived back in camp not a moment too soon. Even from the distance we could see the great assembly of our fellow-prisoners making preparations to go. The sergeant-major was growing anxious, for he thought we had tried to make a sudden bid for freedom, and was wondering how he should explain our

* Mató—dead.

absence to the Japanese if they suddenly checked on our numbers. Strangely enough, the idea of trying to get away had never entered our heads, for both Nunn and I took it that there was no possible chance of securing a boat. Even if we had been fortunate enough to find one undamaged, and to make good our escape from Singapore, we had no knowledge of the tides and currents, and would most likely have drifted helplessly until recaptured by the Japanese. We might have hired the services of some friendly native who knew the waters, and slipped away under cover of darkness, but our combined resources amounted to some thirty dollars only, and no native would have dared his boat or his life for such a paltry sum. To escape northwards over the Causeway into Johore might have been possible, but neither of us had ever been over the Causeway before. We should have had to pass through the Japanese lines to begin with, and, as our arms were now gone, we should have been ill-equipped for such a perilous adventure. Besides, we did not know whether the Japanese had offered rewards for the return, dead or alive, of fugitives from Singapore. In that unknown jungle we would have a very slender chance of eluding native trackers. The odds against our getting clear at this stage in our captivity were tremendous. Later, perhaps, if we got to know the country better, we might make a bid for it.

It was now after eleven o'clock, and we stood in a long, ragged queue, awaiting the pleasure of the Japanese. We were in full marching order. Our kitbags had been loaded on the lorries, and were to follow us to our destination, whatever that might be. There was much speculation as to whither we were bound. Some had it that we were to embark on Japanese transports for Japan; other that we were to march up-country into Johore.

We marched in sections of thirty men each. At the head of each section went one of our officers, and in the flanks Japanese infantry, two to a section. British, Australian and Indian sections were kept strictly apart one from another. Some of our more light-hearted comrades began to whistle, but were curtly ordered by the guards to be silent. I plodded along quietly, with Shaw and Nunn by my side, busy with my own thoughts. Nothing was to be heard but the tramp of marching

37

feet and the occasional clink of a water-bottle. The long line of men seemed to stretch for miles along the white highway. There was little or no traffic on the roads. Rickshaw drivers pulled up as we passed.

Reaching the centre of the city, we struck off in a north-easterly direction, along the broad Serangoon Road which led to Paya Lebar village. By this time the native population had heard of our movements, and began to throng the pavements, excitedly waving Japanese flags. Taunting, scornful words were hurled at us as we passed by. It was an ordeal, but we had prepared ourselves for it. Curiously enough, the Japanese themselves did not appear to be entirely in sympathy with the onlooking crowd. A Malay ran out suddenly from the throng into the roadway and openly spat at Harris, who was just in front of me. I saw Harris' broad shoulders hunch in fury, and he turned his head for a moment to glance at his tormentor. There was murder in his eyes. Just as the Malay was strutting alongside, gathering enough spittle to attack me next, the Japanese guard, without a word, brought his rifle-butt down viciously on the back of the native's head. The Malay fell unconscious, and the Japanese in the column behind us kicked him out of his path. As I turned my head to see the native's fate, our guard smote me roughly on the shoulder with his fist, and ordered me to keep my eyes to the front.

Not all of the bystanders eyed us with contempt. Some stood silently with a great compassion in their eyes, as they watched us go under the Japanese yoke. I saw a woman weep. Perhaps she had already lost some loved one in the holocaust of Singapore, and had no cause to love the invaders. I idly wondered whether there might still be faithful natives, working for our cause underground. From what I had already seen of the Japanese methods, I had little doubt that any uprising or sabotage on the part of the native community would be punished with terrible ferocity. But dauntless souls were already busy in the occupied countries of Europe. Why not in Singapore? In the Chinese war the Japanese had behaved atrociously. There were plenty of Chinese in Singapore, and they would have no reason to forgive or to forget the barbarities which their kinsmen had suffered in China. Our hope of salvation might lie with them in the end.

In Paya Lebar village the long column fell out for an unexpected break of fifteen minutes. A shrill whistle from far in front brought the Japanese guards up to a sudden halt, and I collided with Harris, and he with the man in front of him, like a line of shunting wagons. Our guard turned towards us and shouted "Yasume". This apparently signified 'rest'. It was a word which we came to hail with thankfulness in the subsequent years of our captivity. We all relaxed on a grassy bank which bordered the hot dusty road. Our guards gathered in little groups, smoking. The sun shone brilliantly, and streams of perspiration ran down my back. I took a quick pull at my water-bottle and slackened the laces of my boots. I had never been a wonderful route-marcher, even in the more pleasant English climate, and I suspected that I was soon to develop two lovely blisters, one on the sole of each foot. It was already afternoon, and, in a few more hours, tropical night would be upon us. It looked rather as if the rumour of our marching northwards into Johore might be true after all. Yet I could not understand why we should have been brought this roundabout way. The Bukit Timah road was much more direct.

From where I sat on the bank I could see the house which had for a time been our section headquarters. It was a ruin. The police station which stood opposite was gutted, and its once white walls were blackened. During the action, I had jailed a Malay there, suspected of sabotage. I wondered what had happened to the wretch. Had he been burned to death in a locked cell, or had his friends released him in time?

A long whistle sounded down the roadway and we struggled back into line. Once more the weary tramp of marching feet had begun. I tightened my belt and eased my pack up on my shoulders.

As we went along, the column suddenly made a wide detour round something which lay by the wayside. As we came up I saw that it was the burned-out shell of a motor-car. It was a mere skeleton of twisted steel. Beside it, on the road, lay the charred corpses of three or four human beings. I could see the

D

scene so clearly. The sudden whine of the shell, the screech of brakes, the hurried dash out of the car for shelter, the frightful explosion, the flames, the agonising struggles of the blazing victims. The flies were already busy near the car. For all their callousness, the Japanese did not find the gruesome sight any more pleasant than we. Our guard put his handkerchief over his mouth as he passed.

At Somapeh village there was a fork in the road. One branch led on to Serangoon and Punggol creek on the Straits. I had travelled that road during the action and had found it to be a dead-end. We must, therefore, turn right. And then I saw what a dim-witted fool I had been. For mile upon mile I had been racking my brains, trying to guess our destination. Of course it was the great British barracks at Changi Point. During my whole stay on the island, I had never once had an occasion to visit Changi. As we turned right at the fork, I cast a quick glance at Shaw. "Aren't I the almighty ass!" he whispered, "I was at Changi ten days ago, and it had entirely slipped my mind. Where else could we be going?" "What was it like when you were there, Bill?" I asked. "Very nice," replied Bill, "but you must remember that was ten days ago—before the Japs came."

As darkness fell we were still five miles from Changi. We were all utterly exhausted, for we had received nothing to eat all day. Shaw staggered several times and eventually whispered that he thought he would have to fall out. As we stumbled along, Harris took his pack, Nunn his water-bottle and I his haversack. Thus lightened, he felt easier. Men began to divest themselves of their equipment as they trudged along. But we held to ours like grim death, and followed the white ribbon of a road.

We staggered into Changi Barracks at nine o'clock that evening. I was nearly blind with fatigue, and so sleepy that my eyelids refused to keep open. My blisters had grown to two great agonising patches of raw flesh. I did not see where I was going, nor did I greatly care. The long wailing whistle signalled us to halt. Many men collapsed where they stood. Some of our own men, who had been sent on ahead by lorry from Singapore to receive us, lit the way with blazing torches. Shaw was all-in by this time, and Nunn and I put our arms round him to support him the last few yards, although we were hard put to it to support ourselves. We went along a narrow concrete path and entered a building. Someone shouted that a meal was ready, but I was too tired to eat. All I wanted to do was to sleep. We helped Shaw into a long, dark room, and I felt the crunch of broken glass below my feet. We could go not another step. Nunn and I spread out our ground-sheets anyhow on the floor, and the three of us sank down on them full-length. I did not even take the trouble to remove my boots. I doubted whether I had the energy to do so anyway. With my pack under my head, I fell asleep immediately. We had been on the march for over nine hours, with no food and only scanty rest-intervals. Those eighteen miles from Singapore had seemed like eighty. It had been a gruelling and humiliating experience.

II

The First Year

"Taboleh maso!"* THE MALAY JUMPED FROM HIS BICYCLE and halted only a few feet from me. His dark eyes were full of anger. I grasped my bamboo cane more firmly, and signalled to Nunn to come and join me. The Malay stared at us both for a moment, then spat in the dust. "Taboleh maso!" I repeated, pointing with my cane in the direction of Singapore, from whence he had come. His lips curled in a contemptuous sneer, but he ventured no farther. "Get out of it, emshi, you stupid fool!" shouted Nunn, brandishing his cane, "You're not allowed through this gate, understand?" The Malay, muttering resentfully, swung round his machine, remounted, and pedalled off. Nunn and I returned to our positions.

We stood on guard at the main gate of Changi Camp. We had been prisoners-of-war for exactly a month—a monotonous, unpleasant month, in which we had more or less become accustomed to our new mode of life. In many ways, our condition might have been worse. We might have been crowded into uncomfortable quarters, denied sufficient food, or subjected to constant interference by the Japanese. In times of peace, Changi Barracks had been a magnificent, well-equipped military settlement, with spacious buildings, modern hospital, theatre, canteen and sports grounds. During the action the Japanese had bombed and shelled the whole area, seeking to destroy the massive 15-inch guns, concealed in fortified positions along the fringe of the barracks. Finally the enemy had landed in strength on Changi Point, fighting dourly against stiff resistance. The barracks had been constructed primarily to withstand bombardment from the sea, and most of the blocks ran north and south.

* Taboleh Maso (Malay)—Passage forbidden.

42

This had saved them from utter annihilation by the Japanese artillery, ranged in the north, across the Johore Straits. Much damage had been done, nevertheless. Walls had been cracked, rooms gutted by fire, roofs holed and concrete paths split like crazy-paving.

Under Japanese supervision, we had fenced ourselves in just after arrival. The British, Australian and Indian troops had their separate enclosures or areas. The hospital stood in an enclosure of its own. At regular intervals round the camp perimeter, gates were fixed in the twelve-foot high fence. These were guarded, not by Japanese, but by the prisoners themselves. It was a ludicrous position. The Japanese seemed to be very sure that we would not try to escape. They had very good reason to be, for they controlled the seas, the island of Singapore itself and the hinterland of Malaya. Escapes had been attempted by several dauntless souls, however. We heard that two men had got as far as Kuala Lumpur, before being intercepted by Japanese patrols. Their fate was unknown, but it was rumoured that they had been beheaded. The enemy did not view escape favourably. To him it was all rather like a childish game of hide-and-seek. We had been caught, and had, therefore, no right to take a further part in the game. If we tried to hide again, we were not playing fair, and deserved punishment. In many respects our captors resembled children. They laughed immensely at their own simple jokes; they were fascinated by mechanical toys; they loved to draw moon-like caricatures in the dust with their fingers, and tease their comrades. But as children can be callously insensitive to the sufferings of lesser animals, inflicting agony on some wounded bird or kitten, so could the Japanese be equally irresponsible in their treatment of their prisoners-of-war. We were their playthings, to be fussed over, pushed good-naturedly around, and finally to be cast away in a corner, or torn limb from limb. We could never quite accustom ourselves to this strange, oriental mentality, but we could always be sure that, when those uniformed children began to laugh, it was a sure signal that we might prepare ourselves for some event of diabolical fury, of which we or our comrades were to be the unhappy victims.

Just to remind us that we had not been entirely forgotten, the Japanese set one or two sentries at strategic points in the camp. These patrolled the area by day and night, travelling often in single file, like the dwarfs in "Snow White". We were supervised by an odd, shambling, unwashed trio, whom we came to term Freeman, Hardy and Willis. Occasionally they inspected our billets, our belongings and our persons. Freeman had a taste for Virginia tobacco, so our meagre cigarette supplies had to be carefully concealed on his arrival. Hardy was apparently a non-smoker but liked fountain-pens and wristlet-watches. Willis had a mania for rings and cap-badges. Through crass carelessness, I had already been obliged to deliver to Hardy my much-cherished Parker Duofold fountain-pen. While illustrating to the little thief how excellent a pen it was, I had at least succeeded in breaking the point, but I had no doubt but that it would still fetch Hardy high money in the native 'black market'. I determined in future not to display my watch nor my cigarette-case quite so prominently. Such articles were apparently as much the spoils of war as petrol-dumps and ammunition-piles.

Twenty minutes still to go before the new guards arrived to take over duty. It was mid-afternoon and the sun was hot. Nunn stood opposite me, across the roadway, his back propped against the gate-post. His cane hung loosely in his grasp, his eyelids were half-closed. He was exceedingly drowsy, for he had been awake half the night killing bed-bugs which tormented him. My hide seemed to be rather thicker than his, for I had not been unduly troubled. I had squashed a couple of the brutes on my face, though, and that sickening sweet smell still hung in my nostrils. I made a mental note to borrow a blow-lamp from the store before nightfall. I would burn the little pests out of the wall-cracks.

A long green lalang snake wriggled out of the grass near where Nunn stood, passing within a foot of his leg. Nunn did not stir, for he was a keen naturalist, and would not strike an animal or a reptile, unless it attacked him. Curiously I watched the serpent cross the road. I had no fear of this particular species, for it was not poisonous. It came directly towards me, moving slowly, almost laboriously, as if it had come a long way. Its brilliant green scales glistened in the bright sunshine. I could see the little head darting furtively from side to side, and the forked tongue shooting out like a short black boot-lace. I stepped softly aside, laying my cane down on the ground, directly in the snake's path. It stopped, and the little diamond-shaped head was raised inquiringly. Then it reached the cane. Once more it stopped, drawing in its lithe body in a coil. The little tongue flickered along the cane, and then the reptile changed course abruptly, slithering off into the undergrowth. "I'm glad you didn't kill it, Mac," said Nunn quietly, from the other side of the road. "I didn't intend to," I replied, "I like animals, though I can't say I feel very much at home with snakes." "I like that green, lalang snake," said Nunn, with a laugh, "it eats bugs!"

Still ten minutes to go. I peered across the padang * towards the distant barrack-block. Shaw and Harris should be relieving us soon. To stand idly at that gate for two solid hours was a boring business.

Suddenly, through the trees, I caught a glimpse of a column of men moving slowly towards us. I turned inquiringly to Nunn. "Funeral," he muttered, "we'd better get ready." The cortege came nearer. In front of the procession, quite alone walked the padre, his head sunk forward on his breast. Then followed the stretcher, borne on the shoulders of four men of the Cambridgeshire Regiment. It was draped with the Union Jack. A trumpeter, two officers and some twenty men followed with measured tread, silently, their heads erect, their eyes to the front. One of the officers carried a small Japanese flag, without which no man or party of men might enter or leave the camp.

The cemetery lay without the main gate. As the column slowly passed through, I paid my last silent salute to a young soldier going to his rest. It was tragic that this lad should have survived the perils of war, only to die in captivity. The Union Jack lay over him, softly and tenderly, the proud sad symbol of a mourning nation.

A Japanese staff-car drove in quickly from the direction of

* Padang (Malay)—Grassy plain or meadow.

Singapore. As the procession moved over quietly to allow the car sufficient room to pass, I saw the officer lean forward and speak to his driver. The car stopped. The two Japanese got out quickly, and bowed as the men from England passed them by. The gesture was unnoticed by the marching column. The procession moved on to the burying-place. After a little while, the Last Post was sounded. The soldier had gone on to join his comrades, his fetters unloosed, his broken limbs made whole, his soul rejoicing.

General Fuku was coming to see us. This arrogant Japanese warlord, conqueror of Malaya and Singapore, was reported to have said that he would bring the British soldier lower than any coolie in the Far East. His troops were doing their best to carry out his proud threat, but so far the obstinate British, both in Singapore and in Changi, had shown little repentance for having dared to oppose the victorious forces of Dai Nippon *. They had, in fact, even gone so far as to declare that, when fresh British divisions and aircraft landed on Singapore, General Fuku himself would most probably be pulling a rickshaw through the streets. Such defiance was intolerable. Did those miserable prisoners-of-war not realise that, had it not been for his surpassing generosity, they would have been shot down like pariahs on the Bukit Timah road? They evidently did not. They must be taught a lesson.

Freeman, Hardy and Willis almost performed cartwheels of joy as they told us of the General's coming. Fuku was the greatest man in the Japanese army, Number one Nippon, infinitely greater than Churchill, Roosevelt or Stalin. He had commanded Nipponese troops in China, and had covered himself with glory. In the Malayan campaign he had been as wise as the serpent, as courageous as the lion. His men had died for him without question. Banzai!† We gently reminded the three oriental chimpanzees that Tojo surely was Nippon Number One. They corrected themselves quickly. Tojo was Number One, but Fuku was Number Two. We replied that Churchill was Number

* Dai Nippon (Jap.)—Mighty Japan.

† Banzai—Hurrah! (Literally, 10,000 years).

One and Tojo Number Ten, with Fuku Number Eleven. The trio growled oaths shook fists and brandished rifles.

From an early hour we had been assembling on Changi parade-ground. This was a huge square of tarmacadam and concrete, surrounded by storage sheds. We stood in long, untidy ranks under the hot sun, waiting patiently for the order to move. The Japanese had counted us at least five times, and were now apparently satisfied that their numbers were correct. For the moment they had left us alone. I thoughtfully surveyed the other members of the section as they stood around me. They were rather a dishevelled-looking company. Two months of wood-carrying and latrine-digging had already begun to leave their mark on their faces. The sergeant-major looked much older, somehow, and there were little lines round the corners of Livesley's eyes. Shaw's hair had grown to an unruly mop, and Harris looked as if he had not shaved for several days. Wrigley had a worried look on his face; Ullman appeared completely bored. Dorfman and Bussey were smart enough. Captivity did not seem to have affected them so badly as the others. I glanced quickly at myself. I had always been lean, but I thought I was just a trifle leaner than before. My shorts were soiled with mud and sweat, and the toe-cap of my right boot was hanging off. Nevertheless, I felt fit enough, and was already deeply tanned. I thought of Lemin, Gibberd and the others, and wondered where they might be at that moment. We had heard nothing of or from them since the capitulation of Singapore. A week or so before, a British officer had, we were told, been brought to Changi hospital in a piteously haggard state. He was the sole survivor of a small party of men who had got away just before the fall of the city. They had been driven ashore on one of the countless small uninhabited islands lying off Singapore, and there the Japanese had left them, without water, to die. Racked with thirst and fever-striken, the unhappy creatures had died horribly, one after another. This officer, in desperation, had finally lit a beacon which had been seen by a passing Japanese sloop. A boat had been lowered and the man had been rescued in the nick of time. He lay in hospital, fighting for his life against an attack of blackwater fever. Dorfman had succeeded in eluding the hospital guards and had visited the sick man. It was not Lemin. We breathed again.

A whistle sounded shrilly across the parade-ground. Away in front, the column was on the move. The Japanese guards fell in on their accustomed positions on the flank. We were off, marching down the road which led to Singapore.

After covering a little over a mile, we halted suddenly and fell out by the wayside. The sun was hot, but a cool breeze had sprung up and the air was not so much like the inside of an oven as usual. We seated ourselves on a grassy bank bordering the road, and dangled our throbbing feet in the monsoon drain. It was almost noon. We were evidently to receive no midday meal.

The Japanese guards were more excited than usual. They gathered in little groups in the roadway, chattering together and gesticulating. An officer, armed with his ancestral sword, came slowly past and the soldiers fairly leapt to attention. There was much bowing, much head-nodding, much smiling. It was apparently a great day in their lives. We looked on idly, half-asleep. For the time being, we had apparently been forgotten.

An hour passed. Shaw and I sat back-to-back and we were both almost asleep. Then, suddenly, a small, open Japanese staff-car drew up opposite us with a screech of brakes. Officers jumped out and shouted at the sentries. They in turn shouted at us and we became alert once more. We struggled to our feet and took up our positions in a long line flanking the route. The Japanese guards fell in in front of us, their backs to the roadway. I thought this curious, until I discovered long after-wards, that, though a cat may look at a king, a Japanese private may not look at a general. The minutes passed.

Just in front of where we stood, the road rose sharply, so Fuku was actually upon us before we fully realised that it was he. A car passed first, crowded with high-ranking naval officers. Then another with army 'brass-hats'. Our guards were fairly trembling with emotion. Third in the procession came a magnificent Buick with open hood and gleaming black chassis. The car travelled quite slowly. The chauffeur sat rigidly at the wheel. At the back stood General Fuku, and I gazed curiously at this man whom Freeman had so devotedly described as Number One Nippon.

The General was at least six feet in height—a giant by Japanese standards. He wore a dark-green uniform, peaked cap, Sam Browne and brown leather gloves. He carried a revolver in a holster on his belt and in one hand held a mighty sword, with its hilt bedecked with coloured tassels. He was so broad in the shoulder that he seemed to be bursting out of his uniform.

On the back-seat of the Buick lay a ciné-camera, and just as the car drew abreast of us it halted for a moment. Fuku quickly laid his sword down on the seat and lifted his camera. We were to have our photographs taken. How funny! After pelting us with shells and bombs, Fuku was to put us in the family album! "Smile, Mac," whispered Nunn, mockingly, "the nice General wants this to be a really good photograph." Fuku was sighting along the line of captives. I am afraid I spoilt the snap, for I moved my head at the crucial moment to look at Nunn. My jaw dropped open in amazement. Nunn was very coolly and nonchalantly cocking a snook at the General! It took every effort to keep my face straight. Fuku, gazing through the view-finder, had evidently missed this. What a blessing for Nunn's sake! The General now surveyed us with a cold disinterest, and I thought I had never seen such a bland, merciless face. In his hands our future would certainly be unpleasant. The Buick moved slowly on. I turned to Nunn. "You are a crazy mutt!" I cried. "Oh well, it was worth it," he replied with a grin, "That's one picture that won't be shown in Tokyo."

We did not see the General again. After a quick inspection of the camp and the hospital, he returned to Singapore by a different route.

In May, 1942, a Japanese grammar, complete with vocabulary, mysteriously found its way into Changi Camp. This slim, dog-eared volume had once stood on one of the shelves of the Raffles College in Singapore. It had passed from hand to hand until finally Dorfman, sensing that it might possibly be of some future value to the section, procured it from a British lorry-driver in exchange for two cigarettes.

49

On first examining the little book, we were generally of the opinion that the lorry-driver had had the best of the bargain. Most of us had a passing knowledge of European languages, and had accustomed ourselves, in our study of them, to master the usual preliminary ground-work of simple words and phrases, without which little real progress or facility of expression could be hoped for. Shortly after our arrival in Changi, Livesley, who had been a teacher of Spanish before the outbreak of war, had commenced an interesting conversational class in the language. He had begun his first lesson by giving us a detailed explanation of the subtleties of Spanish pronunciation, and now, after several lessons, we were acquiring several simple, everyday words.

The writer of our Japanese grammar did not, however, favour such a straightforward method of approach. To bewilder us at the very outset, he informed us that there were three distinct forms of the Japanese tongue, each form varying in accordance as to whether we conversed with a common citizen, an elevated citizen or with the Emperor of Japan himself. He passed on quickly to state that, as it was most unlikely that his gentle reader would ever have cause to pass the time of day with Hirohito, The Divine One, the Sun of Imperial Japan, he might safely disregard this third most honorific form of expression. That left the student with merely two forms to master. Was that as easy as it sounded? It was not.

There was the little matter of intonation to be taken into due account. At the end of a word, the voice might be raised, kept level or dropped at will. Should the voice be raised, the word might signify 'bamboo', should it be kept level, the same word would indicate 'young woman', should it be dropped, the word mysteriously meant 'a dog'. In that alone, I could forsee highly embarrassing situations. Then followed a puzzling array of Japanese symbols, differing one from another only by the faintest up or down stroke. Some resembled palm-trees, other pagodas. We were relieved to learn, however, that, in many cases, the old symbolic writing, which was performed with a brush, had now been replaced by a much simplified form, termed 'the running Kana', which could be written with a fountain-pen. I had heard it said that, for a student to master Chinese, he had first to go mad. The same appeared to hold good for the Nipponese tongue. Spanish was veritable child's-play in comparison with this frightful language.

At the end of the grammar I discovered a short list of everyday phrases, and a comprehensive vocabulary. This was more useful, and I carefully mastered some twenty key-words for future reference. These included such terms as 'watakushi' ('I myself'), 'tomadachi' ('friend' or 'comrade'), 'kudasai' ('please'). In my innocence I thought that I had but to string one or two such words together to form a coherent sentence, but I found that, when a Japanese invited you to sit down, he actually said 'Will you condescend to gird your loins over yonder chair?' At that point, I gave the language up as hopeless.

Ullman, however, was made of sterner stuff. I have never discovered whether a Jew's powers of concentration are greater than those of other men, but Ullman certainly did not give up easily. Hour after hour, when the daily fatigues were completed, he sat on his ground-sheet, alone and apart from the rest of us, poring over the pages of the dingy little grammar. He borrowed paper from us upon which to practise the intricate symbols and running Kana. In a month's hard study, he had made remarkable progress.

From then on, John Ullman began to rise rapidly to power as an interpreter. The Japanese could not pronounce the letter 'l' properly, substituting the letter 'r' in its place. Thus Ullman became 'Uruman' for the Japanese. To all sentries in the camp, he was known as 'Uruman san' or 'Mr. Ullman'. None of the rest of us was accorded such a title of distinction. As the days passed into weeks and the weeks into months, Ullman's duties became more and more specialised. He was chief interpreter in the British area, ironing out language problems, settling minor disputes, assisting the Japanese at nightly roll-calls. He received no preferential treatment for his services, no extra pay. He had simply taken great pains to learn a foreign tongue properly, and had found a use for his knowledge. That that knowledge benefited us on more than one occasion, I have no doubt. I know that he insisted we learn, for our own good, the Japanese method of counting from one to a hundred, and by degrees the new numbers were mastered. From then on, at roll-calls, we could shout out our numbers in the line correctly, and thus escape the inevitable buffet with which the exasperated Japanese greeted the efforts of some of our less-enlightened, English-counting comrades.

On 20th June, 1942, we were all permitted, for the first time since the capitulation, to communicate with home. Each man received a blank postcard upon which he was to send a simple message, numbering not more than twenty words. Faced with this awful limitation of language, I racked my brains to think out a suitably worded communication. For every man it was a desperately difficult business. On odd sheets of paper I scribbled out at least twenty trial messages, scrapping them, one after another. One would be too short; another too long; another too vague and cheerless. We had no indication as to how much we were allowed to tell of our whereabouts. Perhaps our folks at home already knew that we were in Changi. Better not mention any place-names anyway to be on the safe side. It would be tragic if the Japanese refused to forward our precious cards just because we had made some innocent blunder. Lemin would surely have told my mother by now that we were prisoners-of-war. But how would Lemin have known? He left us two days before the surrender. We might have been killed after his departure. "I am a prisoner of war." Yes, that was definite enough, surely. If I had been posted as missing, that, at least would relieve their tortured minds a little. It would be but cold comfort to know that one's only son was held captive by such a barbarous enemy, but it was infinitely more satisfying than to continue wondering anxiously whether he were alive at all. What ought I to put next? "I am still with the Section"? No, that was redundant. When the other cards got home, they would take it naturally that we had remained together. Something about my health perhaps? The folks would be worrying about that. "I am fit and well." That would do nicely. That was no untruth. I wasn't like the lad in our hospital who had said the same thing, although one of his legs had been amputated. Yes, I felt fit enough. I was frequently hungry, but so were thousands of my fellow-prisoners. I did not care overmuch for boiled rice, but who did? I could not put that down on my postcard. How many precious words had I used up? Eleven. Including my signature, I had still seven to go. What else was there to say in seven words? Then I remembered that, in every letter that I had ever written to my people, I had invariably concluded with the words "God bless you all, Yours aye." If I said that, they would know for certain that I had written the card. Hastily and anxiously I counted up. Yes, I should just manage it, with one word to spare. Down went the old familiar ending, and I signed my name. The card was collected. I felt happy to think that, at last, a thin thread of contact had been formed with the outside world. Our loved ones at home would not be called upon to endure the burden of anxiety so very much longer. In two months, at the very most, our cards would be joyfully received.

My little card was delivered into the hands of my parents on 12th July, 1943—thirteen long, weary months later. By the time it arrived, I was no longer in Changi. I had made my ill-fated journey to Siam four months before.

On a bright afternoon in mid-August, 1942, I was sent with five other men to collect bags of rice from the central ration store on the parade-ground. We took with us a low, four-wheeled cart to help in bringing the heavy load back to our cook-house. On reaching the main storage-shed, we found a long line of carts from other units all waiting their turn, so we fell in quietly at the end of the queue. We should have at least half an hour to hang on. I sat down, cross-legged on the cart, and glanced down the main road, towards the west gate which opened to Singapore.

A covered lorry was just entering the camp. I paid scant attention to it at first, for lorries entered or left the camp many times during the day. As it slowly approached the parade-ground, however, I saw that a Japanese sentry stood on the running-board, giving the driver directions with his outstretched hand. This was something unusual. In those days of boredom anything unusual made us sit up and take immediate notice. We became attentive.

The lorry circled the parade-ground, coming to a stop just beside our little cart. The Japanese jumped off the running-board and signalled to the driver to get out. The driver was a young Punjabi. At a nod from the Japanese, he ran round to the back of the lorry and shouted something in those strange high-pitched tones, with which we had become so familiar during the action in Singapore. There was a sound of confused movement from within the lorry, and then, one by one, twenty more Punjabis jumped out, falling into two ranks before the Japanese. They chattered and laughed together, until curtly silenced by a quick gesture from the Japanese. "Bango!" (Number!) shouted the Japanese, and the Japanese numbers, 'ichi', 'ni', 'san', 'yong' came trippingly from the tongues of the Indian troops. I hardly heard them. I was staring, fascinated, at the Punjabis, like a rabbit at a snake. Each Indian carried a British Service rifle, and had a brown canvas bandolier of ammunition slung over his shoulder! I must be dreaming it all. I turned my eyes away quickly and then looked again. The Punjabis had now come to a 'For inspection, port arms' position, and the Japanese was walking slowly along the line, examining rifle-barrels. I looked round at my fellow-prisoners on the cart. They were as dumb-founded as I. Having completed his inspection, the Japanese gave a quick order, and the Indians fell out, remaining in a small, excited group round the lorry. They laughed and chattered together, and I could see the flashing gleam of their white teeth. Then I noticed something else. Each Punjabi bore on his tropical shirt, just above the left breast-pocket, a small square piece of white cloth, in the centre of which was a red circle. The Japanese Rising Sun! Then I saw it all too clearly. Those miserable, snivelling traitors had changed sides! There they stood insolently before us, still wearing a uniform to which they had brought nothing but dishonour, armed with rifles which had been held in far steadier and worthier hands than theirs. A great wave of white-hot anger surged over me. I glanced at my fellow-prisoners, and knew by their scowling brows and set jaws that they also fully realised what had happened. "God help those swine if they go out alone on a dark night!" I heard one of them mutter. A quick thrust of a knife in the darkness, the sickening thud of a stone on an Indian skull, the sudden strangling twist of a knotted rope round an Indian throat. One of the Punjabis caught me watching him, and must have seen the contempt in my eyes. He took a quick step towards me, his hand trembling on his rifle, and snarled. It was not quite such a convincing sort of snarl as that practised by his Japanese masters, but he would doubtless improve in time. In Changi camp he would have ample opportunity to try out his new culture. I surveyed the angry Indian coldly. He glanced round quickly, but the Japanese had gone round to the other side of the lorry. This was his chance. He took another menacing step towards where I sat on the cart. "Another couple of paces and I'll wrap that rifle round your neck, you black b——" shouted one of my companions, a burly sergeant of military police. The Indian hesitated at the sound of this voice of authority. There was fear in his eyes. He had changed his coat but not his courage. The sergeant, throwing all caution to the winds, rolled off the cart, his eyes blazing, his massive fists clenched. That was enough for the Punjabi. He turned quickly on his heel and fairly scampered back to join his fellows. Once more the party fell in, and, under the watchful eye of the Japanese, marched off with sloped arms in the direction of the hospital.

Two days later I was on guard duty at the hospital gate. Between the main hospital area and ours lay a sort of no-man's-land, roughly eighty yards wide. On my arrival to take up duty, I discovered two Punjabis on patrol in this intervening area. Although they passed regularly within a few feet of where I stood, they did not look at me, nor I at them. Presently the Punjabis were relieved by two gigantic, bearded Sikhs. The Sikhs had gone over to the enemy as well, had they? It would certainly go ill with them when the British soldier came into his own once more. We had heard it rumoured that the Japanese had been foolish enough to put Punjabis and Sikhs in control of the loyal Gurkha troops, imprisoned somewhere in Singapore. The fierce Gurkhas had said nothing, for they were men of action, not words. Every day at daybreak another Punjabi or

E

Sikh would be mysteriously missing from roll-call. The Gurkhas smiled knowingly—that funny little crooked oriental smile, which I had seen on their faces several months before, when they returned from some grim night patrol, proudly displaying a grisly collection of Japanese ears, upon which the blood had barely had time to dry. They lived for battle, those bloodthirsty little men. Their loyalty was unquestioned. When they were released, their vengeance would be terrible.

A small party of British sick had drawn up at my gate, and waited patiently for one of the Sikhs to come and conduct them across the no-man's-land to the hospital. The Sikh had seen them standing there, white and ill, some leaning on sticks, others supported by their comrades, but he strolled across with maddening slowness of step. With a lazy movement of his hand he signalled to me to let the party through. I stood aside and the men passed me, limping, stumbling, with drawn faces and trembling limbs. One man, hobbling forward with the aid of two walking-sticks, his feet bandaged, began immediately to fall behind the marching column. He would have fallen, but I quickly stepped forward and took his arm. He stood still for a moment gasping. Then he looked up at me and smiled. "Thanks, chum," he said, "my feet are bad, but I've got to make it, somehow. Let me go on alone. I'll catch up with the rest." By this time one of the Sikhs had come quickly across to join us. He stood gazing at the sick man dispassionately. The main party, noticing my sick friend's predicament, had now halted a little way farther on, and two men had turned back to give assistance. I waited quietly, my arm round the man's shoulders. Suddenly the giant Sikh burst into a torrent of words and raised his rifle-butt menacingly. His beard trembled and his black eyes flashed with anger. Then, without warning, he coldly and quite deliberately kicked my sick comrade on the shin with his heavy ammunition boot. The man writhed in agony. This was more than I could bear. Quickly releasing my groaning friend, I turned on the Sikh, blind with fury, reckoning nothing of the consequences, determined to strangle this bearded Goliath with my bare hands. The Sikh, giant though he was, fell back immediately. His eyes were full of fear. Then, quickly, recovering himself, he raised his rifle, his finger on the trigger, the muzzle pointing directly at my breast.

"Curra, bagero!" I heard a shout behind me, and at the same moment received a blow on the shoulder which almost paralysed my arm. Still trembling with rage, I turned to find myself face-to-face with a Japanese gunso or sergeant. He must have come upon us quickly from the British area. The Sikh lowered his rifle like lightning and pulled himself up to attention. The gunso turned inquiringly to me. This was my chance. I pointed to the sick man, whose face was still twisted with pain. "O gomen nasai" I stuttered, bowing to the Japanese, "tomadachi very sick. India man kick tomadachi." I quickly went through the motions of kicking my sick friend and then turned and pointed at the Sikh. The Indian trembled with fear. The gunso indicated with a quick movement of his hand that I was to return to my position at the gate. He then signalled to the two men of the party who had turned back that they were to help their comrade forward. Then he turned on the Sikh. With a sudden forward lunge, he wrested the rifle from the Indian's hands, dropping it on the red earth. He then seized the man by his beard and shook him to and fro as a terrier shakes a rat. There was no mercy in those cold oriental eyes. The Sikh sank to his knees in front of the gunso, his mouth frothing, his eyes bloodshot. The Japanese released his grip on the man's beard, and brought up his knee with a sickening crunch on the Indian's chin. I glanced quickly at the other Sikh, but he was standing stock-still in terror. This was something in which he dared not interfere. The sudden vicious blow had caught the Sikh squarely on the point of the jaw and he rolled back in agony. The gunso picked up the rifle, and for one moment I thought he was going to shoot the fallen man. "Sikh!" snarled the Japanese. The Sikh raised his head. "Curra!" shouted the Japanese, and flung the heavy rifle back at him. The barrel caught the Indian on the side of the head and opened a great jagged tear on his cheek. The blood poured from the wound. Turning on his heel, the Japanese strode off towards the hospital, The party passed through, but still the second Sikh stood as if rooted to the spot. I wondered whether he was perhaps beginning to regret that he

57

had gone over to the enemy. His comrade had less interest in the proceedings, for he lay, half in and half out of the monsoon drain, his face blood-bespattered, his jaw broken. As he rolled his great body to and fro in pain, he whimpered like a frightened child. The Japanese evidently believed in making the punishment more than fit the crime.

Corporal Denis O'Brien—or plain Danny to his many friends—was a bright lad. He it was who first conceived the idea of forming a Prisoners' Dramatic Society in Changi camp, and of constructing a theatre within the British area. Danny was not particularly concerned whether the Dramatic Society performed grand tragedy or strip-tease, provided it helped to keep high the morale of his fellow-men. Entertainment of the prisoners was something which the Japanese regarded as totally unnecessary. If those fools of Englishmen enjoyed dressing up as children or pirouetting round a raised open platform as the Ovaltiney Babies, there appeared to be no real danger in it. True, their idiotic gyrations convulsed their fellow-prisoners with laughter, but that cheerfulness could always be lessened somewhat by extra latrine duties.

Danny O'Brien began most sensibly by laying his theatre plans fairly and squarely under the very nose of Nagewa himself, the Japanese regimental sergeant-major in the camp. Nagewa was a tough campaigner who had served in China and Malaya. He had not been home on leave for seven years, and was beginning to get just a trifle bored. Life in Changi was so unlike anything which he had encountered before. This Englishman with the dark hair and twinkling eyes was rather a comedian. He had an open frank face. What sort of building was this that he sought permission to erect? A theatre? Nagewa had never heard of such a place, but he was interested to learn more. Something new would be something welcome. But wait a bit. Did Englishmen pray in a theatre?

Danny assured him solemnly, by eloquent gesture, that Englishmen normally prayed in a church, and sang, clapped or went to sleep in a theatre. Nagewa was satisfied. Who would build the theatre? Where was sufficient wood to be procured?

Where did the English corporal think he could procure electricity?

Danny was equal to the occasion. His fellow-prisoners would help him to build the new edifice. Some were carpenters, others qualified electricians. Sufficient wood could, with Nagewa's permission, be procured in Changi village, where several wooden native houses still lay in ruins. It would not be difficult to take an electric cable from the camp's power-house. Nagewa considered the matter. He would consult his superiors in Singapore. If they had no objections, he would have none, and the work might proceed. If necessary, the new building could always be used as a rice-store.

Nagewa did not shelve the project. Within a week Danny was given official leave to carry on and his willing band of helpers soon got down to business. Joiner tools were available in the store, loose cable lay around the camp in large quantities. The theatre began to take shape. Nagewa himself was an interested onlooker.

The building of the auditorium was a simple enough matter. Straight poles were driven into the earth and cross-beams secured with strips of coco-nut fibre, instead of nails. The roof and sides were of dried palm-leaves, or attap. The stage was a solid erection, with three short ladders to serve as exits and entrances. Openings were left in the sides of the building for the audience to come and go.

The fitting of a small switchboard, controlling footlights and a single overhead batten was a more intricate affair. The Australians readily came to our assistance with bulbs and floods which they had unearthed in a store-house in their own area. Stage drapes were a headache, but the hospital lent us small quantities of canvas and tarpaulin which we joined together. In a remarkably short space of time, Danny's ideal had come true. We had a theatre. It was not a wonderful theatre, but then prisoners-of-war are not unduly fussy. An audience of two hundred could be accommodated, and the stage measured some twenty feet by fourteen. There was no seating in the auditorium, except for several old benches at the front. These were our orchestra stalls, reserved for officers. Lesser personages squatted on the earthen floor, or, if they were fortunate enough, on wooden boxes, which they brought with them to each performance.

While the theatre-building had been in progress, the drama group had not been idle. Rather ironically, perhaps, the first play to be performed was Sherriff's *Journey's End*,—that sad, gripping work dealing with that other war in which our fathers had died in defence of the same cause for which we had fought. A rather tattered copy of the script had been found in the camp, and casting began immediately. Our own Livesley took the principal role of the hard-drinking but efficient Stanhope, and Raleigh was taken by Bacon, a tall, fair-haired Norfolk lad. Danny himself very appropriately portrayed the cheerful Trotter. Although I had little skill as an actor, I was given the part of the German prisoner, having knowledge of the German tongue. We all used the same copy of the script. Rehearsals were begun.

From the very start the play went with a swing. It was a man's play, and we all felt at home in our parts. Stage properties did not present such a problem as we had anticipated. We borrowed wooden bedsteads from the barrack-rooms and empty boxes from the cook-house. Tunics, greatcoats, trousers, leather belts, revolver holsters and steel helmets were readily available in the camp stores. Danny was quite ready to ask Nagewa for real weapons as well, but on thinking the matter over, we decided to run no risks and make our own from wood.

As the German prisoner I had to have a distinctive uniform, but this matter was speedily arranged through the kindness of certain Dutch prisoners who had by then arrived in our camp from Java. They lent me a faded green outfit, which was an excellent substitute for the German field-grey.

Our stage-manager, electricians and carpenters had done their job well. By a cunning system of suspended cords and pulleys, the final collapse of the overhead beams of the dug-out was effected most realistically. As my part in the play was a relatively small one, I had also a hand in producing sound-effects. For the distant rumble of gunfire, we beat with our fists on the base of an empty 50-gallon petrol drum, and for the occasional chatter of the machine-guns we brought hinged pieces of wood smartly together. To produce the final shattering explosion in the third act, six of us, standing round the petrol drum, hurled into it simultaneously an armful of large stones and pieces of broken concrete.

By permission of the Japanese, Australian and Dutch prisoners from other areas were brought in parties to see the play. We opened on a Monday evening, somewhat nervously perhaps, but nevertheless determined to do our best. The performance was excellently received. On Tuesday evening all our senior officers attended. They applauded vociferously. We had found our feet and were much more confident of our lines. Wednesday's performance was given to a house so packed that men were almost sitting on the front of the stage itself.

We had hoped to make Thursday's performance particularly good, as our audience was to be an all-Australian one. We had no front curtain on our stage, changes of time being indicated merely by the switching on and off of footlights. As the play opened that Thursday evening, I peeped through a hole in our sky backing and saw the usual great sea of upturned faces beyond the glare of the footlights. It was another full house. I felt sure the Aussies would enjoy this play.

Raleigh had just made his first entrance when the rain began. At first it was but a tiny, flurrying patter on the roof, and the audience, so intent on the play, hardly heard it. As the play proceeded, the noise grew to a steady drumming. Important lines were lost, and at the back of the hall our public were already beginning to show signs of restiveness. The play began to sag in a most disturbing fashion. Our uncertainty emboldened our impatient audience. I heard a few distant catcalls and not a few oaths. This was terrible. The second and third acts were still to be played. We did not look forward to them.

At the end of the first act, we all had a hurried consultation back stage. What was to be done? Were we to bow our heads in submission to the elements and bluntly tell our audience to go home, or were we to carry on this travesty to its bitter end? Danny was magnificent. "To blazes with the weather," he said, "we'll put on the last two acts, whether the Aussies go home or not. This is a play worth doing and we're jolly well going to do it." Thus encouraged, we began the second act.

The rain had eased a little, but the damage had been done. The Australians were not a particularly tolerant audience. Suddenly the drumming on the roof died away as quickly as it had begun and we threw ourselves into our parts with renewed enthusiasm. It was too late. The audience did not like the play. If they had simply withheld their applause, we should not have felt so badly, but their animosity took a more active form. They commenced to pass humorous asides which were not at all in keeping with the general atmosphere. These began with the excellent scene where Hibbert, the shirker, attempts to go sick before the big enemy attack. "Go on, Stanhope!" said an encouraging voice from the hall, "kick the little joker." "Give him M. and D." cried another. Stanhope controlled himself wonderfully well, ignoring this unexpected interruption. The play went on. Osborne read his lines from *Alice in Wonderland*. He could barely be heard for the storm of jeering laughter. "Oh, go home, Grandpa!" came a voice. Osborne did not falter.

Before the third act began, Danny went out alone on stage and made an honest, good-natured appeal for fair play from the unruly audience. His words were hardly heeded. He came back disappointed and angry. "They won't listen to a word I say," he said furiously. "These ill-bred swine don't deserve to see a play like this." "Are we scrapping the third act, Danny?" I asked. "Are we heck!" he shouted, "we'll play the third act or bust!" The third act began.

By the time it had gone a little way, I was really wondering whether the play was being performed on the stage or in the hall. As I made my brief appearance as the German prisoner, there was a great roar of applause, and for a moment I stood, dumbfounded, wondering for whom this ovation was intended. Then I realised that it was intended for me! The sympathy of the audience had apparently gone over to the Boche. I was listened to attentively, and without comment. As the sergeant-major searched me and relieved me of my precious letters, much against my will, the audience growled and booed. As I made my exit, I was given another round of applause. Then Raleigh entered, slowly and wearily, and received the colonel's congratulations for his dash and daring. The audience were not impressed. "Well done, my boy!" cried the colonel, "I'll get you a Military Cross for this!" "Aw, go and get stuffed!" came a voice from the hall. "Give him a D.S.O., give him a V.C.!" "Give 'im a kick in the pants!" cried another voice. The play gradually reached its climax with the death of Raleigh. Stanhope went to fetch another blanket to put on the dying boy. When he returned Raleigh was dead. "My God—he's dead!" cried Stanhope bitterly. "My God, so he is," cried the audience, "wrap up the show!" And we wrapped up the show, angrily, miserably, revengefully.

In our little play the principals all perished in the final act. The German prisoner did not die. By August, 1945, those same principals had died—not on the boards of Changi theatre, but in the tangled jungles of Malaya and Siam. The prisoner alone survived.

The Japanese were angry. Several prisoners had attempted to escape from Singapore and Changi, and it was rumoured that one of these at least had succeeded in eluding all patrols and had actually reached India. This had to be stopped somehow. It had been always said that an Englishman's word was his promise. A pledge of non-escape would, therefore, require to be obtained. It was remarkable that the Japanese could be so simple-minded as to credit a beaten enemy with such uprightness.

Nagewa called a conference of senior officers from the British, Dutch, and Australian areas. A Japanese officer from Singapore was also present. After evening roll-call was over, our officers visited us in our barrack-rooms. We listened attentively. The Japanese demanded that every man sign an official non-escape form immediately. Should we refuse, action would have to be taken in the matter. What further action could the Japanese take? We sought out John Ullman and asked his opinion. After all, he understood the strange minds of those orientals better than we.

Ullman was far from optimistic. The Japanese were not bluffing, he thought. They believed implicitly that, if they once obtained our written promise, they might rest assured that no further bids for freedom would be attempted. He suspected that the enemy desired to withdraw certain of his forces from Singapore, and was prepared to trust our word, backed up by only a thin garrison. The Indians, perhaps, might even be left in sole charge. Would it not be best to sign the form, and then patiently await the right moment to strike?

We considered the matter at length, weighing the pros and cons carefully. Finally we decided that the Japanese were bluffing. We would call their bluff. We would not sign the form. We told our officers that we weren't interested.

The next day passed without incident. We carried out our normal camp fatigues. Freeman, Hardy and Willis were no different from what they had been the day before. We had successfully called their bluff. They would have to think up something better next time.

Ullman was right and we were wrong. That evening, after roll-call, we were harangued in Japanese by a young officer in the parade-ground. He stood on a box the better to be seen, and spoke volubly for nearly ten minutes. His speech was translated. We were to sign the forms immediately, otherwise on the following day, severe penalties would be imposed. What could these penalties be, we asked ourselves. Starvation diet? That would not be much different from our already meagre ration. Solitary confinement? That couldn't be done with so many prisoners. Extra fatigues? They could be borne. Disturbed sleep? The bugs already saw to that most effectively. We would not give in so easily. We returned the form unsigned and lay down to sleep. Our officers did likewise.

I was awakened at dawn the following day by a tremendous clattering from our cook-house. I immediately rose and went along to find out what was afoot. On the broken concrete path which led past the cook-house there stood two large rice-carts, upon which the kitchen staff were piling all their pots, dixies and other utensils. I hurried up to the first man I met. "What's up?" I asked. "We've got to be out of here in an hour," he said gloomily, "Japanese orders." "But where are we going?" I stammered. "God knows," the man replied, shortly, and turned away. I ran back to break the news to the other members of the section. They were as mystified as I.

In less than half an hour, we were all called out on parade. We took our possessions with us and scrambled across the rough ground to the parade-square. There was no breakfast for anybody that morning. What new frightfulness had those little devils in store for us now?

We fell in under the baleful eye of a Sikh sentry and were counted. We were all there and the great parade-ground was black with men and carts. The Japanese moved excitedly through the throng, shouting, gesticulating and occasionally kicking men out of their way. Then, a little after eight o'clock, the order was given to move, and the mighty column began to march down the road to Singapore. What was to happen to us? I racked my brains to find a possible solution to the question as I swung along. Surely we were not once more to make that terrible march to Singapore? I doubted whether I could walk those eighteen miles again. I was certain that many of my less fit comrades couldn't. Shaw, for one, was suffering from the most violent attack of diarrhœa, and simply couldn't go far without having to fall out. Livesley had a pick-wound in his right foot which was quite evidently giving him plenty of trouble already, judging by his pursed lips. Nunn had a raw wound on his shoulder, and was carrying his pack in one hand like a portmanteau. He would not go on like that for long. I hitched my pack higher on my back and set my teeth. This was going to be a hell-march, in comparison with which our trip up from Singapore would seem to be little more than an afternoon stroll.

We had passed the spot where we had stood several months previously during Fuku's visit, when we arrived at a sudden fork in the road. A narrower road led off to the right in the direction of the Selerang barrack-block. These barracks lay roughly a mile west of Changi, and had previously formed part of the Changi military settlement. We had never been at Selerang before, as our infrequent excursions outside our wire, under Japanese escort, had mostly been in a southerly direction. The marching column turned off to the right.

As we approached the new barracks, my anxiety grew apace.

The building was in the form of a square, with a central parade-ground. At one time it had been a fine, roomy billet—for a limited number of men. Now triple-apron barbed-wire fencing ran round the outside of the building at a distance of only a few feet from the walls. This fencing was heavily patrolled by armed Sikhs and Punjabis. As I passed through the only entrance into the white parade-square, I could not help thinking of the old nursery rhyme about the spider and the fly. We were walking into the Japanese parlour easily enough. Would our exit be as simple?

It was evident, of course, from the very beginning that we were to be overcrowded. One glance at the limited accommodation around us and at the great surging throng of Allied prisoners-of-war sufficed to show us that. Only the Changi hospital cases had been left behind. We thanked God that they at least had been spared this horror. In comparison with Selerang the Black Hole of Calcutta faded into insignificance.

We fought our way into the barrack-rooms. A room which, in normal times, would have held forty men comfortably was made to hold four hundred. Each man had a space of roughly three feet by two to call his own. One solitary cook-house was to serve this multitude. There were no sanitary arrangements whatever. We settled down gloomily to await the next move by the Japanese.

During our first day over twenty men went down with dysentery. It was not to be wondered at, for there were no latrines and although we worked like demons to dig them in the open square, we had to break our way through solid concrete. This took time, and in the meanwhile, men lay dying. Flies were everywhere, the busy messengers of death. By evening on the first day, our dysentery victims had risen from twenty to over two hundred. It was an epidemic. A young lad went down with a burst appendix. An immediate operation was called for, but, though Changi hospital could actually be seen across the padang, the Japanese refused permission for the sick boy to be moved. Despite desperate and heroic efforts by the doctors, he died in the night.

We still refused to sign. The dysentery epidemic grew worse.

We received only plain boiled rice to eat, without salt or sugar. We had a meagre ration of water, quite insufficient for our needs. We did not shave, nor did we wash. We slept in agony or not at all. On the second day over eight hundred men had contracted dysentery.

By the third day it was all too apparent that, unless we signed the form, only a miracle could save us from death. Things had reached a truly desperate pass. Our slender rice supplies had given out and the Japanese had refused us any more rations. There had been plenty of trouble with the Sikhs and Punjabis too—much face-slapping, much rifle-butting. Two men, wandering over the square during the night, had fallen headlong into the twelve-foot deep latrines. One had been rescued with a broken leg, the other had perished in the foulness of the pit. We still refused to sign.

On the morning of the fourth day, a new threat by the Japanese changed the whole picture. We were informed that, unless the non-escape forms were signed by noon, all our sick comrades in Changi hospital would be brought over to share our misery. The Japanese were not bluffing. The very thought of those thousands of pitifully maimed and suffering creatures being subjected to the barbarous treatment of Selerang filled us with absolute horror. Before noon our Australian G.O.C. signed, under duress, on behalf of all prisoners. We waited anxiously while the Japanese were being informed.

A few minutes after noon, we received the order to fall in. We did so silently. There was no laughter in the ranks. Our cook-house staff gathered together their pots, pans and dixies. The barbed-wire was rolled back. The sentries stood clear. We marched out. That night we slept once more in our old places in Changi barracks. We had capitulated a second time.

After Selerang, the Japanese left us alone for a bit. One might almost have thought that they were sorry for what they had done, but we all knew better. During those three terrible days and nights of close confinement, we had all seen the enemy for what he was—an oriental thug who would stop at nothing to gain his ends. The mask had slipped for a brief spell, and we had seen a raging, untamed beast behind it. Selerang stood out as a grim signpost of danger in our forward path. At some future time in our captivity, those dark passions would again be revealed, perhaps in an even more ruthless form. We had to see to our defences.

Shortly after our return to Changi, our sergeant-major went down with dysentery. I awoke one morning early to find him groaning in bed, his limbs trembling, his face an ashen grey. Wright often left his mess-gear exposed, and sometimes even unwashed, between meals. No man who valued his life dared to be so careless, for the tropical heat brought out myriads of marauding, disease-ridden bluebottles. These loathsome flies settled on the slightest particle of uneaten food, spreading their hideous germs over everything they touched. The sergeant-major was removed to hospital for treatment, and Nunn took over temporary command of the section.

A fortnight later, a consignment of Red Cross supplies arrived unexpectedly in camp. Unfortunately the Japanese had opened many of the packages before we saw them, and had removed for their own selfish use packets of cigarettes and tins of corned beef. They had the lion's share; we received merely the crumbs from the feast. We were exceedingly grateful for small mercies, however, believing that bigger and better supplies would soon be on the way. But nothing more ever came. It was not the fault of the International Red Cross, for that organisation worked tirelessly and magnificently on our behalf. The blame lay wholly with the Japanese who, refusing to succour us themselves, snapped and snarled, like dogs in a manger, at the outstretched hands of more Christian men who would have done so.

The sergeant-major was fearful lest he had missed his Red Cross supplies. We assured him that they were quite safe. On his return we handed him his portion, which included, besides cigarettes and bully beef, several tins of condensed milk. We had given those up from our own parcels, believing they would speed his recovery to health. He thanked us, but began to open a tin of beef. Nunn very sensibly took the tin from him, handing him a tin of milk instead. After an illness which had perforated the lining of his stomach, Wright would most certainly not benefit from a tin of bully beef. Wright was an obstinate man. Although he took the milk meekly enough, I found an empty corned-beef tin next morning outside the barrack-room window. I taxed him with the deed. He told me curtly to mind my own business. Two days later, he was back in hospital, this time with a severe internal hæmorrhage.

On this second occasion his recovery was not so rapid. At last he came back to us, a mere shadow of his former self. From then on he went warily, paying more attention to his diet and to the cleanliness of his mess-gear.

A keen game of hockey was in progress on the padang. It was an Officers versus Other Ranks match. Sergeant-Major Blinch was on the right wing and I was his inside man. There had been no scoring, but the Other Ranks were pressing hard.

A long raking pass came towards me. I flicked the ball out to Blinch and raced down towards our opponents' circle to be ready for the return pass. I was enjoying this game immensely, for it was well over a year since I had had a stick in my hand. Blinch cleverly eluded the opposing left-back and smacked the ball across in my direction. It was a perfect pass. Eagerly I lunged forward, my stick raised to strike.

Then, quite suddenly, the unexpected happened. The sparkling white ball, rolling towards me, vanished before my eyes and reappeared against the toe of my right foot. I swung at it at once, but the back tackled and I lost possession. I stood for a moment blinking in amazement. It had been most extraordinary, just like a conjuror's trick. I had never had the slightest bother with my eyes before. It must have been the sun.

The ball came towards me again. I swung fiercely at it and this time I missed completely. The final whistle blew, but I stood stock-still, as a man in a trance.

Blinch ran over to me. "That was a good game, old chap," he said, "but what came over you in the last minute? I thought you were a cert to score." "So did I," I replied, "but something happened to my eyes. Sergeant-Major, would you please roll a ball towards me from about thirty feet?" Completely mystified, Blinch did as I bid. It was no good. At about eight feet from me, the ball simply vanished. I looked at Blinch's face. He was some twenty feet away at the time. "I can't see your features clearly, Sergeant-Major," I announced. Blinch was worried. "Look around at the trees," he said, "and see if there's any difference." I looked steadily at the nearest clump of tall bamboo, but instead of distinguishing each branch clearly, I could see only a punched-out mass of leaves. It was strange, this perforated appearance everything had. "Better go sick right away," said Blinch. "I'll take your stick back."

I walked slowly and alone to the M.I. room. Surely this sudden freak of vision would right itself soon? It was most inconvenient, all the same. The M.O. was out when I arrived, but a young Eurasian orderly examined my eyes. "They look all right to me," he said, "take a dekko at that wall-chart." I turned to face the chart, covering one eye with my hand. "Can't even see the first line clearly," I announced, after a moment's concentration. I tried the other eye. It was just as bad. "I'll take a note of your name," said the orderly. "See the M.O. first thing tomorrow."

The next day there was no change for better or worse. The M.O. was kind but mystified. "Better see the eye-specialist," he said, "I'll give you a chit."

In Changi hospital the eye-specialist gave me a long, searching examination. He peered into my eyes with an opthalmoscope. He turned back my eyelids to investigate their inner surface. He asked me to read from a wall-chart. He tried me with a dozen different types of spectacles. It was no good. Eventually he asked me to sit down before him. "When you came here just now," he said quietly, "I honestly thought you were just malingering. We get lots of folks doing that every day. Now I'm convinced that your eyesight is affected. Your lateral vision is there all right, and will probably remain, but your focal vision has gone, just flickered out like a candle." This was a terrible blow. I did not answer for a minute. "With luck," the specialist went on, "your central vision might return in England with decent treatment, but frankly, I think you've 'had' it."

He was brutally frank, but then those were not days for quibbling. "Can't you do anything here, sir?" I asked. "Not a chance," he replied, "we haven't got the stuff." "What do you think caused it?" I inquired. "Oh, I could only guess," said the specialist. "The rotten food probably, coupled with a touch of sun. Anyway, I'm going to recommend you for a permanent inside job out of the direct rays of the sun, and remember—don't worry." As I left him, I hoped that I might be able to follow his advice. It was a most grievous blow.

My mother had always been a prolific letter-writer. From the day I left home to join the Army, she had written regularly twice a week. Like so many other mothers, she had received the unwelcome news that her only son had been posted 'missing, believed prisoner-of-war' after the fall of Singapore, but this did not prevent her from sending off her bi-weekly budget. Not for one moment during those dark, uncertain days did she believe that I had perished. She did not write about the war for she hated war, deeply and instinctively. Instead, she described minutely the apparently insignificant things which went on at home from day to day—how the garden grew, how Dad looked in his fire-watcher's helmet, how Peter, the cat, was faring, what they had all had for lunch. They were innocent, homely epistles which would have passed the most ferocious censor. Yet, reading between the lines, I could easily sense the anxiety which lay behind the words of cheer. But there was also hope and an unswerving faith in the mercy of God.

The last letter I had received had been at the Maldive Islands on my journey out to Singapore. I was hungry for news, but month after month passed and still nothing came. Now it was November, 1942. Surely there would be a letter before very long. This constant waiting was hard to bear.

Then, suddenly, the first mail arrived in camp. The excitement was intense. The letters were given out one evening at roll-call. Every man stood with bated breath, straining his ears to catch the names and Army numbers. As each name was called, a happy beaming man would step eagerly forward, his hands outstretched, his eyes shining, his whole body trembling with joy.

Some unfortunates received nothing. It was a bitter blow. They passed it off with an unconcerned shrug of the shoulders and a quick smile. "Better luck next time," they would say. I knew how deeply disappointed they were. It was so cruel to be forgotten at such a time.

The mail had been arranged in alphabetical order. I was far down on the list. There was still a large pile of letters to be delivered. I hardly dared to breathe. They had come to the N's. Already Harris and Livesley had received several letters each, and now Nunn went forward. Paterson, Pearson, Pressley, Would they never reach the S's? The voice droned on. Rammidge, Robertson, Sampson, Shaw . . . Shaw? I nudged Bill who stood beside me, but I need not have taken the trouble. Bill had not missed his name, and fairly leapt forward. Simpson, Smith. "Which one?" came the excited chorus from the ranks. "1608138, Lance-Corporal, J. D." said the voice. I stepped quickly forward. There was a groan from the other Smiths. "You seem to be a popular sort of fellow," said the voice. I had received no fewer than thirty-five letters!

That night we read and re-read our precious mail. Days afterwards we were still reading it during rest-periods. For some men, their letters told of joyful things, of renewed love and steadfastness; for others, they were the grim messengers of disaster and grief, bearing tidings of broken homes or dead friends. The rough had to be taken with the smooth, and the sad heart was not worn on the sleeve of one's shirt. But I could read the news on the faces of my comrades.

A central office of information was established in one of the barrack-rooms, and any scraps of general news which had eluded the eagle-eyed censor were posted up for all to see. Watling Street had won the Derby! I smiled as I read the brief note in the sports column. I thought of the Singapore race-track as I had seen it nine months before, pitted with shell-craters, bestrewn with dead.

My thirty-five letters were more valuable than I had ever imagined. By the time they came, our supplies of cigarettes had given out, although loose native tobacco was available. This required to be rolled, and, as packets of cigarette-papers could not be had, except at an extortionate price, thin paper of any type was at a premium. My mother, sensible person that she was, had written on airmail paper. Her letters were sufficient, when carefully cut into small portions, to give each man in the section a good reserve of cigarette-papers. We blessed her as we all enjoyed my mail.

The New Year brought a worsening of conditions in Changi camp. When the Japanese entered Singapore, they had taken possession of considerable stores of food with which they supplemented our daily ration of boiled rice. After eight or nine months, supplies of beef had given out, for there were many hungry mouths to feed. We then went on a diet of chilled mutton. That lasted almost till Christmas. From then on we became the lean kine.

Our cooks did everything humanly possible to make the bleak rice ration more appetising. With finely-ground rice-flour they made pasties and cakes, frying them in coco-nut oil. Fresh fish began to arrive in the cook-house daily. These varied in size from dried whitebait to armour-plated monsters of the deep sea. Baby sharks were not an uncommon delicacy. Sometimes we received portions of berlachang, a sort of salty native fish paste. For vegetables we had occasional supplies of yams and green tapioca shoots. Boiled rice remained our staple food—plain, unsweetened and often unsalted boiled rice of an inferior grade. True, it was also the food of the Japanese and of the bulk of the native population. They did not take rice as we were obliged to take it, however. They ate it in more or less the same proportion as we in England take potatoes—as a subsidiary part of the meal. We, on the other hand, ate rice in huge, unbalanced quantities to satisfy our ravening appetites. It would have the desired effect, but only for a short space of time after every meal. Then we were hungry again.

I had always been used to rice, but in a more palatable form. Nevertheless I settled down fairly quickly to the monotonous diet. Some men found it exceedingly hard to do this. Dorfman, in particular, detested the stuff.

In its unpolished state, rice still possesses certain vitamins necessary to bodily health, but when the rice is polished, those vitamins are lost. We soon discovered that our supplies were of the polished variety. Although we had not sufficient knowledge to tell one type from the other, our bodies were not slow to react. By January, 1943, every man had contracted stomatitis.

This disease generally begins with a slight rawness and tenderness on the surface of the lips. At first there is little more than a certain discomfort when drinking hot or cold liquids. In a few days, however, the tongue, the inside of the mouth, the back of the throat and other parts of the body are horribly and painfully ulcerated, and it is agony to eat and drink.

I suffered with the rest from this unfamiliar malady. My lips and tongue were so swollen and painful that the passage of food became a daily torment. Speech was difficult, and, in the mirror, I saw that the surface tissue had begun to peel off my tongue, leaving raw, throbbing, cherry-red flesh below. It may have been my imagination, but I fancied my eyesight was also getting worse. Every day hundreds of men went sick. The doctors prescribed rice-polishings, a sort of greyish-brown bran, which looked and tasted not unlike burnt sawdust. This unpalatable substance apparently contained the much-needed vitamins. Supplies were rushed from Singapore. I spread the stuff over my rice ration and swallowed it painfully with copious draughts of water. In a remarkably short space of time my bleeding tongue and mouth began to heal. The new medicine had been effective in my particular case.

There were many worse cases than mine. The really bad ones went to hospital, where a temporary riceless diet, containing Marmite was given. We heard of one poor individual who, never having seen Marmite before, thought it was a new type of ointment and carefully rubbed it into his ulcerated thighs. The result was agony, for the salty extract burned like ten thousand fires.

The vitamin deficiency showed itself also in a particularly acute form of neuritis, mostly affecting the soles of the feet. Livesley was one of those worst hit by this ailment. Night after night he lay for hours awake, grinding his teeth in pain. Finally he discovered that the only way in which he could hope to sleep was with his feet immersed in a bucket of cold water. Despite his extreme suffering, however, he did not complain, nor cease to sympathise with the rest of us in our misfortune.

As 1943 began, we all longed to shake the dust of Changi from our feet.

Towards the end of 1942, it had been widely rumoured in Changi camp that parties of British, Australian and Dutch prisoners, working on the docks of Singapore, had been hastily assembled by the Japanese and sent by train northwards into Malaya. A British lorry-driver, bringing rice into the camp, had spoken to a Dutchman who had spoken to an Australian, who had spoken to somebody else who had gone on one of the parties. The lorry-driver favoured us all with a sly wink and a knowing smile. He had had the information, so he said, straight from the horse's mouth. The Japanese had apparently a big job on in the Kra Peninsula. A road was being built straight across the narrow neck of Malaya from the Gulf of Siam to the Andaman Sea. It was being constructed by parties of Allied prisoners-of-war. The work was hard—pick and shovel mostly—but there was plenty of food, and the prisoners were living like fighting-cocks. The lorry-driver gave us this last important piece of news wistfully. Nourishing food was no more plentiful in Singapore than it was in Changi apparently. We listened with interest to the lorry-driver's tale. Part of it at least might be true. Nunn, whose knowledge of Far-Eastern history was fuller than ours, said that he had once read somewhere about a project to cut a canal through the forty-mile wide Kra Peninsula. Before the project was begun, German engineers had been called in to give their advice. They had declared that the job couldn't be done except at colossal expense. The plan had been dropped. Could it be possible that the Japanese were intending to reopen the project? There would certainly be no lack of cheap labour with thousands of prisoners-of-war available, but what good would it serve? Nunn suggested that it might, perhaps, be a short-cut, by which troops could be transported to Southern Burma. The Japanese might be considering an invasion of India. The idea seemed preposterous, but then this war was full of surprises. We asked Ullman to make tactful inquiries the next time he saw Nagewa. Ullman did so, but Nagewa knew nothing—or would not tell.

There was no doubt that large numbers of men were leaving Singapore regularly. As they departed for an unknown destination, more and more men were being withdrawn from Changi camp to replace them. The Australian area was half-empty and many of the Dutch in our area had also left. I could not think that so many men would be required simply to drive a road, or even a canal, across a forty-mile strip of land. It looked as though something on a much more ambitious scale was being attempted. We had heard before that there were several disused tin-mines somewhere in Northern Kedah. Perhaps the Japanese had decided to operate them again.

In late January, 1943, the withdrawal of men from Changi camp suddenly and mysteriously ceased. We were sorely disappointed, for living conditions in the camp were becoming so unbearable through lack of adequate food and medical treatment, that we had been hoping our turn would come soon. We had heard such wonderful tales of Malaya as a land of plenty, where fresh meat arrived daily, and eggs could be bought from the natives for a few cents each. It must be a veritable Paradise on earth.

February brought fresh developments, however. Japanese doctors and medical orderlies suddenly arrived in Changi, and a general inspection of all prisoners, except those who still lay in hospital, was systematically carried out. It was not difficult for me to conceal my eyesight disability from the Japanese, for eyes were not examined. It appeared, in fact, that if a man had his normal quota of legs and arms, and had not suffered from dysentery, he was fit. This curious habit which the Japanese had of judging a man's ability or inability to work purely by his outward physical appearance was to be seen in a much more merciless form at later stages of our captivity. We went to our medical inspection in Changi blithely enough, fearful lest we should be turned down. A year later we dreaded these inspections like the plague, for to pass them very often meant to die.

We learned from our comrades in Singapore that the February 'up-country' party from Changi had spent only half an hour in

Singapore before entraining for the north. Although nobody from our section had gone on this party, several of my friends in other units had departed. Perhaps, as 'kempi', we were to be kept in Changi till the last. We all fervently hoped not.

In mid-February, 1943, lists of names appeared of those who had been selected for the various parties. Each party numbered approximately a thousand men. Eagerly we scanned the lists, and then, one day at the beginning of March, I saw my name. I was furious. The section had been divided between two parties, one leaving on 20th March, the other on 2nd April. After all that we had successfully come through together, the battle of Singapore, the Changi march, Selerang, a whole long year of captivity, we were to be separated! It was infamous. Nunn, Harris, Wrigley, Bussey, Shaw and I were down for the first party. The sergeant-major, Dorfman, Ullman, and Livesley were noted for the second. We protested loudly to the sergeant-major. He promised to see Blinch in the matter. Blinch was sympathetic, but could do nothing. He had his orders from Nagewa like the rest of us. The Japanese had made the selection and it would have to stand. As the days slipped past inexorably and the 20th March drew near, we redoubled our efforts to find a way of staying together. We even planned to go sick *en masse,* but Blinch pointed out very sensibly that the Japanese would not look favourably on such an action. Besides, there would be more parties, and we had no guarantee whatever that we would not be separated again. Blinch advised us most earnestly to let matters remain as they stood, and to attempt a reunion at some near future date in the new country to which we were all bound. We had, of course, no assurance that we were bound for the same place, but that was a risk which had to be taken. After all, we had been taking risks ever since we arrived in this forlorn island. Sorrowfully we decided that nothing further could be done.

On 18th March we received a cursory kit inspection from the three chimpanzees, Freeman, Hardy and Willis. Having been forewarned, we carefully hid our more private possessions from the crafty trio. But their main concern seemed to be whether we had boots, water-bottles, and mess-gear. After all, if a man's strength was to be used to the utmost, he would require those things before adequate clothing. It was a warm country so what did a shirt matter? If a man were bitten to death by mosquitoes and perished with malaria, that was a chance which had to be taken. Prisoners-of-war were expendable.

On the morning of 20th March we paraded in Changi square, complete with blanket, ground-sheet, pack, haversack and water-bottle. The four members of the section whom we were to leave behind stood back as the roll was called. I could hardly bear to look at them, for I had already seen the sadness in Livesley's eyes. During my service I had been parted from comrades before, but this was the grimmest, bitterest parting which I had ever experienced. Desperately I fixed my gaze on the long line of lorries which the Japanese had sent for our transport. This time we were to ride to Singapore. I prayed for a speedy departure.

Suddenly we were on the move. We clambered aboard a lorry. I moved forward behind the driver's cabin and resolutely set my face for Singapore. I did not look back.

III

Task Force

It was two o'clock in the morning. The sliding doors of the covered cattle-truck were tightly closed, but a chill breeze blew in across my face, and I shivered. Somewhere in the darkness near me, a man stirred restlessly in his sleep. The head of a sharp rivet pressed into the small of my back, and I wriggled cautiously into a less cramped and uncomfortable position. As I did so, Nunn rolled over dreamily, striking me on the chin with his outstretched elbow. Gently I pushed his arm away. The train rumbled on through the night.

It was three days since we had left Singapore. We were travelling steadily northwards, and had halted only for brief periods at little wayside stations for a quick meal of rice and to stretch our aching limbs. The names of the stations meant nothing to us, for we had no maps, and could only guess as to our whereabouts. The countryside around us was changing, however. At first we had journeyed through dense jungle where tall trees and bushes brushed lightly against the steel sides of the truck. Now it was more open country. On either side of the track lay wide stretches of grass and heathland, dotted with clumps of pine and rubber trees. It appeared that we were still in Malaya, for we had passed through a little valley the previous afternoon, and had seen from the truck door a circular gun-position, protected by barbed-wire entanglement, in which still stood three forlorn field-guns of British type. Their muzzles pointed drunkenly skywards, and the surrounding trees were shattered and torn. We could all see the grim little drama so clearly. The dauntless gunners firing over open sights until their last shell was gone. The last desperate fixing of bayonets. The screaming, murderous charge by hordes of Japanese. The last cool order to fire from a young artillery officer. The fierce surge over the barbed wire. The last eddying swirl as the gunners went down before wave after wave of Imperial Guards. For us, the curtain had gone down at Singapore, but here, in this place of bitter memories, an unseen hand had lifted the hem as we slowly passed by, revealing once more for a fleeting moment the tragedy of former things.

We travelled thirty to a truck. We were miserably uncomfortable. We sat upright, our backs pressed against the sides of the truck for support. During the day, the sliding doors were left open, but we travelled so slowly that the breeze was not enough to cool the oven-like interior. At night the doors were closed, and we shivered in the bitter cold of tropical night. Escape was not to be thought of. In daytime an armed sentry sat at the open door of each truck, rifle in hand, legs dangling over the side. We had the unpleasant company of an unshaven lugubrious Japanese, whom we soon nicknamed "Happy Harry". Not once during the long journey had he as much as smiled, either at us or at his fellow-sentries. For mile after mile he sat silently huddled by the open door, apparently asleep. Let one of us make a sudden movement, however, and he was instantly and watchfully awake. Happy Harry was definitely not to be trifled with. At the slightest sign of trouble he would shoot to kill, and even he could hardly miss in the narrow confines of that steel trap. We might, with luck, have overpowered him in a quick rush from behind, and gained possession of his rifle and ammunition, but a quick glance along the train at Kuala Lumpur showed us such a move had already been anticipated by the Japanese. Every second truck in the long line had an open, observation car, as one finds in American and Continental trains. In this place of vantage sat several sentries, grouped round a light machine-gun. With one rifle only, we would stand little chance of shooting it out against these hawk-eyed watchers, and we would be riddled with bullets before we could scramble a dozen paces from the train. At night our immediate chances of escape seemed rosier, for Happy Harry left us alone at the first approach of dusk to join his comrades in the observation-coach. But at night the steel doors were closed tightly, and could be opened only with an ear-splitting screech, distinctly audible above the rumbling of the train. At night also, speed was increased considerably. In the inky darkness we might well have launched ourselves out over a cliff down into some rocky ravine, there to lie, bruised and broken, until picked up and shot by some Japanese patrol, or murdered by an unfriendly native. If we were to escape, then our getaway would have to be scrupulously planned down to the very last detail. We would need arms, compass, maps, money, warm clothing, food and a fair supply of medical stores. For an escaping prisoner-of-war the jungle was not neutral. It was a grim, merciless enemy.

Early in the morning of the fourth day we pulled into a tiny station with the name of Cha Wong. The train jolted to a standstill. On the low dusty platform stood a long line of covered dixies, and Happy Harry signalled to us to get out. We queued up for breakfast sleepily. The sun shone down from out of an almost cloudless sky.

As we moved slowly forward, with mess-tins in hand, Nunn nudged my arm. "Mac," he said quietly, "take a look at that sign-board over there." I glanced at the strip of wood. "Cha Wong," I replied. "It doesn't mean a thing to me." "Yes, but look at the native writing above it," said Nunn. I looked, but could distinguish only a blurred mass of weird hieroglyphics, which might have been Malay, Hindustani or Arabic, for all I knew. After a weary, restless night I was in no mood for language puzzles. I glowered at Nunn, but he would not be shaken off so easily. "That script isn't Malay," he said, "Malay is full of whirls and half-circles, but that is mostly straight lines and dots." "Perhaps it's Morse Code," I said, with a feeble attempt at humour. "Don't be stupid," replied Nunn severely. We had reached the head of the queue. A dark-skinned native, clad in sarong, ladled out my ration of rice. Nunn was next to be served. As I turned away, I heard him speak to the native. "You Malaya?" he queried. The native shook his head. "Thai," he replied. I looked at Nunn. "What's Thai?" I asked. "Siamese," he replied, "we're in Siam."

By late afternoon we had entered much more cultivated country. Well-tended padi-fields ran alongside the line, and we passed several native villages. In one I could just make out the gilded roof of a small pagoda. For several miles we skirted a long, flat seashore, and I could see the sun gleaming on the distant water. It was a quiet, peaceful countryside, unravaged by war. My spirits began to rise. Perhaps this was the promised land of milk and honey, where meat was plentiful and eggs only a few cents each. We could not be very far now from the Kra Peninsula, where the other up-country parties had gone. By evening we should have reached our journey's end. We halted at a station called Ban Kra. This must be the place. But we had halted only for water, and did not get out. Night came and we were still rolling northwards.

I awoke with a start on the morning of our fifth day to find my fellow-passengers rolling up blankets and stowing them away in packs and kitbags. "This is it, Mac," said Shaw, getting out his mess-tin, "Happy Harry has just told us to pack up." I began to get my meagre belongings together. It was a blessed relief to think that at last we had come to the end of the road. Another day in that foul truck would almost have finished some of us. I felt shockingly grimy and longed for a nice cool bath. I glanced at my face in a mirror, and started back at my horrid, unshaven, bleary-eyed visage. It had been an exhausting, soul-shattering journey.

We left the train at a siding and marched about two hundred yards to a distant platform. The name of the place was Ban Pong. Reaching the platform we fell out to await breakfast. There was no sign of life in the little station. In the distance, however, I could hear a train shunting and the high-pitched sound of native voices. The place was evidently a railway junction, for I could see our train puffing off empty along another line leading to the east. We had not quite reached our destination then. We sat down on our packs and kitbags to await further developments. Two of the sentries had gone off, probably to make arrangements for breakfast. I dozed in the hot sunshine.

Suddenly there was an excited babel of voices—British voices. I opened my eyes and looked about me. A long line of brown-skinned men, clad only in shorts and boots approached us from the direction of the siding. They were bearing dixies with them, and as they came they sang, lustily and unmelodiously. The song was "The Holy City". I was on my feet in a moment, listening in rapt amazement to the old familiar chorus. We had sung it so often at Changi as we marched out with the wood-carts. This was no band of Thai workmen, lisping their un-familiar oriental music, but British soldiers roaring a refrain which had almost become the signature-tune of British prisoners-of-war. "Jerusalem, Jerusalem" they sang, "lift up your heads and sing," and we joined in spontaneously, eagerly, as we had always done before. "Curra!" yelled Happy Harry, furiously brandishing his rifle. "Hosanna in the highest!" we chanted, ignoring him completely. This was a joyful reunion in which Happy Harry had no share. We were captives in Babylon, but we had not forgotten that we had been once free men. Some day, God willing, we would be free men once more, and return to England's green and pleasant land.

We surged forward to meet our comrades, hugging them, clasping hands, pouring out questions. How long had they been there? What work were they doing? How were they being treated? Had they any news of the war? Breakfast was temporarily forgotten as we thronged around them excitedly.

They had been there for the past two months, in a camp nearby called Nong Pladuk. There were over 1,500 men in the camp, and they were engaged in loading sections of railway line and sleepers, and in repairing damaged engines and rolling-stock. The Japanese were treating them reasonably well, and food was much better than it had been in Changi. There was fresh meat at least twice a week, and the camp had a canteen where one could buy eggs, coffee and cigarettes. We licked our lips in greedy anticipation. Of the progress of the war there was little or no definite information. One of the lorry-drivers in the camp had had it from a Chinese that the tide of war in Europe was now flowing for the Allies, and that increasing numbers of men were being diverted to the Far East. The Japanese, of course, had their own version which they pumped into their prisoners at every available opportunity. According to them, Japanese forces had now set foot in Australia, and were preparing for a big offensive in Burma. But that, of course, was enemy information and not to be trusted.

Then we heard, with increasing uneasiness, of the type of work which we had been brought all the way from Singapore to do. The job in hand was the building of a single-track railroad from Ban Pong straight across the country in a north-westerly direction to Moulmein, on the Lower Burma coast. At first the going had been fairly easy—through padi-fields mostly—and the Japanese had been in high spirits. Now the railway gangs had struck rock and roaring mountain torrents, and progress had been held up considerably. The job had apparently a time-limit set on it, and work was already falling behind schedule. The Japanese were constantly showing their fangs and jogging the prisoners on to greater efforts. Several men who had been sent back sick to Nong Pladuk had spoken of long hours, back-breaking toil and vicious treatment. The entire distance from Ban Pong to Moulmein as the crow flew—or as the railway ran—was roughly 250 miles, but it was difficult to say how much of the track had been already laid, as gangs were working in separate sections, spread out across the countryside. Australian gangs had been sent from Singapore direct to Moulmein and were working towards us.

I asked one of the men, an R.A.S.C. corporal whom I had known in Changi, if this railway was intended for military or merely for civilian use. He looked at me for a moment, and then laughed derisively. "Civilian?" he cried, "not on your life! Good God, man, the whole place is hiving with Jap front-liners. Every train that comes here is crammed with troops, guns, ammunition and high explosive. From what I can see there's one helluva push coming in Burma soon, and it's not our boys that are going to do the pushing. If this God-forsaken railroad isn't finished in time, then heads are going to fall—yours and mine, probably." I looked at him anxiously. "Only last night," he continued in an undertone, "a Jap trooper drew in here and stopped for about an hour. I was on a party taking some rice along to them and I met a Jap officer. He was only a kid and he asked me if this was India! Would you believe it?" I nodded, and asked him to go on. "Well," he said, "I told him it was Siam, and then he made me draw a map on the ground and show him exactly where he was!" "Didn't he have a map of his own?" I asked. "Nary a one," replied my friend, with a laugh, "and neither did any of the other officers." "What were the troops like?" I asked. "Oh, tough," he said, "tough as blazes—not a bit like our Changi gang. They don't talk so much, somehow, but I found out a lot of them's been in China, all through the Malayan do, and in Java as well. When I gave them their tea, they said 'arigato'. Fancy thanking me! It's more than I ever got from Freeman, Hardy and Willis anyway." "Would you do something for me?" I asked him with a smile. "Sure, chum. Anything you like," he replied readily. "I'm as bad as the Jap officer," I said, "would you mind drawing a map for me too?" Cautiously he bent down and traced with his finger in the dust a map of the country which would have done credit to any teacher of geography. "There's where we are now," he said, "and there's Moulmein, away over there in that corner, see?" I saw clearly. He drew a long thin line, with a thick smudge crossing it at right angles. "That's the railway we're building," he said, pointing to the line. "And what's the smudge?" I asked. "That's the mountains," he replied, grimly, "the tail-end of the Himalayas. The railway's got to go over that." "Heaven help us!" I cried, "they must be well over 4,000 feet high!" "They are," he replied, straightening his back, "I told you it was a fair devil of a job we're on." I thanked him and wished him good luck.

I saw it all so clearly now. I saw why the Japanese had not mown us down as we waited in massed assembly at the Bukit Timah road away back after the surrender. I saw why Fuku had boasted that he would bring the British soldier lower than any coolie in the Far East. This was the superhuman task for which we had been spared our lives. We were to build a railway over gorges and through solid rock so that our enemies might be brought within striking distance of India. Flagrantly disregarding all recognised principles which forbade of prisoners-of-war being used on military undertakings, the Japanese, without reckoning the cost in human life, were to hurl us into this desperate project until we dropped dead from sheer exhaustion. We had certainly come as lambs to the slaughter. I smiled grimly as I remembered Nunn and his canal across the forty-mile wide Kra Peninsula. There was more than a slight difference between 40 and 250 miles. Bitterly I prayed that, while there was yet time, the Allied air-forces might get wind of this accursed railway and blast it into oblivion. But the skies were empty of aircraft, Allied or Japanese. They had been so for weeks and months past. We were the truly forgotten of men, the pitiful flotsam and jetsam of war, tossed and flung hither and thither by the angry, roaring tide of barbarism.

A long train of low, open wagons drew in and stopped at the platform. At a sign from Happy Harry we clambered aboard. The train started off with a sickening jerk which flung us headlong on the wooden floor. We were off along the road the prisoners had made.

We travelled very slowly, for in places the line had been bent into a switchback by the extreme heat of the sun. The way led across padi-fields and under huge trees. For a time we ran alongside a mighty, tumbling river which we came to know later as the Menam. As we proceeded at a leisurely ten or twelve miles an hour, we passed several bamboo camps by the side of the railroad, where other prisoners ran out to wave us on our way. I noticed that many of them wore bandages wrapped round their legs and arms. One man had only one leg, supporting himself on crutches. Despite their deep tan, many looked drawn and weary.

Just before darkness descended, we halted at a little station called Whanpo. We all got out and the cooks lit a great fire of dry bamboo. As the wood crackled and the flames leapt fantastically, we sat down and had a meal of rice and tea. We were parched with thirst and exceedingly drowsy. Then the Japanese marched us down to the river-bank and halted us for the night. There were no huts, no tents, no covering of any kind overhead. The last sounds we heard were the rushing of the river and the gentle rustle of the breeze in the tall lalang.

"Ichi, ni, nessai-yo, nessai-yo!" It was a stupid little refrain, but we kept time to it, hour after weary hour, as we heaved the great wooden logs into position. For a moment I took one hand off the heavy tow-rope and wiped the sweat from my eyes. Ukemi had turned for a brief second to speak to one of his henchmen. I cautiously straightened my aching back and glanced around me.

The tropical sun blazed down pitilessly from out of a clear blue sky. From where I stood, on the very edge of the embankment, the ground dropped down almost perpendicularly to the rocky shores of the brawling Menam river. The steep slope was strewn with enormous jagged pieces of granite which had been blasted away from the cliff-face that morning by the dynamite gangs. At the far side of the river the land rose steeply in a tangled mass of dark-green jungle. Above me the great cliff loomed menacingly. The whole valley shimmered with light, and the river wound through it like some silver python.

For a full mile behind me the rocky slopes were black with men. Some stood in a long chain, passing baskets of sand and rubble from the river-bed to where the cement-mixers were at work; some carried pails of water; some staggered along under massive burdens of railway-sleepers and long iron bolts; some laboriously piled thirty-foot sections of steel line. Pick-and-shovel men were everywhere, striking, pulling, digging, levelling. A huge embankment was being slowly but steadily thrown up against the foot of the beetling crag. Along the top of this the railway would shortly run.

It was five days since our arrival at Whanpo. We had left camp that morning at seven o'clock, and, except for a fifteen-minute break at eleven, had been toiling solidly for five hours. In charge of our particular section was Ukemi, the most dreaded Japanese in the camp. Ukemi was not a regular soldier but a civilian engineer in uniform, and bore the rank of 'gunsuko'—an honorary title carrying powers equivalent to those of our Company Sergeant-Major. Ukemi's ill fame had spread further than Whanpo. Some said the man was mad. Having seen him several times in action already, I was inclined to believe it. In stature he was small, but he was as agile as a monkey. In nature he was tigerishly sadistic. For hours he would sit cross-legged on some flat rock, coiled up like the little cobra he was, watching the prisoners at work. Suddenly he would call one of the sentries over to where he sat and point languidly with the tip of his bamboo cane at some unhappy man who appeared to be flagging. The sentry would nod grimly and suddenly descend ferociously upon the flagger, raining blows and curses on his bowed head. Sometimes Ukemi would handle the matter personally, dragging the prisoner forth from his working group, and making him stand in agony on some razor-edged piece of granite, with a heavy stone held above his head. In a short time the prisoner's arm-muscles would weaken with the strain, and the stone would sink. That was a signal for Ukemi to bring his cane viciously across his victim's shoulders. As he did so he laughed, hideously.

It was one o'clock in the afternoon, and in the distance I could hear the clink of dixies as the camp-orderlies brought out our rice. At noon one of our gang had very nearly lost his life. My blood still ran cold as I recalled the incident. Ukemi had desired a heavy pulley and block to be fixed at the very summit of the overhanging cliff to aid us in heaving the gigantic teaklogs into position as supporting piles for the railway. One of our gang had been selected for the hazardous job of scaling the rock-face, with a thick rope tied round his waist. On the top of the crag, fully eighty feet above our heads, grew a gnarled tree which had withstood the storms of centuries. Round the trunk of this tree the rope was to be knotted.

The man had stood, open-mouthed in amazement, and had finally shaken his head. The cliff could not be climbed by him or by any other human being. Examining the sheer face carefully, I thought I could just trace a way whereby he might reach the top. It would be a horribly risky way, but it was the only one. Ukemi had apparently seen it too, for he indicated it with one hand, while, with the other, he brought his cane whistling down on the prisoner's bare back. I saw an ugly red weal arise on the man's flesh. He started off grimly, his jaw set, his eyes averted from the rushing river below.

We stood in silence as he ascended, fearing that the slightest sound would unnerve him. The seconds seemed like hours. Ukemi stood looking upwards, a faintly contemptuous smile on his lips. If this man fell to his death, there were plenty more prisoners to replace him.

Slowly and painfully the man struggled upward, gingerly testing every slippery foothold as he went. He was little more than five feet from safety when the cursed rope fouled on the branch of an overhanging bush. Cautiously the climber braced himself against the rock-face and began to shake the rope clear. "Curra, bagero!" shouted Ukemi, jerking the rope suddenly from the bottom. Precious time was being lost, and this miserable wretch of a prisoner was slower than a tortoise. At the sudden twist of the rope the climber swayed forward perilously, and I closed my eyes, expecting to hear him thud down the awful precipice. But with magnificent grit and courage he held on, his hands clinging to the ledge like limpets. Life was sweet even to a prisoner-of-war. Then he turned again and safely reached the top. Quickly knotting the rope round the tree-trunk, he tugged it twice and then hauled up the heavy iron pulley from the bottom. This secure, he unloosened the rope which he had carried with him and passed the end through the pulley. We caught it at the bottom and made it fast for him to descend. He came down hand-over-hand, steadying himself with his feet against the cliff-face. As he jumped clear at the foot, he turned and looked at Ukemi. It was but a brief glance. I shivered involuntarily. Ukemi would do well to say his prayers to his Shinto gods that night, for he might not be alive on the morrow. Here at his very elbow stood a man who would pursue him like an avenging fury to the uttermost ends of the earth there to destroy him utterly. If Ukemi saw the look, he gave no sign, however.

We sat down for a blessed hour in the hot afternoon sunshine and ate our rice dinner. Ukemi and his minions withdrew themselves from us and sat in a little group, smoking and laughing together. We would begin work again at two o'clock and go on till nine at least. For the past two days we had been working on by the light of flares. This was a rush job and we were slightly behind time. The task would be completed in time, however, if Ukemi had anything to do with it. He drove us like galley-slaves.

"Oro men starto!" The shrill voice was Ukemi's, and wearily we rose again to our feet. There would be no more rest-breaks that afternoon. A party of Dutch moved over to the pulley-rope. We were to have a change by going on pick-and-shovel work. I carefully selected my shovel, for I should have it as a companion for the next seven hours, and it would be merely courting disaster to pick a broken or bent one. These Japanese picks and shovels were hopeless for heavy work like this, for they were too short in the haft, and seemed to be made of scrap-iron. The pick-heads chipped on striking rock, and the shovels crumpled like tin-foil.

"Ichi, ni, nessai-yo, nessai-yo!" I glanced round as the Dutch gang took up the refrain, tugging together on the heavy rope. Ukemi had left us in charge of a dreamy-eyed sentry, and was back on his perch on the flat rock. I did not envy the Dutch the company of this maniac for another seven hours.

Pick-and-shovel work had one great advantage over every other type of occupation. While the pick-man was busy, the shovel-man had a brief respite and vice versa. Not, of course, if Ukemi were looking, but he could not be looking everywhere at the same time.

It must have been about three o'clock when the tow-rope twisted. Shaw had just completed a metre's hard picking and stood clear as I began to shovel out the rubble. As I bent my back, I heard Ukemi give a sudden angry shout, and glancing quickly towards the flat rock, saw that he was on his feet. The Dutch had stopped pulling, as the twisted rope had wedged itself fast in the pulley and could not be shaken loose. I wondered which of those unfortunate Dutchmen would be selected to climb the cliff-face again and ease the rope clear, but Ukemi apparently considered that a sharp, quick tug on the rope would get it running smoothly again. He gave an impatient signal, and the Dutchmen bent their backs.

Curiously I looked upwards to see what would happen. The action may have saved my life. Simultaneously with the quick tug on the rope came a sudden horrible tearing sound from the cliff-top, and I saw the tree which had withstood the storms of centuries, slowly begin to topple over the edge. The Dutch had let go the rope and flung themselves against the side of the rock. I do not think that during the action in Singapore I had ever moved faster. With a yell Shaw grabbed my arm and together we flung ourselves headlong behind a huge boulder as the great tree, with tons of earth clinging to its roots, hurtled down on top of us. I shut my eyes and fairly hugged the shelter of the boulder. For a moment the whole world went mad around me. Branches crashed and splintered, stones sang past my head like pieces of shrapnel and clods of earth rained down on my shoulders. I heard a man scream but dared not raise my head.

All was quiet again, except for the faint patter of small stones falling from the face of the rock. I looked cautiously around me. Everywhere men were peeping from behind boulders like frightened rabbits. By throwing themselves against the cliff-face, the Dutch had saved their lives. The tree had fallen clear of them and now lay in a tangled mass, with pieces of rope still wound round its trunk.

I looked round for Ukemi, but the flat rack upon which I had last seen him standing was empty. One of the massive branches of the fallen tree lay across it. The Dutchmen were jabbering together excitedly as they pointed to the edge of the embankment. I ran across and looked down the steep slope.

Thirty feet below me, across the jagged tooth of a mighty granite boulder, lay Ukemi. At that distance I could not see his face, but I noticed his legs writhing in agony. His must have been the scream I heard as the great branch swept him like a ninepin over the edge of the embankment. As I stood staring at the man below me, three of the sentries rushed frantically to his aid. Tenderly they lifted him in their arms and brought him up to the top. We stood silently watching. As they passed me, I looked on the face of mine enemy. It had been mutilated almost beyond belief. As the sentries gently laid him down on the hot earth, I saw his body sag and suspected that every bone had been broken. As four men were sent off to make a rough stretcher, one of the sentries uncapped his water-bottle and knelt by the side of the gunsuko. It was too late for water. Suddenly Ukemi gave a throaty rattle and the blood gushed from his mouth, his nose and his ears. I turned my face away. When I looked again Ukemi was dead. Without warning, the hammer of God had fallen and destroyed this cruel man. As he had lived violently, so had he also died. But his blood was not on our hands.

The Whanpo section had been scheduled to take ten days. We completed it in nine, working shifts far into the night. On the tenth day we rested. The Japanese were well satisfied.

The work had not been done without injury to our men. Legs and arms had been torn and bruised by stones, hands lacerated by constant picking and digging, eyes blinded by hot creosote. Three-quarters of our company were sick. My eyesight had deteriorated to a marked degree, and I had the beginnings of an ulcer on my right leg. I limped as I walked, but was still on my feet. So were the other members of the section, although Shaw had twice threatened dysentery.

The river-bed camp was not a camp at all in the strict sense of the term, for only the Japanese had tents. The camp orderlies had constructed a rough bamboo shelter for our food supplies, but night after night we slept out in the open, exposed to wind and weather. It was an uncouth existence. During the night, while the Menam rushed by, mosquitoes pinged past our drowsy heads and scorpions came along to share our blankets. These devilish creatures favoured the inside of a boot as a resting-place, and Harris had found one one morning a shade too late. He was still limping with a swollen foot. Being duly warned by our friend's misfortune, we carefully shook our footwear upside down every day to dislodge such unwelcome guests. Whanpo camp seemed to be the habitat of every creeping and crawling thing known and unknown to man, and our sudden arrival had been bitterly resented. Snakes wriggled unwillingly from under our very feet, scorpions walked nonchalantly past us, centipedes measuring a foot in length waited for us on top of our mess-tins and ferocious armies of ants assailed us in a determined and ceaseless campaign. These were not the little brown ants one found in the Scottish woods, but huge black creatures with bodies half an inch long. When cornered, they would stand up on their hind legs and fight viciously back, like negro heavy-weight boxers. They marched forward, millions strong and it was a foolish man who tried to hinder their passage. In close battle formation they went, their spear-head ready for action, their flanks protected by a long line of seasoned scouts. Twigs placed in their path would be swept aside with astonishing force. Some-times they met another army head-on. Battle would be joined immediately and unquestioningly, provided the opposing force were more or less of the same strength. Let a small army of black ants meet a larger one, however. Forward, with extreme caution, went the little scouts. Back they hurried to the main body to make their report. The smaller army would halt for a brief moment, then swing off quickly in another direction, avoiding battle. We watched those little creatures whenever we could, learning lessons in tactics and strategy which might have availed us much, had we been free men. But we were prisoners-of-war and less than the ants.

We had built a rough shelter under the trees to act as a make-shift hospital. One doctor and two orderlies tended as best they could to the scores of sick men. The Japanese did not visit the sad place unless to order more men out to work. Ukemi had been a devil for this barbarous method of recruiting extra labour, but now Ukemi was dead, and the other Japanese were a shade less callous—or so it appeared to us.

On the tenth day we were actually on holiday. It was un-believable. We splashed deliciously in the cool river, ridding ourselves of the solid layer of grime which had covered our bodies for over a week. I did not dare to venture too far out, for the current was swift and deep, but contented myself by sitting in the shallow water and kicking my legs out while I held firmly to the sandy bottom. After a while I returned to the bank, and after clearing a small space of ants and other crawling things, sat down and gazed out over the sparkling river.

About twenty feet out in the stream there lay a large flat rock, and a sudden movement on top of it attracted my attention. I called Nunn over and pointed to the rock. "There's something moving there," I said, "but I can't quite see what it is." Nunn stared for a moment and then turned with a shout to the other bathers. "Hi there! Keep away from that rock. There's a python on it!" There was an instant scramble to get ashore as quickly as possible. I watched spellbound as the great snake slowly raised its head. What I had taken to be a large stone lying on the top of the rock had actually been the coiled serpent. It was a truly monstrous creature, far bigger than anything I had seen before, even in the Zoo.

Unlike the lesser denizens of Whanpo valley, the python had not the slightest interest in our presence. Lowering its head again into its shining coils, it calmly went to sleep in the hot sunshine. I shuddered to think of what might have happened had one of our men swum out to that rock. Shaw had suggested it. That stealthy terror would have moved like lightning and before the swimmer realised his peril, he would have been enveloped in those mighty coils. A reptile which could reduce an ox to a shapeless pulp would make swift work of a man.

Nunn and I stayed on to watch the beast, for we were both deeply interested in all God's creatures. I am very glad we did, for, in little more than ten minutes, we had a ring-side seat at one of the most breath-taking jungle battles either of us had ever seen. It was a battle between two giants, grim, silent, relentless.

Until Nunn pointed out the little black snout moving through the water like a miniature torpedo, I had not realised that even land snakes make excellent swimmers. I had never given a thought as to how the python had reached the rock, for I was too much taken up with its movements. We sat spellbound, straining our eyes.

The little black snout reached the overhanging shadow of the rock and for a moment the surface of the river was unrippled. On the top of the rock the coiled python slept on, unaware that an intruder had come to disturb his peace. Suddenly, from out of the coils, a flat, diamond-shaped head reared up in alarm, as a second flat, diamond-shaped head appeared over the edge of the rock. The newcomer was still semi-submerged in the river, but, from the little we could see of him, he was the big brother of all pythons. Without more ado, the battle was joined.

As my eyesight was not good enough to enable me to witness every move in this fierce struggle, I had to rely on Nunn's exciting second-by-second commentary. The second python had swum out to the rock with one purpose—to get on top of it. The first python was equally determined to stay where he was. There was room for only one python on the rock. One of them had to go.

The first python prepared for battle by swiftly unloosening its coils until its tail hung over into the water. Then, as foot after foot of the second python appeared, it hung back, poised, waiting for that moment to strike. But the second python, watching its opportunity, lunged forward first and threw a massive coil round its opponent's throat. The first python seized the tail of the other snake in its mouth, attempting vainly to swallow it. Then the two bodies became inextricably locked, writhing, tugging, pulling, one against the other. It was a truly fearsome sight, one to make the blood run cold in sheer horror. For a full two minutes the conflict raged on the rock, and from the shore I could see great gleaming, rope-like bodies thrashing to and fro. It was impossible to tell which body belonged to which python so closely were they locked in battle. Round the base of the rock the water churned and boiled furiously, throwing up white spume. Then, as suddenly as the fight had been joined, it was broken off. The first python had been dislodged and slithered into the water with a faint splash. The second python swiftly coiled itself up on the rock. It had won the day and was now un-disputed king of the castle. We watched the beaten python heading out into the open river. Then we went back to camp.

It was strange how that ulcer on my right leg developed so quickly. It had begun one evening just after my arrival at Whanpo. We were returning from work at the time, utterly exhausted, and somebody had lurched into me in the growing darkness. I lost my balance for a moment on the narrow path, and stumbled into a clump of young bamboo. There had been a quick stab of pain as one of the needle-like shoots had penetrated my bare leg, but I had thought nothing of it. After all, we were being gashed and bruised constantly while at work on the railway. By the light of the camp-fire I had examined the wound, but it looked little more than a pin-prick. I washed the thin trickle of blood away and forgot the incident. Next day I had a definite limp.

While Nunn and I had been watching the python fight I had felt a sudden sharp twinge shoot up my leg as far as the thigh. An egg-shaped gland was rising steadily in my groin. I eventually had to report sick.

The medical officer was hideously overworked. By the fitful gleam of the camp-fire he gave my leg a quick examination, handed me over to the care of an orderly, and turned to tend a more serious case. After all, I looked fit enough and was on my feet. These dysentery victims were not. The orderly washed my leg and painted the wound with iodine. I refused to be bandaged.

On the eleventh day I awoke to find my whole leg so painful that I could barely hobble along. My groin swelling had gone down a bit, but the little pin-prick hole was red and angry. Harris had a shell-dressing in his pack and gave it to me. I tied it loosely over the wound. Then I crawled up to the hospital to show myself to the doctor.

I found the place in a state of chaos. All but the most serious cases were packing kitbags and haversacks. The medical officer and his two orderlies were busily engaged stowing away meagre supplies of medicine, cotton-wool and bandage in a long wooden box. I sat down on the sandy earth to await the doctor's attention.

As I waited, a Japanese officer approached. He was a newcomer to the camp, having probably been sent to replace the dead Ukemi. He was a trim figure in his gleaming white shirt, khaki riding-breeches and brown boots. He wore spectacles and carried a note-book and pencil in his hand. As he saw me sitting there at the hospital entrance, he came across and stood looking down at me for a moment in silence. I looked up at him and smiled ruefully. "No goodterna," I said, "bamboo no good." The young Japanese bent down quickly on one knee beside me, and I swayed backwards, expecting an immediate blow. After all, prisoners-of-war did not usually address Japanese officers. He did not strike me. There was a look almost of compassion in his eyes. I stared at him for a moment, completely nonplussed. Then he signalled to me to withdraw the shell-dressing from my wounded leg. I obeyed in silence. The pin-prick had widened to the size of a sixpence and was oozing a thin yellowish pus. The Japanese made a wry face and shook his head. "Bamboo no goodterna," he said, standing up, "you Englando sojo-ka?" "Hai," I replied. "You no worko," he said, "you Chungkai." "Arigato," I murmured, for it was not every man who was excused work by a Japanese officer. The Japanese held his note-book in his hand. "Namo," he inquired, his pencil ready. "Smith," I said, "Englando kempi." "Kempi-ka?" he asked quickly. "Hai," I replied. Once more this magic word had come to my aid. The officer gave a slight bow and turned into the hospital. I sat on in wonderment. What had he meant when he said "Chungkai"? Was this another term for 'sick'? It sounded almost like the name of a place, but the only names I knew were Whanpo, Ban Pong and Nong Pladuk. I gave it up. He had distinctly said that I was not to work anyway, so I might as well get back to my bed. Wearily I crawled back to my ground-sheet. On my return I told Nunn of my encounter with the Japanese, but he had never heard of any place called Chungkai. I fell asleep in the hot morning sun. The pain in my leg had died down to a dull ache.

I awoke with a start some ten minutes later to find Nunn packing his belongings into his kitbag. I scrambled to my feet. "What's up?" I inquired, "are we moving again?" "Yes," replied Nunn, "we've been ordered to parade with our kits right away outside the Jap tent." I rolled my kit together and limped along with Nunn to the place of assembly.

Every single man in the camp was on parade. As we fell in I saw with horror that even the worst dysentery cases were there too, lying full-length on the sand. It was a pitiful company. Some stood, pale and shaking, holding to comrades for support; some had grimy bandages around their limbs; some coughed rackingly; some gazed forward as if in a dream. I could hardly believe that this was the same company which had left Changi only a little over a fortnight before. The long hours of back-breaking toil, the interrupted rest, the bad food, the vicious treatment of Ukemi and his thugs—all had left their hideous scars on the bodies of my comrades. Although many were in desperate straits, however, their spirit was still unbroken. They could still smile and make light of their terrible sufferings. That spirit had carried them through Singapore and Selerang. It would carry them through to the end.

The tent-flaps parted and the Japanese officer, who had spoken to me shortly before at the hospital, came out, accompanied by three sentries. Our medical officer stepped quickly forward and joined the group. Together the two officers, British and Japanese, inspected the prisoners.

I had seen examples already of the swiftness with which the Japanese mood could change, but the sudden transformation which had taken place in the Japanese officer staggered me completely. I could hardly believe it was the same mild individual who had questioned me about my leg. Now he scrutinised every man in a cold, contemptuous manner, even those whose injuries were all too apparent to the eye. As he slowly walked along the line, he murmured "worko" to each man in turn, despite our medical officer's frantic protestations that the men were mortally ill. It was pure, cold-blooded murder. Half of the men whom he had so calmly passed as fit for work had dysentery or bronchitis. They would, if unduly strained, collapse immediately. The Japanese was inexorable.

Shaw stood on my right, Nunn on my left. We did not move as the two officers approached. The British officer pointed to Shaw. "This man very sick—dysentery." "Dysentery-ka?" growled the Japanese, eyeing Shaw from head to foot, as if he were some prize steer, "dysentery nye. You worko." The Japanese gazed at me without the slightest sign of recognition. "This man very sick—eyes and ulcer," said our doctor. The

Japanese looked me squarely in the face. I met his gaze as coolly as I dared. He motioned me to remove the shell-dressing from my wounded leg. I did so as quickly as possible. "You Chungkai," he said briefly, and moved on to examine Nunn. Nunn was ordered to work. So were all the other members of the section. My heart stood still with dismay as this cruel farce of an inspection continued. Having finished, the Japanese officer returned to his tent. I was relieved to find that he had not, at least, passed the worst dysentery cases as fit. A mere handful of us had been selected for Chungkai.

What was Chungkai? I still did not know. As the Japanese officer had made his callous selection, one of his sentries, following closely on his heels, had carefully noted the Chungkai cases. Now the same sentry ordered us to fall out and form up in a separate party from the workers. For yet another time we were to be parted, and I could not as much as raise a finger to prevent it. I hung on to my position between Shaw and Nunn, hoping against hope that I might be overlooked, but the sentry had seen me. He rushed across, his rifle in his hand, and with a heavy heart I silently fell out and followed him.

The workers moved off first under armed escort and took the northern trail. I felt like a caged beast, and turned my head constantly from one side to the other as my comrades marched past, trying desperately to seek an opportunity to slide into their ranks, but the sentry, as if anticipating such a move, placed himself directly in front of me, his rifle at the ready. I simply could not argue with a loaded gun. I had to let them go. It was Changi all over again, but this time I had been left alone. As my friends marched away, I turned my back. I looked out over the river with a great lump in my throat. For me, the tumbling water had lost its sheen, and the jungle was cold and colourless.

I looked round at my companions af the Chungkai party. The workers had gone. The camp was quiet and deserted. I saw a handful of tired, sick men, and realised suddenly that they also had lost their friends. Somehow I felt that I had been rather selfish in my misery. I turned to a young Dutch boy who sat near me, his arm swathed in bandages. "What's Chungkai, chum?" I asked, sitting down on the sand beside him. The Dutchman smiled in a friendly way. "Hospital—I tink," he said. "Back the line—towards Ban Pong?" I asked. "Ja," he replied, quickly, "I tink so." "What's wrong with you?" I asked, pointing to his bandaged arm. "Ulcer," he replied, indicating, with his free hand, that the wound stretched from shoulder to elbow. I lowered my eyes in shame, for mine was such a small, insignificant flea-bite in comparison with his monstrous sore. He must be suffering agony. I handed him my tobacco box, and offered to roll him a cigarette. But he thanked me and shook his head.

The sentry came past and ordered us to our feet. I took my Dutch friend's pack, for he had difficulty in carrying his belongings with only one free hand. There were six stretcher-cases in the party, but the two hospital orderlies had been left behind. We were to move to the nearby railway-line, there to await transport. For once, the Japanese sentry did not hustle us along, but let us make our own speed. I toiled up the steep slope from the camp to the line and left my kit. The Dutch lad promised to keep an eye on it for me. Then I returned to give a hand with the stretchers. It was a tricky job getting those sick men up that slippery slope, but at last we succeeded. Although it must have been agony to be jolted backwards and forwards, they did not cry out.

We waited till noon by the line. Then we ate a meal of rice which had been left over from breakfast. This was what Nunn would have jocularly termed 'the unexpired portion of the day's rations'. About one o'clock a short train of open wagons came puffing up from the direction of Ban Pong. The engine was pushing, back-to-front, at the rear. The train halted. Our party moved into the empty wagons. The sentry jumped aboard, with a quick wave of his arm to the driver. The train moved slowly off towards Ban Pong. Whanpo camp was no more. We had left it again to its rightful owners—the centipedes, the ants, the scorpions and the snakes. My heart was not on that train but with a long marching column, plodding ever northwards.

It is said that elephants, on feeling their end to be near, seek out a quiet valley and there lay themselves down to die. It took me exactly twenty-four hours to realise that Chungkai was the quiet valley where prisoners-of-war came to die. It was no hospital camp, but a dark, tragic burial-ground.

Things went ill with us from the very moment we arrived in the place. Just outside the main entrance gate stood a small bamboo pavilion which was the Japanese orderly-room. On a narrow bench, at the door of the pavilion, sat four unkempt Japanese soldiers, their rifles in their hands, their heads bowed as if in sleep. At a sign from our sentry we halted just in front of the four guards. We were very weary and swayed on our feet. Our sentry stood for a moment as if hesitating to speak, and then suddenly burst into a torrent of Japanese. The guards, with one accord, raised their heads and gazed at us without interest. They seemed to be in some sort of oriental trance. Then one of them languidly rose to his feet and advanced towards us. A low conversation followed between him and our sentry. I could only pick out the words 'Whanpo' and 'Chungkai'. Gradually the voices of the two men were raised in anger, and I saw our sentry grasp his rifle tightly as if preparing to strike. The other three guards came over to support their comrade, and all five men stood in a circle before us, arguing and gesticulating violently. There appeared to be some misunderstanding about our arrival. The camp had not been notified, and there was no room for us. I several times caught the word 'mato'. This was certainly an unpleasant welcome.

The harangue finally subsided and the four guards returned to their bench. Our sentry saluted them and motioned to us to proceed. We entered the camp.

From the very moment I first set eyes on the place, my spirits began to fall. The camp was surrounded by a twelve-foot high bamboo stockade, and contained a large number of long, rectangular huts, roofed with attap. The huts did not appear to lie in any definite pattern, but were spaced out at random across the area, some with their backs to us, some with their sides. In some unaccountable way, the roofs of the huts seemed to have sunk so low that they almost touched the ground. Each hut had four entrances, set roughly one on each side. The whole place bore an air of overpowering gloom and misery. Involuntarily I shuddered. It was almost as if we had entered a cold dark mortuary. As we moved farther into the camp, we passed little groups of prisoners, British, Australian and Dutch. They showed but scant interest in our arrival. Some raised their heads questioningly and gave us a listless smile; others sat on with their backs to us. All looked horribly emaciated and ill. One man stood up near us, grinning vacantly. Then he raised a bony hand and pointed derisively at us. "Chungkai, Chungkai," he chanted, "That's where the Englishmen come to die!" The poor creature was mad. I turned my head away abruptly. It was horrible to look at those wide-open, staring eyes and to listen to that high-pitched cackling laugh. What tragic place, in Heaven's name, was this that we had been brought to? My Whanpo comrades were sick, but at least they were sane and moderately cheerful. These broken-down skeletons of what had once been Allied soldiers terrified me by their strange looks and dumb, silent suffering. I shivered again, although the sun was warm.

Our sentry halted us in an open space, surrounded by huts, and after signalling to our two orderlies that the stretcher-cases were to be removed elsewhere, indicated by gesture that we were to make our own arrangements for the night. Then he left us alone.

I stood for a moment, undecided, and then, judging that it would be best to find some sleeping accommodation first before trying to seek food, I moved over with my kit to one of the least dilapidated huts. I had to crawl under the overhanging roof to enter.

I stood in shocked amazement when I surveyed the inside of the place. The hut was roughly fifty yards in length by six yards in width. When first built, it had been a spacious, airy house, with a roof of freshly-cut attap, supported on thirty-foot long bamboo poles. The hut had a central earthen pathway, flanked on either side by a continuous platform of thin laths, raised three feet off the ground. This platform constituted the prisoners' sleeping-accommodation, each man possessing a bed-space of roughly two feet by six.

That was how the place had once been. Now it had vastly changed. Through wind, weather and general neglect, the central supporting poles had sagged to an angle of some thirty degrees, allowing the roof to drop almost to ground-level. In places the old attap was hanging in shreds, exposing the interior of the hut to every sudden rainstorm which blew over it. The sleeping platform was no longer level, but humped and wrinkled, with laths missing or displaced everywhere. The whole place smelt foul.

It was not so much the hut itself but its occupants that made me draw my breath in horror. From one end of the building to the other, the sleeping-platforms were crammed with men, some lying almost on top of others. As I passed slowly along the central pathway, littered with withered attap and cigarette-ends, I examined each man in turn. Gaunt eyes, hollow cheeks, pitifully emaciated bodies—all bore mute and awful testimony to the ravages of disease and the bestial treatment of the Japanese. These creatures did not live; they merely existed. I saw bearded Dutchmen with angry, untended sores, haggard Englishmen with their thin legs curled up in agony, skeleton-like Australians deformed and fever-ridden. As I walked, I looked desperately from side to side, hoping to find at least one reasonably fit man. Not one was to be found. Everywhere was suffering, misery and silent despair. This was a doomed company, the shattered remnant of a lost cause, the withering flower of humanity itself, the forgotten of God. I, who had already seen suffering in so many evil forms, could hardly bear to look.

At one end of the hut, not far from a door, I found a narrow empty space between two ground-sheets. Not a head was raised as I quietly laid down my kit. The space was little more than eighteen inches wide, but it would suffice my needs. I unrolled my ground-sheet.

Two men entered the hut by the open door and came towards me. In comparison with the other occupants, they were fit and well-fed. One had a dirty bandage round his wrist, but the other had no marks of illness. They jumped nimbly on the ground-sheets which lay on either side of my little bed-space, and sat cross-legged, surveying me in a most resentful way. I smiled at the man with the bandage, but received only an ugly scowl in return. Undeterred by such a hostile reception, I quietly began to lay down my blanket. The man with the bandage spoke for the first time. "Here, mate," he said angrily, "what the blazes d'ya think you're doing?" I turned to face him in some surprise. "I'm moving in," I replied curtly, "so what?" The man looked at his plump companion. "You can't get that space," he said, "it's booked." "Who by?" I asked. "By us," said the bandaged man, and laughed jeeringly in my face. This was a bit thick. After all, I was no Japanese. These men were my comrades-in-arms and fellow-prisoners. I swallowed my rising anger and spoke as quietly as I could. "Look here, chum," I said, "I don't know who you are, and I don't greatly care, but I've come here and I'm jolly well going to stay here, whether you've booked this space or not." With that, I flung my kit to the top of the bed and straightened my blanket. "Like hell you'll stay," cried the unbandaged man, and with this, he gripped the corner of my ground-sheet and tossed it, together with my blanket out into the dusty, central pathway of the hut. As I bent to retrieve my possessions, my other belongings were thrown out as well. I turned furiously on the two men, my fists clenched. This was too much.

As I made for the unbandaged man, his companion picked up his heavy ammunition boot in his undamaged hand, and struck me a vicious blow on the shoulder which temporarily paralysed my arm. I staggered backwards and knocked my ulcerated right leg against the sharp end of a bamboo lath. The pain was excruciating. I gasped, and felt suddenly giddy and sick. I looked at the two men again. They had now moved closer together like a couple of Siamese twins. One still held the boot in his hand, but the other had now possessed himself mysteriously of a heavy iron spanner. In my present damaged state, I could no sooner argue with an iron spanner than I could with a loaded rifle. I quietly rolled my scattered kit together again under the cold and watchful eyes of the two tyrants and turned to leave that accursed hut. "We'll maybe meet again some day, you and I," I said quietly, "when I haven't an ulcer in my leg and you haven't a boot and a spanner. It'll be a bit more even then." "Oh go to hell!" growled the man with the spanner. "No, I'll just go outside," I retorted, "where the air's a bit cleaner than it is in here." I left the hut immediately, and, after seeking around for a flat space on the open ground, laid out my kit a second time. In the distance I could just make out a line of men moving forward, mess-tins in hand. I hastily unpacked my mess-gear and went off to join the queue. After all, I had to eat, even if there was no room for me in the hut.

I had some little difficulty in securing my ration of rice and stew, as no one knew where I had come from and I was thus an extra unwanted mouth to feed. I crept back to my blanket, feeling miserably unhappy and alone. My travelling-companions from Whanpo had moved into other huts, and were nowhere to be seen.

I had just finished the last grain of rice, when I discovered that someone had stolen my water-bottle. I had left it under my kitbag while I was getting my rice, and now it had gone. I looked round quickly, but there was not a soul in sight.

"Chungkai, Chungkai. The place where the Englishmen come to die." I could not forget the stupid rhyme. If I did not get out of this camp quickly, I should never leave it alive. I had been denied a lodging by my own men, I had been treated as an unwelcome stranger in the rice queue and now, to crown all, my water-bottle, my most precious companion, which had travelled with me all the long way from England, had been stolen, and I should never see it again.

This was no hospital camp. This was a vile, wicked place where men who had once marched shoulder to shoulder in a common cause could strip their very comrades and leave them for dead. There was no good Samaritan in Chungkai. Men passed by their brothers on the other side of the way, their heads averted. I had never believed that I could become so bitter as I was that night as I lay down to sleep. But I managed to keep bitterness out of my prayers.

I awoke next morning, stiff and cold, to find that the ulcer on my leg had grown to the size of a half-crown. That encounter with the bamboo lath had not improved its appearance. I bundled my kit together and limped across the square with it towards a long hut which I took to be the hospital. One of our orderlies stood at the entrance. I moved inside to have my leg dressed. There was nothing in the place but permanganate crystals and cotton-wool. I carefully bathed the ulcer, wiping away a thick greenish layer of pus which had formed overnight. If this open wound were not treated properly soon, I should have gangrene. Tearing a strip off a clean white vest which I had in my pack, I made a fresh bandage and fixed it over the wound with a layer of fresh cotton-wool. Then I tied Harris' shell-dressing once more over the place, and tied the ends tightly. My leg felt easier. The orderly seemed relieved to see that I could manage to look after myself. I thanked him grimly for his cotton-wool, and went out into the sunshine.

After breakfast was over, the first funeral of the day passed me by. I stood stiffly to attention. A man standing near me looked across at me curiously. "You just come here?" he inquired. "Yes," I replied, without moving my head. "I thought so," said the stranger, "we've stopped standing to attention now." "Why?" I asked, puzzled. "Oh, if we did, we'd never have done," replied the man, carelessly. "Yesterday there were twenty-one deaths in the camp, and eighteen the day before that. In the first week of this month alone, nearly a hundred men were buried!" "I see," I replied slowly. "They come here on their last legs," continued the man, with a shake of his head, "and, before you can say Jack Robinson, they're gone." "What, in Heaven's name, is wrong with them all?" I asked, shocked to the depths. "Oh, lots of things," said the man, "dysentery, malaria, beri-beri, heart-trouble, pneumonia. Some of them just die of broken hearts." I stared at him for a moment in horror. "And does anybody ever leave this camp alive?" I asked. "Oh yes, plenty of folks do," said the man. "Every day there's working parties going down to Nong Pladuk." I pricked up my ears at the name. "Where do they leave from?" I asked. "From the hospital over there," said the man, with a nod of his head, "you see the M.O. if you want to go." With that, he turned and left me.

It took me a full minute to realise that I was being given an opportunity, a golden, heaven-sent opportunity to escape before nightfall from that sad place. I had prayed for deliverance, and here was my chance. Would the M.O. pass me as fit to work? I should very shortly find out. I went back to the hospital.

"Hallo, you back again?" The orderly regarded me curiously. I nodded. "Look, chum," I said earnestly, "I want to go to Nong Pladuk on today's party. Can you fix it for me?" The orderly eyed me with suspicion. "Nothing doing," he said with a shake of his head, "you can't do heavy work with that hole in your leg. The M.O. would never pass you." I would not be shaken off that easily. "Is it a Jap M.O.?" I asked. "No, British," the orderly replied. "Well," I said, "you put me down for inspection this morning, and I won't tell the M.O. how you left me to bandage my own leg." The orderly smiled. "Wise guy, eh?" he said, "O.K. I'll put you down, but don't blame me if you're refused." "I'll take that risk," I replied. "When's the inspection?" "Ten o'clock," answered the orderly.

At ten minutes to ten, I was back at the hospital. A small group of men had already gathered to await the medical officer, and I noticed at least three of my Whanpo comrades in the party. They, like me, had evidently had enough of Chungkai.

The M.O. was punctual. He slowly passed from man to man, pronouncing his judgment. "You can go. You can wait another day. No, you're not going." The orderly came at his heels, making notes. I could not help thinking of that other inspection at Whanpo only twenty-four hours before. It seemed like an eternity. I waited in suspense.

"What's wrong with your leg?" The officer looked at me keenly. "Ulcer, sir," I replied, "but it's only a small thing." "Let's have a look at it," ordered the officer. I undid the bandages, and held out my leg. "Does that hurt?" asked the officer, pressing with his finger just above the edge of the wound. I did not wince, though it hurt abominably. "No, I hardly feel it, sir," I replied, untruthfully. "Are you fit otherwise?" he asked. "Yes sir," I answered. "Well, you don't look so fit to me," he said, glancing at my lean arms and legs. "Oh, I've always been thin, sir," I replied quickly, "but I feel O.K." The officer gave me a quizzical smile. "All right," he said, "you can go." I could have hugged the man. I had been most fearful lest, by some mischance, he had seen me before and remembered my eyesight, but he was a stranger to me. All was well.

Immediately the parade was over I sought out the orderly. "I'm awfully sorry to trouble you again," I said, "but last night some heel pinched my water-bottle. I'll be lost without it. Could you help me?" The orderly looked at me for a moment, as if sizing me up. Then he turned to a big medical chest which stood in a corner. He rummaged in it for a moment, and returned with a new water-bottle. He handed it over to me silently. I thanked him most warmly. "It's a spare one I had," he said quietly, "I wouldn't have given it to you, but I liked your guts out there just now when the M.O. was prodding your leg. It must have been darned sore." "How do we get to Nong Pladuk?" I asked him, "we don't have to hoof it, do we?" "No," said my friend, "you go by lorry, in about an hour's time." "It's supposed to be a pretty good camp," I remarked, remembering what my R.A.S.C. friend had told me at Ban Pong. "Oh, fairly good," said the orderly, "the best on the line, I should think. But remember this: Nong Pladuk is a place where they make you work darned hard. If I were you, I'd go sick with that leg whenever you get there. Otherwise you'll end up without it altogether. Cheerio, and good luck." I thanked him again and took my leave.

This was assuredly my lucky day. Nong Pladuk might be no place for weaklings, but, whatever its unknown rigours, they were infinitely to be preferred to this nerve-racking, soul-destroying moribund existence which was to be found in Chungkai. As the lorry drew slowly out at the main gate, I looked back for one brief moment. Broken-down huts, dilapidated roofs, sagging walls, shattered men. I prayed never to set foot in that accursed camp again.

Before the Japanese invasion of Siam, Nong Pladuk had been

an obscure hamlet, lying some fifty miles due west of the capital, Bangkok. Its inhabitants quietly tended their padi-fields as their fathers and grandfathers had done before them. They lived in bamboo huts clustered round the little railway station, through which the great express trains thundered southwards on their long journey to Malaya. They were kindly country folk, venturing but seldom beyond the narrow boundaries of their little village. Few strangers passed that way, for the white dusty road leading from the neighbouring village of Ban Pong ended abruptly in a banana plantation. A wandering Chinese pedlar might visit Nong Pladuk, laden with the latest Bangkok novelties, but he would tarry only long enough to display his cheap wares to the shy, curious community. He would carry native tobacco, gaily-coloured sarongs, sticky sweetmeats for the children and gilded effigies of Buddha—all the varied bric-à-brac of the oriental colporteur. The children of Nong Pladuk played in the sunshine, or stalked an elusive lizard; the young men boasted and laughed; the old men sat by the wayside, dreaming dreams; the women sang as they bent their backs in the flooded rice-fields. Around the hamlet grew in profusion the juicy fruits of the countryside—mangoes, durians, guavas and mangosteens.

When the Japanese came to Nong Pladuk there was no more singing. All but the old women hid themselves indoors, for they feared the bold eye of the invader. The young men were silent and sullen. The children shunned the stranger in their midst. Only the old men sat on calmly, having no fear. They had reached the winter of their days and only waited to die.

The Japanese were not disturbed by the unfriendliness of their reception. Their eyes were fixed on a distant horizon beyond the northern hills, where victory would bring them rare reward and the joyful plaudits of their people and their Emperor. Had not their leaders already promised them that, before the coming of the next monsoon, they would stand before the very gates of Calcutta itself? They would travel by the new way the prisoners were making, and their attack would be sudden as the lightning and swift as the tiger's claw. Burma would soon be aflame, from Rangoon to Mandalay.

So the fate of Nong Pladuk was sealed. From a sleepy, sun-bathed hamlet it rose, almost in a night, to become the key-point in a gigantic network which stretched from Singapore to Moulmein. The organisation of the new railway supply and repair centre at Nong Pladuk was entrusted to three leading Japanese officers—Hachi Moto, Saki Moto, and Kani Moto. The Motos carried out their orders to the letter. They were ruthlessly efficient, and unswerving in their loyalty. Every man and child in Nong Pladuk was dragooned into cutting down and piling bamboo. The children, of course, thought it was all part of a game, but the young men scowled and whispered together as they slaved for their arrogant enemy. The Siamese were a proud nation who had fought dourly for their independence.

As the first Allied prisoners-of-war arrived from Malaya, they were set to work immediately on the establishment of a base-camp and the construction of numerous bamboo huts to act as store-sheds and light repair units. The thickly-wooded country-side gave excellent cover for such work, and comparative freedom from aerial detection. The three Motos each supervised an area of about two square miles, and the hut building went on apace. No nails were used, as the prisoners soon learned the trick of fitting pieces of bamboo together like a jigsaw puzzle, and of lashing the rafter-beams with long strips of wet, tough tree-fibre. As soon as accommodation was ready, the great grim rush began. By day and night trains drew in from Malaya with all the much-needed supplies of sleepers, line-sections, drills, welders, forges, picks, shovels, bolts, screws and dog-spikes. What the Japanese could not pillage from Malaya they requisitioned from the Siamese. Loop-lines and special sidings were built, and the broad fan-like leaves of the banana-trees barely concealed the thousands of sleepers which had been piled beneath them. This railway job had to be pushed on with the utmost speed. There could be no delay, and failure would mean death to the Motos. It would also inevitably mean death to the prisoners.

In their lay-out of Nong Pladuk prisoner-of-war camp, the Japanese had been devilishly cunning. Fearing that their sidings and supply-sheds might, though heavily concealed, become the target one day for a vigorous Allied air attack, they deliberately built the camp in the open padi half-way between Nong Pladuk and Ban Pong, ringing it around with searchlights and Bofors gun-positions, manned by Punjabis. Thus, should the expected air attack come by day or by night, the camp would be pin-pointed as a fortified area, and liable to suffer instant bombard-ment. It was true that the camp housed, besides the prisoners, a small detachment of Korean guards who would assuredly perish in the rain of death, but Koreans were untrustworthy, ignorant soldiers, whose passing would be little mourned. As for the prisoners, they deserved their fate. It would be grimly amusing to stand back and watch the British destroy the British.

Despite its evident perils, I took an instinctive liking to Nong Pladuk base-camp. It was so different in every way from Chung-kai. Around the central parade-ground stood spacious, well-constructed huts, each raised fully four feet off the ground on wooden supports. This would prevent flooding during the monsoon. Floors were made from strong planking, and a little staircase of sleepers led up to the entrance of each hut. At the back of the camp stood a tiny church and a long, low hospital. The hospital was tolerably well-equipped, although it possessed no real surgical facilities whatever. At Nong Pladuk, men worked hard, but received payment every ten days. It was a mere pittance, of course, but it meant little extras at the camp canteen which could eke out the daily diet—eggs, coffee, tobacco, brown sugar and nutty toffee. One was not paid if one were sick. Consequently the hospital was not over-crowded—not until the men who had been working farther up-country began to come back. At the back of the canteen-hut, a thriving shaving and hairdressing business was carried on by one, Harry Carnell, a genial Londoner and experienced barber. The Japan-ese also employed prisoners in camp as cooks, tailors and general fatigue-men. Okasaki was the Japanese Camp Commandant, but he preferred to leave much of the internal administration to the senior British officer, Colonel Toosey of the Artillery. Okasaki showed more than usual wisdom in doing this, for Toosey was a skilful, efficient officer, fair-minded in all his dealings, both with the British and the Japanese. It was not, therefore, surprising that he gained the trust and respect of both nations.

At the main entrance to the camp stood the Japanese guard-room and living quarters. On a little veranda in front of the guard-room a three-piece orchestra played stirring airs every morning as the long line of workers moved out to Hachi Moto's goods-yard, about a mile away. The Japanese had unearthed a violin, a saxophone and a piano-accordion, and three prisoners played the instruments. Sousa's marches were most popular, although "The Road to the Isles" was a firm favourite. As soon as the column of workers had passed through, the orchestra dispersed and the veranda was again taken over by the camp sentries.

Although certain of the Nong Pladuk guards were Japanese, the majority were of Korean extraction.

The Japanese despised the Koreans, and would not tolerate them in their battle-lines. It was not very hard to understand their reason for so doing. At best, the typical Korean soldier was simple-minded and loutish; at worst, when drunk with crude native whisky, he was a cruel fiend, in comparison with whom an angry gorilla would have seemed almost gentlemanly. There were no limits to the Korean's brutality, although there were definite limits to his courage. It was foolish to give such apes a loaded rifle, but it was criminal to allow them a bayonet also. In their ignorance, they frequently used this latter weapon as a sword or dagger, inflicting grievous injury on prisoners and Siamese alike. In Nong Pladuk, the nicknames by which the Korean guards were known gave ample proof of their character. There were Black Sam, Killer Charlie, The Butcher and The Undertaker. One could not reason with a Korean as one some-times could with a Japanese soldier. He would merely grunt like a pig, or snarl like a cross-tempered dog. In physique the normal Korean was much stronger and tougher than the average Japanese, but he had the mind of a moron and the heart of a devil unchained.

I arrived in Nong Pladuk from Chungkai on 6th April, 1943,

and reported sick immediately. The ulcer in my right leg had widened to an angry suppurating wound, three inches long and two inches broad. Through the middle of the festering hole ran a narrow, blackened spar which I realised with horror was the central bone of my leg. It was now agony to move the injured limb in any direction, and as I lay on my blanket on the hospital floor, I wondered fearfully whether the whole leg would have to be amputated. If gangrene set in, it would be touch and go with my life.

Major Smyth was no ordinary surgeon. With but the most primitive instruments he had already healed worse cases than mine, and he set to work on me as if I were the only patient in his charge. With his calm face and strong, deft hands, he could not but inspire confidence in any man. First the ugly wound was cleaned and finally exposed in all its hideous tenderness. Then, to halt its spreading, a carbolic solution was carefully applied every day through an old-fashioned fountain-pen filler. The acid burned like many needles and the infected flesh whitened and dropped off from the edges of the wound. The gathering pus was swabbed from the face of the ulcer with a piece of cotton-wool, or, if that failed, scraped off with a spoon. Drastic diseases demanded drastic treatment.

I watched the hole every morning and gleefully saw it slowly diminish in size. By the end of a month it had shrunk to the size of a sixpence. In six weeks it was little more than a pin-prick, and I could walk again freely. In two months it had healed completely, and I felt fitter than I had done at any time since the surrender of Singapore. While in hospital, I had fared exceedingly well on an almost riceless diet. I had eaten eggs, liver, sweet potatoes and Marmite. My eyesight also seemed to have improved with the better food and enforced rest.

I was discharged from hospital during the first week in June, and by the middle of the month I was out at work with Hachi Moto. I had joined an honourable company of fellow-prisoners and was a wage-earner once more.

I suppose it really was Galloping Gertie's fault that I came to be beaten up that day. Galloping Gertie, or plain Gertie to her many acquaintances in Hachi Moto's yard, was an open railway truck which had seen many years' faithful service in Malaya before being trundled northwards to Nong Pladuk.

Shortly after her arrival, Gertie deliberately developed a mysterious twist in one of her wheel-axles. At first the defect was not detected, for Gertie's daily trip between Nong Pladuk and Ban Pong was along a comparatively straight stretch of line. One morning, at Ban Pong, Gertie met a sharp bend, just where the main Bangkok section was joined by the prisoners' railway. This was her opportunity to engage in a little bit of private sabotage. Without warning, she cantered joyfully towards the bend with a Japanese clinging grimly to her hand-brake. Gertie cared nothing for brakes, and much less for the Japanese. She hit the bend at a gallop, but simply refused to follow the line. Over she went on her side with a screech of delight, effectively blocking the prisoners' railway and upsetting her load of sleepers all over the line. She had done her little job very well, but not just to perfection. The Japanese had jumped clear in time, and had, unfortunately, escaped with his life.

It took several hours to lever Gertie back on her wheels. The Japanese had lost valuable time through her little escapade, and were in an ugly mood. From that day, Gertie was never again permitted to travel to Ban Pong. She was relegated to purely internal duties in Hachi Moto's goods-yard, rumbling backwards and forwards between gangs of prisoners with loads of empty petrol drums and rusty iron bolts.

But Gertie, though disgraced, was by no means penitent. At every available opportunity she would leave the line and wait cheerfully to be put back on it again. The Japanese hated Gertie and ran from her path when they saw her approach. The prisoners liked her, but they too moved cautiously out of her way. After all, one could never tell precisely what Gertie would be up to next.

I was working with a sleeper gang that morning when Gertie jumped the catch-points down by the railway-crossing. There was a chorus of oaths from her Japanese attendant, and a distant, encouraging cheer from another gang of prisoners working down the line. It would not be long before some of us would be taken off the sleeper party to lend a hand in levering the wagon back into position. I could see that our guard was already making up his mind as to whom he would send.

"Ju men—wagon-o." The Japanese pointed down the line in Gertie's direction. I was determined that I should be one of the ten men required, for it was heavy work trotting to and fro with those massive greasy sleepers all day. At first it had been three men to a sleeper, but now it was two. If more demands were made for up-country workers, I could see it becoming one. I stepped forward quickly.

Working with a 30-foot section of line as a lever, we slowly righted the fallen wagon once more. She went back on the line with an angry crash, and we straightened our backs, just as the lunch-time whistle blew. We hurried off to join the marching column which had already begun to move back to the camp.

When we had gone to Gertie's aid in the morning, our sleeper gang had been brought up to strength from another group, and on our return that afternoon, we found our places filled. But there was no idleness in Hachi Moto's yard. We were directed to another gang. The Japanese who had been in charge of us in the morning had been tolerably cheerful, and had not interfered with us. In the afternoon, however, we came under the supervision of a sulky-looking guard, and grimly began to prepare ourselves for possible trouble.

The task which had been allotted to us was the cleaning-out of a small store-shed, containing boxes of nuts and bolts, rolls of wire and hanks of thin cord. We joined the gang which had been on that particular job that morning. It was not a heavy task, and, with luck, we might make it last until the closing whistle. We usually tried, as far as was possible, to work in twos, for that gave an occasional chance for quiet conversation. That afternoon, however, the Japanese removed me early from the main squad, setting me to work straightening out coils of rusty barbed-wire. We were given no tools to do this properly, having to rely merely on the strength of our hands and fingers.

As I sat alone on an upturned box a few yards away from the hut, pulling and wrenching at the bent wire, I fell to studying our guard as he squatted cross-legged on a pile of sleepers near at hand. He wore a forage-cap, gleaming white singlet, khaki shorts, socks and rubber-soled boots. Across his knees he carried a light bamboo cane, the recognised token of his authority. He appeared to be almost asleep in the hot afternoon sunshine. His eyes were closed, but his lips still wore a sulky, contemptuous sneer. A sly fellow this. He would pretend to be asleep until one of the squad, falling for the trick, would quietly slip off for a moment to gather a couple of ripe mangoes.

Then the little oriental devil would explode with a shout and a curse, and the fat would be in the fire. It happened several times each day, and yet our boys never seemed to learn a lesson. The sleeping guard never slept.

The Japanese suddenly opened his eyes, and with a single lithe movement, was on his feet. He strode across to the hut as if struck by some passing fancy. Curiously I watched him go, wondering what was going on in that unpredictable, suspicious little mind. He entered the hut, and emerged after a few moments with an angry glint in his black eyes. By this time, all the stores had been neatly replaced in the hut, and our men were strolling aimlessly to and fro, giving the impression that they were still busily occupied.

The wailing hooter sounded shrilly across Hachi Moto's yard. I gathered my bundle of wire together gingerly, for the barbs were sharp and my fingers ached. Having stowed it away in the shed, I turned to fall in with the squad for the usual evening count. This generally took little more than a minute, and then we were off, helter-skelter, to join the main column marching back to camp.

As I fell in at the end of the line, I could sense that something was wrong. Our guard eyed us coldly and suspiciously, and would not give us the order to go. Other gangs hurried past us, but we still stood rigidly to attention. Another Japanese came past, and a long, low conversation took place between him and our guard. In one hand our guard held a hank of thin cord which he brandished as he spoke. The other Japanese, nodding his head and muttering "Hai" several times, hurried off in the direction of Hachi Moto's guard-room. We waited on in suspense. What was up? I glanced uneasily at the faces of my comrades, but they were apparently quite as mystified as I.

A few moments later we saw the long line of workers move out of the yard and swing off along the white road which led to the camp. We had been kept behind. I began to have that unpleasant feeling in the pit of my stomach which I always had at the first hint of approaching trouble. It was quite apparent that the Japanese suspected one or more of our particular gang of some misdeed, something connected with that hank of cord. Had one of our men stolen a hank? It looked rather as though that might be the answer. If such were the case, then we might as well prepare ourselves forthwith for a barbarous cross-examination. Hachi Moto's private army of Korean kempi were a prize gathering of merciless thugs.

Suddenly the chief of the kempi arrived, in company with a Japanese officer. Our guard waxed eloquent once more, drawing in his breath through his clenched teeth with a whistling sound in the peculiar way in which Japanese soldiers addressed their officers. There was much bowing on both sides. The hank of cord was again brandished. The officer turned to face us, drawing himself up stiffly to attention. Then he began to speak haltingly, in English.

"Thees morning," he said softly, "my sojo say forty-eight pieces of cord in little store-house. When oro men yasume at lunch-time, only forty-five pieces left. Now my sojo say only forty-tree left in house. Where other pieces, plees?" His voice was now shrill, like that of a child, but his eyes were those of an animal. He held out his hand towards us. "Geeve me back cord, plees," he continued, "then you all go home." I glanced at the face of the chief of camp police. He was a tall, raw-boned Korean, as powerful as an ox, as intelligent as a stone. His teeth were bared in tigerish expectation, and his hand clasped and unclasped his rifle in sadistic frenzy. It would indeed go ill with us if we were left to the pleasure of this bloodthirsty ape. He would think as little of bludgeoning us to death as he would of standing on a cockroach. I looked cautiously along the line of my fellow-prisoners, but the face of each man was completely expressionless. I honestly began to wonder whether, in a sudden fit of forgetfulness, I myself had stolen the beastly cord.

The officer began his preliminary investigation with me. Looking me straight in the eyes, he held out his hand and said quietly, "Geeve back cord, plees." I wore only a forage-cap, shorts, socks and boots. I took off my cap and shook it upside-down, then turned my pockets outside-in to show that I did not have the cord concealed on my person. The officer watched me coldly as I did so and then pointed in silence to my boots. Bending quickly, I slipped off my boots and my socks. Then I stood up again and shook my head. "I haven't got your cord," I said.

The officer moved so quickly that I had no time to intercept the blow. With all his strength he struck me a stinging smack across the face with his open hand, and I fairly rocked on my heels. My eyes were watering badly. The blow had been struck in complete silence. The officer had not shouted or cursed at me. Then it was the next man's turn. Another shake of the head and another shattering blow. On it went down the line of a dozen men. Nobody had seen the missing cord. The officer hesitated for a moment. "One man steal cord," he said brusquely, "one man tell truth, oro men go home."

But nobody would own up. Matters had reached an impasse. Dusk was falling and we still stood before our harsh inquisitors. Then, quite suddenly, one of our gang stepped forward. He was a thin, fair-haired lad whom I had not met till that afternoon. The officer fairly leapt forward. "I have your cord," said the lad, "now let the other men go." "Bagero!" shouted the officer, "where ees cord?" The lad quietly moved across to the pile of sleepers upon which our guard had been sitting that afternoon, pulled a sleeper over on its side, and returned with two hanks of cord which he handed to the officer. "I have the other three hanks back at the camp," he said, "I took them with me at lunch-time."

The officer stood quietly turning the cord over in his hand. Then he turned to face us again. "Engleesh sojo go back camp for cord," he announced, "oro other men guard-room." He nodded to the waiting Korean. In company with our Japanese guard, who had been a silent bystander throughout the investigation, the fair-haired lad set off back to camp by a short-cut past the railway-station. On an angry shout from the Korean, the rest of us left-turned and marched down to the guard-room. This was Hachi Moto's torture-chamber. The officer turned on his heel and left us to the tender mercies of the Korean kempi.

Darkness had fallen and it was beginning to rain as we fell in in two rows facing the guard-room entrance. Six more Koreans were there. One of them went off and shortly returned with four blazing Tilley lamps which he proceeded to hang in a row from the low roof of the outside veranda. The beam shone out half-way across the road, brightly illuminating the two silent ranks of tattered prisoners, and throwing grotesque shadows on the now muddy ground. We waited grimly for our cord-pilfering comrade to return. At last he came back, still accompanied by the Japanese guard, and handed over the last three hanks of cord to the Korean. Then he fell in with the rest of us. He had been hurrying, and I could hear his heavy breathing.

Suddenly the Japanese officer returned and took up his position on the top step of the guard-room, facing us. He had prepared quite a little speech for our benefit. "You all very wicked sojos," he said in his high-pitched voice, "you steal from Nippon sojos, and then you tell lie. Nippon sojos do not steal and do not tell lie. You all very lucky men. Korean kempi will punish you, but you will not die. After you punished, you go back campo." With a curt order in Japanese to the waiting Korean, he turned and left the guard-room. The show was about to start. "This is going to be good," whispered the man next to me, "and I *don't* think!"

The Korean ape stepped forward and ran his eye over us speculatively. In the glare of the lamps, I could see his evil face working horribly. He was deliberately stirring himself up to a mad temper. This beast would not know when to stop. The Japanese officer had said we would not die, but we could be so maimed that death might appear almost desirable.

The Korean seized me by the arm and dragged me forward to the veranda steps. The Japanese generally selected for punishment the tallest man in a squad, and I was the tallest man of our little assembly. The Korean then mounted to the highest step when my head was on a level with his chest. Then, with one hand, he gently teed up my chin as though it were a golf ball. My legs shook under me, but I succeeded in keeping erect.

The blow started right at the Korean's toes. Every muscle in his face and neck stood out like whipcord as he summoned up every ounce of strength in his body. Then he struck me a truly fearful blow with his clenched fist on the left side of my face. I swayed backwards and forwards like a tree in a gale, but one thought kept hammering through my mind. I must not fall. God grant that I do not fall. For a fallen man was kicked, and a kick on my so recently healed ulcer would nearly kill me.

I did not fall. Coloured lights danced before my eyes, my head thumped like a trip-hammer and the side of my face had gone absolutely numb. Twelve times that vile Korean hit me, but after the first blow, I hardly felt the rest. My cap had fallen off and lay in the mud, but I was still on my feet. The Korean motioned to me to replace my hat and to get back into line. I staggered into position once more. Then the cord-stealer was similarly manhandled. Only he received twenty-four vicious blows and his face was cut open. On the last blow he fell to the ground and the Korean leapt upon him with a snarl and kicked him murderously in the small of the back. The fallen man groaned but struggled to his feet, with difficulty.

Then our enemy had a brainwave. Why should he tire himself out buffeting those miserable prisoners? Let them buffet themselves. That would be most amusing. We were paired off in twos and ordered to buffet one another and not to stop until ordered to.

This was the most degrading experience of all. For fully

half an hour we stood facing one another in twos in the now teeming rain, smacking the faces of our comrades. The road was so slippery underfoot that we were hard put to it to keep our balance. The Korean had joined his comrades on the veranda bench and the whole group roared with laughter at our antics. We were the poor, chained dancing-bears.

Try as I would, I simply could not persuade my sparring-partner to keep his temper. He was a short, dark fellow, broad in the shoulder. I had the longer reach, however, and although I merely patted his cheek, I could see his eyes flash with anger. Cautiously I began to steer him away from the near brilliance of the lamps towards the outer circle of darkness, hoping to make a pretence of the whole disgusting business, but the pig-headed fool would not budge. "Move over a bit, man," I whispered urgently, "get back to the dark patch and we won't be seen." "Oh, to blazes with you," he muttered hoarsely, and I realised that he had lost his temper completely. This was too much. After the hammering I had taken from the Korean, even my own comrade meant to continue it in earnest. The short dark man lunged viciously at me. We were both sadly out of breath. His blow missed and as he came forward he slipped and met my bunched fist squarely between the eyes. It was not a hard blow, but meant merely to be a quiet deterrent. It caught him off his balance, however, and he fell heavily at the Korean's feet. "Very goodterna," shouted the Korean, surveying the fallen man. Then he motioned to me to sit down on the veranda step. I had apparently given an excellent performance.

The show was over. Twelve grimy, bedraggled men fell in silently at a signal from the kempi. Every man was almost spent. I was gasping for breath, but was otherwise in fairly good shape. We marched back to camp. The band was not there to play for us, but we received double rations that night from a kindly cook. It had been a trying evening.

In planning the new railroad to Burma, the Japanese had sadly underestimated the primeval force of Nature. Perhaps their maps of Siam were inaccurate or out-of-date; perhaps the reports of their surveying teams were over-optimistic; perhaps they had staked too much on this fateful throw, and could not afford to lose. With powerful Australian gangs working in a south-easterly direction through the province of Amherst on the Burma coast, and mixed groups of British and Dutch prisoners pushing steadily north-west from Ban Pong, there was every reason to hope that the new line would be in operation well before the coming of the monsoon.

For the first few weeks, progress had surpassed all expectations. The Japanese were jubilant. The prisoners, freshly arrived from Singapore, seemed to be working well in their new surroundings. It was true that they argued constantly amongst themselves about the most trivial matters, but that seemed to be a characteristic of these stupid British soldiers. The bamboo cane or the rifle-butt soon settled those arguments. The British had an unhappy habit of maligning their cooks, and accusing them of undercutting rations. The Dutch were lazy, and needed constant watching. They too carried a chip on their shoulders regarding their cooks. On the whole, however, things were going exceptionally well.

It was at Whanpo that Nature gave her first clear hint of unwillingness to co-operate. As a grim warning, she threw great boulders and brawling streams in the path of the advancing workers. But the boulders were blasted aside, and the streams were bridged. This meant delay, of course, but the Japanese had reckoned on certain occasional setbacks, and it was still many days before the monsoon was expected. The work proceeded.

Nature smiled sardonically, and added tough bamboo clumps, teak forests and sheer walls of rock to her defences. Even these difficulties were laboriously surmounted or by-passed by the ant-like forces of man. The job would be finished in time. It was rumoured that the Australians, meeting fewer obstacles, had reached the Three Pagoda Pass on the southern slopes of the Dawna Hills, and were working in a downward rush through Siam. The meeting could not now be long delayed. The British and Dutch teams, now reinforced by press-ganged Tamil labour, were pushing on resolutely, and their vanguard had reached a place called Kinsyok, at least 100 miles north-west of Ban Pong.

Nature was being slowly conquered. Every day the forces of man won a new victory against her, but Nature was ever a grim loser. She had saved two mighty weapons for a last desperate thrust, and the time had now come for her to launch them furiously against her dogged but tiring enemy. These weapons were monsoon and cholera, and both were as unexpected as they were terrible.

The forces of man broke and began to wither away before such fearsome wrath. As the premature monsoon lashed down on hills and valleys, turning mountain streams into foaming, rushing torrents and dusty jungle roads into knee-deep quagmires of black, glutinous mud, the lonely outposts at Kinsyok, Kanu and Nikki Nikki were almost obliterated. The Japanese, seeing their magnificent dream melting away before the force of the wild tempest, went mad with anxiety, driving on their unhappy prisoners to tasks far beyond the normal powers of human endurance. Day after day, the tattered battalions, once allied in the cause of freedom, went out gallantly to their lonely Calvary in the northern hills. With rain streaming from their hideously emaciated bodies, they tugged and heaved at iron and stone, while their vicious little galley-masters howled at them like fiends above the roaring fury of the elements. For thousands of men a railway sleeper became a Cross, and a dog-spike a nail of crucifixion. But the die had been cast, and the railway still went on, with a dead man under every sleeper. The junction of the Ban Pong and Moulmein lines was now long overdue, but the line would be completed to the last prisoner, and even to the last Japanese.

After three long weeks, the ferocity of the monsoon began to subside a little, and the sun would appear for brief periods behind a ridge of black, lowering cloud. Many of the so-called working prisoners were desperately ill with dysentery, beri-beri, malaria and tropical ulcers, but, with the easing in the weather, came a new hope that the Australians could not now be so very far distant. A last mighty spurt, and the junction of the two lines could still be made.

Reserves were rushed north from Singapore to Ban Pong. This ill-starred, unhappy company included our sergeant-major,

Dorfman, Livesley and Ullman, but before we at Nong Pladuk knew of their arrival, they had passed through Ban Pong. For weeks past, lorries had lain hopelessly bogged in the jungle roads, and already the monsoon had exposed gaping breaches in the new railway. So the prisoners had to proceed on foot. There were many tales of tragedy and heroism on that grim march. Exhausted, sick men were carried prodigious distances through the jungle on the backs of their fellow-prisoners; water-rations were given up to help dying comrades; doctors worked till they collapsed in their tracks. Few of these men had been fit enough to make the long train journey from Singapore in the first place, for, after our departure, rations at Changi had grown steadily worse. The Japanese had summoned them, however, and they had to go. Dauntlessly the column marched northwards to the relief of their brothers at Kinsyok.

They had barely reached that stricken camp when Nature struck her last appalling blow. She sent her cholera, that giant of all diseases, the most dreaded killer of the East. The attack came so suddenly that neither Japanese nor prisoners were prepared. During the monsoon, it had been difficult enough to transport meagre rice supplies to the northern outposts, let alone vital medicines and serum. Without medical supplies, it had been argued, the prisoners could still struggle on, but without food they must assuredly perish.

A Tamil labourer collapsed one day in agony at Kinsyok, with a thin trickle of rice-water flowing from his lips. In four hours, he was dead. Then the white men were struck down, not singly, but in their scores. The slender medical staff were swamped, but worked magnificently to save precious lives, assisted only by a sketchy knowledge of the disease, and a small supply of saline solution. The solution was injected directly into a vein to counteract the coagulating effect of the disease on the blood-stream. The treatment was agonising. Many survived it and triumphed; but thousands died. The doctor himself finally contracted the terrible disease, but, with outstanding devotion, he continued to tend his patients, sometimes crawling on his hands and knees in agony from man to man.

The cholera germ does not die when its victim dies, but lives on virulently in the ground where the body lies buried. Only fire can kill the killer. So, while the vile epidemic raged at Kinsyok, a great bonfire of bamboo was kindled to cremate the dead. The men who bore their comrades to the place of cremation lived lonely, empty lives, dwelling apart from their fellow-prisoners. Each of those men knew the terrible dangers of his daily task, but he had offered his life willingly in the service of his friends. By day and night the great fire burned on Kinsyok hill, a grim beacon for the living, a red holocaust for the dead. Returning workers saw the light from afar off, and wondered who would be the next to die. The fiery monument only mocked them in their misery.

At the time, we at Nong Pladuk knew little of such disasters. We lay without the cholera belt. Every now and then, during the monsoon, parties of sick would arrive in camp, but they came from places near at hand, and had little information of what was happening north of Whanpo. As each party moved in, I eagerly sought news of the rest of the section, but nobody knew their whereabouts. They had not come back to Chungkai anyway. I was assured of that fact by a man who had known us all at Changi. The days slipped by.

One morning in early October, 1943, we suddenly ceased loading trucks with sleepers and rail-sections. Tactfully we questioned our guard about the unexpected stoppage. With many gestures, he explained that no more supplies were now required, as the railway had been completed. It would not be long, he said, before we were reunited with our lost comrades, for large parties of British, Dutch and Australians were on their way back, leaving Tamil gangs to maintain the line.

So the Japanese dream had become a reality at last. The railway work was over. From now on every available truck and wagon would be needed for the transport of men and materials to the Burma front. The long-awaited push had started. Soon the invading hordes would descend on Rangoon and Mandalay in their furious westward drive to the gates of Calcutta. We unhappy captives could do little to impede the immense Japanese effort, for we were too closely guarded. Nevertheless, in our own small way, we did what we could.   Steel filings mysteriously found their way into piston-shafts, sand appeared in petrol-tanks, rifles, left for a moment untended, suddenly lost firing-pins and even bolts, sections of spare line went up-country inaccurately or insufficiently drilled.   We guessed that there were no steel drills north of Chungkai.   We were quite right.   In due course the offending sections would come back to Hachi Moto for further adjustment.   We adjusted them as best we could, and they were then sent back once more with apologies—but they were still useless to the enemy.   This sabotage was our humble contribution from behind the enemy lines.   It was unlikely that it would have more than a pin-prick effect on the Japanese, but it gave some feeling of satisfaction to engage in it.   After all, a rail-section which could not be fitted into position at some vital point on the railway might hold up a train, a lorry with sand in its petrol-tank might have to be finally abandoned by the wayside, a rifle without a firing-pin could not destroy a British life.

All the time, of course, our hope lay with our free allies in India.   It was rumoured that the Chinese intelligence service operating widely through Siam and Indo-China, was a first-class organisation, maintaining regular contact with British forces in India.   Our comrades-in-arms would not be caught unawares as we had been in Singapore.   The free armies would be massing in Assam and Bengal, and the advancing Japanese would find themselves confronted by a mighty wall of steel over which they could not pass.   The guns would roar and the warplanes would dive and the shattered, mauled remnants of Imperial Japan would pull out desperately before the grim assault.

On a morning in mid-October, we marched out of Nong Pladuk camp with a curt 'eyes right' to the Japanese guard, and a cheerful wink to our Sousa-playing orchestra.   As usual, the marching column turned left on the road which led to Hachi Moto's yard.   Suddenly our guards halted us.   Had somebody failed to salute the sentry?   Had somebody fallen out so early in the day?   Had the Japanese left his ammunition behind?   We stood quietly on the muddy road, awaiting further instructions.

The column was turned.   We were not going to Hachi Moto's

today. Perhaps it was an unexpected rest-day, and we could go back to our blankets for another hour's slumber. How very pleasant!

The guard moved slowly along the column, laboriously counting off a party of some thirty men. On reaching my file, he stopped, motioning the men behind me to proceed to Hachi Moto as usual. Our small party was apparently required for another job that morning. We were marched back into camp, finally halting outside the hospital. Several stretchers lay piled up against the hut wall, and our guard ordered us to pick them up. Then we marched out again, but turned right at the camp entrance and struck off towards Ban Pong.

The sun shone fitfully, but the skies were overcast. The ditches were still flooded after the recent monsoon, and the road was a sea of mud. During the monsoon, my boots and I had parted company. They had served me faithfully, and I was sorry to see them go, but they were no longer wearable, even as sandals. For several days I had walked gingerly on my bare feet, carefully avoiding sharp stones, but now my soles had become accustomed to the hard going, and were steadily assuming the texture of leather. The barefooted natives, who padded softly past us every day at work, had regarded me at first with no small amusement, but now that several of us had been obliged to discard our foot-wear, they hardly glanced at us. Compared with them, we were still raw novices, but we were learning fast. I could now march over the granite chips at our camp entrance without as much as a twinge. My toes had begun to spread out, like talons, as I walked, but without socks and boots, I was no longer troubled by small footsores or blisters. I stepped forward easily and lightly.

The long platform at Ban Pong was deserted when we arrived. This was the first time I had been there since I came up from Singapore in March, and I looked round curiously, remembering every detail of that fateful morning. My thoughts turned auto-matically to my comrades of the section. For over six months I had tried every possible means to get news of them, but the jungle had swallowed them up completely. At Whanpo they had apparently marched out of my life.

A troop train rumbled in from Bangkok, and stopped at the opposite platform from where we were seated. It was full of Japanese soldiers. Some of them got out and strolled along the permanent way, smoking and laughing together. They almost seemed as if bound for a picnic. Most of them were tough, bearded front-liners, but there was a sprinkling of young men amongst them. I studied the faces of these lads, going to their first battle. They looked tired and listless somehow, and did not join in easily in the good-natured chaff of their more seasoned comrades. I almost pitied them as I imagined them cast suddenly into conflict with some ferocious Gurkha or Senegalese. The kukri would flash and the young men would die where they stood. They would be very afraid to die. The seasoned Japanese were a different proposition though. These men would not fire at their shadows, for they were practised in the art of war. They were brawny infantrymen, armed to the teeth, and ready for trouble. But even as I gazed at them milling round the train, I knew in my heart of hearts that they were going to lose this war.

The Japanese had returned to their trucks, in which they seemed to be as crowded as we had been on our journey north from Singapore. They sat with their legs dangling out over the side, and one of them threw us over a handful of native cigarettes. Perhaps they pitied us as we squatted there like beggars in the sunshine. We shouted 'arigato' and smoked their cigarettes. Tobacco tasted no different even if it came from an enemy. It was more than our Nong Pladuk guards had done in the past six month anyway. They were a sulky crowd.

In the distance another train was approaching down our railway from the north. It hooted mournfully as it neared the platform. It was coming in on our side, and we all rose to our feet at a signal from our guard. At the same time, the Japanese trooper moved off to distant Burma. The trains passed each other just outside the station.

The second train pulled up beside us with a screech of brakes, and we moved forward with our stretchers unrolled. I think I had expected to find the trucks full of Japanese wounded, for I could see no other reason for the stretchers, They would be sullen, vindictive patients if they had just been in action against our forces. We could be on our guard for kicks and face-slappings aplenty.

As I looked into the first truck, I stopped still in my tracks, shocked and sick. Then, involuutarily, a groan burst from my lips. The truck was full of Dutch prisoners and not Japanese wounded. They lay mutely propped up against the truck walls or stretched full-length on the grubby floor. Their limbs were twisted, their bodies broken, their faces sunken and old. Disease had ravaged them frightfully, and my mind flew back to the terrors of Chungkai. Chungkai. That was it. The Japanese were evacuating Chungkai. I should have thought of that in the first place, whenever I saw those pitiful wrecks of humanity. Chungkai was not the only place where the Englishmen, or the Dutchmen either, for that matter, came to die. They were coming to Nong Pladuk also.

We tenderly brought out the first of these living skeletons and laid them down on the platform to await transport. Our Japanese guard eyed them distastefully and quickly moved aside. "Cholera!" he grunted, and spat on the ground. Cholera? I looked at the nearest Dutchman inquiringly, but he shook his head with a faint smile. "Not cholera," he whispered, for he was very weak, "Dysentery—and Kinsyok." "You haven't come down from Chungkai, then?" I asked. He shook his head. "Kinsyok," he repeated wearily, "Kinsyok, bad camp." In my excitement I shook the poor wretch by the arm. "Tell me, mate," I asked quickly, "were there any British with you up at Kinsyok?" He nodded his head slowly, his eyes rolling. "Many British," he replied, "tausands of British. They all die —almost. Tausands die. Cholera, you know—terrible, terrible." He grasped my hand. "Me no cholera, me dysentery. British on train." He pointed with a shaking finger towards the truck from which we had brought him.

I was off like a flash. From truck to truck I wandered down that hell-train, past sorry little groups of Dutch and Australians, until finally I came upon them, my own kinsmen, in the last two trucks. I recognised them one after another as they were half-led, half-carried from the train. There were men of the old

18th Division whom I had known in Changi, men of the Signals, of the Service Corps, of the Military Police. There were Scottish countrymen of the Gordon Highlanders and the Argylls. All were hideously emaciated, with great ulcers on their limbs, swollen legs, and bowed shoulders. Only those eyes were the same. Full of suffering though they were, they still looked at me steadily and without fear, brave and resolute to the end.

Then Nunn walked off alone from the last truck. He strove to appear jaunty, as had ever been his way, but his legs quivered under him. He carried a pack and his rolled ground-sheet on his back, and had a bamboo staff in his hand. I ran towards him with a glad cry, and flung my arms round his thin body. His shoulder-blades stood out like knives. He could hardly speak for joy. "Oh, Mac, Mac," he said over and over again, "My God, am I pleased to see you!" I put an arm round him or he would have fallen, and led him across to a pile of sleepers which lay on the platform. There we sat down together.

I did not press him to speak. At last he raised his eyes, and the old familiar quirk was still at the corners of his mouth. "I feel like the prodigal son," he said, quietly, "it's been a long time." "It has that," I agreed, "but at last you've come to a decent camp amongst real friends." "Not before time either," he murmured. "My God, Mac, you don't know how lucky you were to leave us at Whanpo. We went on to Kinsyok, and some of us went even farther up to Nikki Nikki. The Japs were simply bloody to us and hit us with everything from a rifle-butt to a dog-spike. Then the monsoon came and the cholera after that. The men began to die off like flies. I think there are six thousand dead at Kinsyok alone." I stared at him, utterly stupefied, for I could scarcely believe such horror. Nunn went on with his tale. "The railway's finished, you know. What's left of the old Changi brigade are coming back by degrees, but many of them are too ill to travel yet." He gripped my hand for a moment. "The sergeant-major's gone, Mac," he whispered, "so's Stewart Livesley." For a moment I was too stunned to speak. My voice had sunk to a whisper. "This is awful,"

I stammered, "what happened?" "I wasn't there," said Nunn, "but I understand the sergeant-major died of dysentery, and Livesley—well, I think he died of debility." "What's debility?" "Another name for a broken heart," said Nunn quietly, looking away. There was a silence. My heart was too full. "What about Shaw?" I whispered at last. I had been dreading to ask about Bill, for I had remembered how ill he was the last time I had seen him. "Oh, Bill had his ups and downs like the rest of us," said Nunn, with a smile, "but he's all right. He came through the Kinsyok mincing-machine like a hero, and now he's at Kanchana Buri, about twenty miles from here up the line. He's pretty fit—considering." "What about the others?" I asked, "Harris, Bussey, Wrigley, Dorfman and Ullman?" "Only rumours," said Nunn, "but I think they're all O.K." He turned and surveyed me with interest. "Gosh, you look fit enough now," he said, "they must be feeding you on bully beef every day!" "Not quite," I replied with a smile, "but it's quite good here at Nong Pladuk. Thank God you've come. I've missed you badly." "Thank God I have," said Nunn, "we'll maybe manage to stick together this time—and once Bill comes down the old trio will be complete."

Nunn limped along beside me as I helped to carry a stretcher back to camp. I took his meagre belongings on my back. As we went, he talked about the railway and I listened in silence. Somehow I could not get Livesley out of my mind. I remembered him as I had last seen him at Changi before we left for Siam, standing alone, watching us sadly. Now he had died of a broken heart in some lonely jungle camp in the northern hills. It was a terrible blow to learn of the death of this Heraclitus whom we had all loved so well. Nunn had been the messenger of bitter tidings, but, for himself, I welcomed him at Nong Pladuk like a man who had returned from the dead. For that was, more or less, what he had done.

Nunn was a slimly-built man, but he had an iron constitution. He had, moreover, learned the trick of not overtaxing his bodily strength, no matter what rigorous work he was called upon to undertake. Several times, as we toiled together at

Whanpo, I had noted how carefully he expended his physical reserves, taking full advantage of every available opportunity to rest his limbs. The very moment a 'yasume' was announced by the Japanese, he would instantly drop whatever implement he held in his hands, and stretch himself out full-length on his back on the hot earth, closing his eyes and breathing deeply. At first I made the mistake of thinking that he was utterly exhausted, but I soon realised that it was all part of a deliberate plan, which would undoubtedly prolong his life. Then I asked him to teach me the trick. In a short time I became quite an adept at this Yogi-like method of self-restoration. The lesson was simple to learn, but not always so easy to practise. "Watch the Jap, Mac. Never take your eyes off him, whatever you're doing. The moment he turns his head away, slow up—not suddenly, you know, for that's too obvious, and doesn't really help you—but gradually, like a wheel easing down. If you're asked to lift a weight that you know is beyond your strength, make a pretence of straining every muscle in your body—but don't lift the weight until the Jap sends somebody else to help you. You may get a wallop with a bamboo cane for being such a weak workman, but don't worry about that. Then, whenever you get a yasume, don't just sit down cross-legged. Lie down and that'll rest your heart. And don't, for the love of Mike, get on your feet again until you're ordered to." At Nong Pladuk, I had discovered that this sage counsel could be put into effect without hurting my fellow-prisoners. I never carried it out unless there were obviously too many men available to do a particular job. This happened more frequently than one might have supposed, especially after the railway had been completed. I never once left my share of work for a fellow-prisoner to do, but, at the same time, I never rendered the Japanese any un-necessary service. Brawnier prisoners than I sometimes vied with one another in producing prodigious feats of strength while at work. They would demonstrate to an admiring audience how they could, unaided, carry up to four sleepers on their broad backs, or move a section of line with a single tremendous effort. More often than not, this performance was their undoing, for not only would they have wasted vital physical reserves, but also distinguished themselves, before the watchful eyes of the Japanese guard, as very strong men, who in future could always be selected for tasks requiring more than average human powers. A lorry which had toppled into a ditch would have to be set back on its wheels, a giant tree-stump torn out by the roots— then the strong men were immediately summoned to the task. As time went on, many of them ceased to be strong men, falling an easy prey to dangerous diseases. Then, one day, we would hear in shocked amazement, that they were dead.

Nunn did not stay long in Nong Pladuk hospital. Every day I visited him, and was astonished at the uncanny speed of his recovery. He had a big ulcer on his thigh, but it healed much more quickly than mine had done. Although he had nursed his strength most carefully at Kinsyok, he had arrived at Ban Pong utterly exhausted. Yet, within three weeks, he was out at work in Hachi Moto's yard. Fearing that he had not fully recovered, I suggested that we pool a part at least of our meagre earnings as a sick fund to be drawn on at will by either of us in the event of a recurrence of sickness. He fell in with the plan willingly, and became my banker. It was little enough that we could hope to save, but it might purchase an egg or a hand of bananas, when most urgently required. I felt fairly sure that Nunn would be the first to draw on our emergency capital, but, as it turned out, I was.

One morning in November, 1943, Nunn and I were at work in Hachi Moto's yard. Our task was the clearing of a small hut containing empty fifty-gallon petrol drums. Our guard that day was a comparatively lenient Japanese, who talked to us constantly about his wife and family in Kyoto, and did not supervise our work too closely. We were taking things easily, for, with luck, the task could be made to last the whole day.

About ten minutes before the lunch-time hooter went, how-ever, it became evident even to the most dull-witted of us that, once more, the sly Japanese had caught us all napping. His kindly talk about Kyoto had been a blind, for he had even counted the number of empty drums which we had moved that morning. Purring like a cat, he suddenly showed us his claws. The task would be finished by lunch-time, otherwise the kempi should hear all about our laziness. There still remained over a hundred drums to move. We looked at one another, and then, to the accompaniment of an angry snarl from the Japanese, began to work like demons. It meant a terrific spurt from every man, but we could just make it.

Nunn and I, temporarily discarding our 'go-slow' tactics, bent our backs and fairly tore into the work. By the end we were hurling the heavy drums from one to another like footballs along a human chain which stretched out of the hut to the nearby piling-dump. As the hooter sounded, the last drum was just being thrown out. Quickly it bounced from man to man until it came to me. As I put out my hands to grasp it, a strange feeling of giddiness suddenly came over me, and I swayed on my feet. With what seemed a tremendous effort, I managed to toss the drum on to the next man. We fell in in two ranks. The task was done.

But our Kyoto-loving Nipponese was of a vindictive nature. He was rather annoyed that we had completed the work in time, for he was secretly looking forward to calling in the kempi to punish us. Deliberately he kept us standing there until the main column of workers had begun to move back to the camp. To tag on at the end, we should have to run. At last he let us go.

We all immediately broke into a gallop to catch up with the rest. Without the slightest warning, my legs suddenly collapsed under me, and I fell headlong in the middle of the yard. How stupidly clumsy I was, tripping over my own big feet! I scrambled up quickly, but found that my legs seemed to have turned to rubber. They swayed and wobbled under my weight, and would not obey my will. I felt exactly like some grotesque puppet, moving forward by wires and strings. This was awful. What had come over me? Surely I was not becoming paralysed? The marching column was drawing steadily away from me. I could not catch up, no matter how I tried. Nunn, who was in the last file, looked round and beckoned urgently with his hand. I raised my arm in response, but again collapsed heavily. I felt terribly weak as though all my strength had suddenly ebbed from my body. The column had now passed the guard-room and turned left for the camp. I should never catch up now. I lay on the hot earth and gasped for breath.

Suddenly I felt a strong arm round me, and I was hoisted to my feet. Nunn had returned, as I knew he would, and with him had come a stranger. The newcomer was a veritable giant, well over six feet in height, and enormously broad in the shoulder. I thought I recognised him as having come down with Nunn's party from Kinsyok, but could not be certain. "Get him on my back, Sergeant," said the giant to Nunn, in a cheerful Cockney voice, "I'll carry him back to camp." I was raised like a feather on the stranger's shoulders, and the three of us passed the guard-room. I think the kempi actually saluted, but I was not greatly interested.

After a few moments of this pick-a-back journey, I began to feel much better, and whispered to the giant to set me down again. "Not on your life, mate!' he replied, "you see, we both know what's wrong with you." I looked questioningly at Nunn, and he nodded his head. "We were at Kinsyok together," said Nunn, turning to the broad stranger, "and we've both seen this kind of thing before. In fact, Joyce here has had it before himself." "Joyce?" I inquired. "Yes, mate," said the giant, "Don Joyce is the name. I'm in the Gunners—135 Field Regiment." "I'm another Donald," I replied, "Same section as Nunn here. Now, tell me, what do you both think I've got?" "Beri-beri," said the giant quietly, "had it myself at Kinsyok. I was as weak as a kitten, but I swelled up like a balloon, and the Japs thought I was as strong as four men. They gave me four men's work to do anyway." For a moment I was silent. I had heard of this strange disease before, but had never known very much about it, except that it was a form of dropsy, caused by eating too much rice. I had been eating quite a large amount of rice lately, for I was always so hungry. We were now half-way to the camp. "I don't know what I'd have done without you both," I said, "for I don't think the Japs would have carried me back to camp." "Sure, they wouldn't," said the giant with a laugh, "they'd have left you there, or the kempi would have kicked your face in." "Thanks very much, anyway, Joyce," I said. "Aw, shut up!" said the other, rather uncomfortably.

"And don't call me Joyce, will you? That's a girl's name. Call me Don, like the other fellows." "O.K., Don," I replied. "Is this beri-beri dangerous?" I inquired. "It can be—very," said Nunn, "you've simply got to rest with it, and try not to eat too much rice." I smiled grimly. "Looks as though I'll be digging into our sick fund," I said, winking at Nunn.

Although I twice asked my large friend to set me down, he insisted on carrying me not only into camp but into hospital as well. There I was left until Major Smyth could see me. After lunch, Nunn brought my bedding over from our hut, and Smyth arrived on his heels. His examination took only a few seconds. "Beri-beri," he said quietly, "Get yourself a bed-space farther down the ward and I'll see you again later. Got any money?" "Yes," said Nunn, before I could utter a word. "Good," said the Major, "buy a couple of eggs and a hand of bananas at the canteen, and get them inside you quick. And lay off rice in the meantime." "You're lucky," said the Major, suddenly. "Yes, sir?" I said inquiringly. "Yes, you seem to have two very good friends at least. By carrying you in, they've probably saved your life. You'd never have made it otherwise."

As I lay back on my blanket, half an hour afterwards, after a lunch of two boiled eggs, four bananas and a piece of nutty toffee, I felt most humbly and eternally grateful, not only to those two great-hearted friends who had snatched me back from the jaws of death, but to God for His everlasting mercy. It was up to me to try to get well again quickly, for I owed that service both to my friends and to God.

There are two distinct forms of beri-beri. There is the dry variety, which is characterised by an excruciating neuritis, but little swelling. Then there is the wet variety, where the victim's body begins to swell up, like a giant balloon, with an excessive amount of fluid. The swelling generally starts at the feet and ankles, gradually moving up the legs to the abdomen, and finally affecting the whole frame. Wet beri-beri, though painless, is much the more dangerous of the two forms, and by far the more frightening. Things can come to such a pass that the unhappy sufferer, hideously bloated, loses all semblance to a human being, becoming like a giant football with two small legs and a face roughly scrawled on it. In such terrible cases, the patient usually dies, unless the liquid, which is fast smothering his heart and lungs, can be drawn off artificially, and in large quantities. As this fluid results from an over-consumption of rice, the sudden stoppage of the rice diet has usually marked effects for good. The swelling begins to decrease, and the patient improves, but it is many days before he regains anything like his former strength.

It was the New Year before I left hospital. I was put on the camp's permanent sick-list, and thenceforth, my duties were light, in-camp fatigues. Work out at Hachi Moto's yard had dwindled by then, but Nunn and Joyce still went out every day. I racked my brains to find a way of augmenting the sick fund. Then I entered the 'tobacco racket'.

The man who set up the first tobacco factory in Nong Pladuk camp had a keen eye to business and a shrewd knowledge of the inherent weakness of human hature. Even before our one and only consignment of Red Cross provisions reached us at Changi in 1942, every tobacco-loving prisoner had provided himself with a small tin box in which he stored his precious supply, together with a quantity of roughly-cut cigarette-papers. Next to his blanket and water-bottle, his tobacco box speedily became the prisoner's dearest possession. Immediately he received his miserable wages at the end of a working-period, he would be off hot-foot to the camp canteen to lay in fresh reserves.

At first, it was far from easy to accustom ourselves to the taste of native tobacco. Our palates, gently nurtured on mild Virginia weed, rebelled violently against the new and powerful mixture, which entered the lungs like a whiff of strong ammonia. Heads swam and eyes watered. Many men became total abstainers on the spot. The majority persevered, however, and quickly discovered that the new blend, ferocious though it was, contained practically no nicotine when treated properly, and gave a satisfying smoke.

Native tobacco was sold by the kati, in compressed block form. In colour, it varied from black to a golden brown. As only the richest prisoner could afford to buy a whole kati at a time, the blocks could be purchased in halves or quarters, depending on the means of the customer. The weed had to be 'doctored' before use. This treatment was eventually brought to a fine art, particularly by our Dutch comrades from Java, who knew the tobacco of old. First, the compressed block was thoroughly teased out and rubbed by hand, until a great mountain of loose strands emerged. The pile was then immersed in water which instantly turned a jet black. The sodden mass was then carefully wrung out, like a wet cloth, and removed. Then followed the drying process. A ground-sheet was spread out in the sun, and the tobacco laid out on it in neat rows. In that great heat the stuff did not take long to dry, but the rows had to be turned regularly. This was done by the owner who sat jealously guarding his precious possession from the stealthy hand of the predatory passer-by. At last the process was complete and the tobacco was carefully gathered together again. It had now lost its extreme virulence, and was smokable.

There still remained a thorny problem to solve. This was to secure an adequate quantity of cigarette-papers. In Siam, packets of Rizla sheets were obtainable, but only at fantastically high prices. A packet cost nearly as much as a kati of tobacco. Letters from home were quickly used up. At last we began pilfering paper at every possible opportunity from the Japanese. Sometimes it was too thick to roll properly, but a group of Australians cleverly solved that difficulty by setting up a paper-splitting business. I never ceased to marvel at the way those keen-eyed experts did their job, armed only with a short piece of bamboo and a razor-blade. The paper was rolled over the bamboo at one end and held firmly in position, while a deft cut was made with the blade. A quick flick of a finger-nail and the first layer was peeled off surely and steadily. Air-mail sheets could be sub-divided into two or even three distinct layers, post-cards into seven or eight. Of course the Australians kept back a sheet or two every time for their own use. That was only their due reward for their trouble.

The Nong Pladuk tobacco factory really came into being through the sheer inability of many of us to roll cigarettes in the dark.   With our ungummed papers, it was often a trying enough business even in daylight.   When darkness fell, it became an absolute impossibility, except for the most experienced roller. What would appear to be an evenly-rolled cigarette turned out to be a ragged trumpet of tobacco, either half-filled, or over-flowing.   Valuable supplies dropped out of the tin and were lost. We turned in desperation to the crafty factory-owners, as they knew all along we would.   They could provide us, at their price, with the neatly-finished product.

The factory began in one of the huts, amongst a group of sick men.   With great patience they invented simple rolling-machines of bamboo and strips of rubber, and with their pooled resources, purchased large supplies of tobacco and Australian-made cigarette-papers.   Having enlisted the services of a British lorry-driver, whose daily duties took him to places as far distant as Ban Pong and Kanchana Buri, they bought their tobacco at cost price, which was considerably lower than the Japanese-controlled prices pre-vailing in the camp canteen.   The lorry-driver was, of course, taking a big risk in smuggling the stuff in, but he was quite prepared to run that risk in return for a share in the firm's profits. The Japanese, ever on the alert, suspected that something of the sort was going on under their very noses, but could find no real proof, for the lorry-driver was much wilier than they.   The tobacco came in concealed under a driving-seat, behind a tail-board, or at the bottom of a vegetable crate.   Once it had passed the guard-room, of course, the chief danger was over, for a kati of tobacco looked the same, whether it had been bought at the canteen or outside in Ban Pong.

There were no sleeping partners in the tobacco firm, each member of the group having his particular job.   One man treated the raw material, two men rolled, while another prepared papers, smearing each sheet with a thin film of rice-paste which acted as a strong adhesive.   On an average, 150 cigarettes could be made from a kati.   The enterprising company slung a placard at the end of their bed-space, between two mosquito-net uprights. This bore the well-known name of Salmon and Gluckstein, and was an excellent advertisement for their wares.   Trade was brisk from the very start, for prices were moderate.   Soon another

he brandished his rifle, but this time he had stumbled on a place where men were too busily occupied paying a nobler, higher service than to him. The padre, with hands folded and head bowed had just commenced his closing prayer. The Korean growled angrily and strode through us towards the altar. The quiet, steady voice of the padre continued without as much as a tremor. The prayer came to an end and we all stood up to receive the benediction. As I rose to my feet, I could see The Undertaker standing at the altar quivering with anger, his small pig-like eyes fixed menacingly on our padre. The quiet voice went on unmoved. "And the blessing of God, The Father, God, The Son, and God . . ." "Curra, bagero!" the Korean screamed, smashing his bunched fist into the padre's face. We stood stock-still in silence. The padre had staggered, but regained his balance. "The Holy Ghost be with us all, Amen," he concluded in the same quiet voice. We raised our eyes. The Undertaker had gone berserk, standing with his rifle and bayonet quivering at a 'charge' position. Any moment I expected to see our padre run through. Suddenly, with a supreme effort, the furious Korean pulled himself together, and grasped the padre by the arm. Then he led him roughly out of the chapel in the direction of the guard-room. The service was at an end.

When we first heard, early in 1944, that a model prisoner-of-war camp was to be constructed at Nakawn Patom, a small village lying some fifteen miles east of Nong Pladuk, we treated the information cautiously as yet another stratagem of the Japanese. The new camp, it was stated, would be laid out on recognised Red Cross lines, its position notified to the Allies, and its perimeter fence illuminated at night with powerful searchlights. There would be plenty of good food at Nakawn Patom, and ample medical supplies. In due course, all prisoners-of-war in Siam would be housed there, and receive regular wages although they performed only the lightest duties. We took the mention of this Utopia with a large pinch of salt. Having denied us Red Cross supplies for over two years, the Japanese were unlikely to treat us at this stage with such consideration.

But, as time went by, the Utopia looked like becoming a

reality. Every morning, parties of prisoners left Nong Pladuk
for Nakawn Patom, returning in the evening with the news that
the new camp was going up quickly. Nunn, who was on the
job, told us personally that the huts were the largest and most
up-to-date that he had ever seen, and that the whole settlement
was being laid out with the most careful attention to detail.
There was to be no central kitchen, as there was at Nong Pladuk,
but a number of small cook-houses, each serving a limited
number of huts. During a yasume, Nunn had spoken to a
Siamese workman who was giving expert advice on the construction of the new huts, and had learned that the much-heralded
Japanese push in Burma had misfired badly. Apparently the
enemy had been halted on the banks of the Irrawaddy by vastly
superior Allied forces, and was now beginning to retire before
their determined assault. What was even more heartening was
the whispered information that a Japanese convoy, nearing Bangkok, had been bombed by American aircraft, and that American
submarines had appeared in the Gulf of Siam. There was also
an interesting rumour that the Americans had begun to strike
back in the Pacific, and had recaptured the islands of Mindanao
and Luzon in the Philippine group. If this were true, then the
joyful day of our deliverance was coming steadily nearer. A
feeling of quiet optimism began to spread through Nong Pladuk
camp. Our little concert-party which frequently gave perform-
ances on rest-days, had a new song to sing, or rather, an old
song with new words. The air was the familiar "Good night,
Sweetheart", and the last verse pulled at our very hearts.

> "Good night, comrades, now our show is ending,
> Good night, comrades, on your way you're wending,
> One day nearer to the day of our returning,
> Goodnight, comrades, goodnight."

We joined in the refrain lustily, but the day of our returning was
fated to be somewhat delayed.

One morning, in the middle of 1944, Nunn told me that his
Nakawn Patom party was a man short, and that I could go with
him, if I so desired. I had been put on the Nong Pladuk
permanent sick-list, but felt quite fit and had so far recovered
from beri-beri that only the tips of my toes were slightly numb.

I was most curious to see this new Red Cross camp, so asked Nunn to count me in. The Japanese guard raised no objections. I set off with the party by lorry.

Despite what Nunn and the others had told me, I was amazed at my first sight of the new camp. It was a magnificently spacious place, with large huts set in streets. It would easily accommodate all prisoners in Siam. Concrete had been used in the construction of the cook-houses and of certain of the main roads. I could not help comparing this clean, neat settlement with the sprawling shambles which had been Chungkai.

I worked all day carrying bamboo poles and lacing roof-beams. I enjoyed the task, for it was not arduous and the Japanese guards did not interfere with us. I had just completed the last quick knot on the roof of one of the huts, and was glancing idly round me from my thirty-foot high place of vantage, when I suddenly saw something which disturbed me greatly. Round the perimeter of the camp ran a high bamboo stockade, on the outside of which lay flat, open country. During the day a long, low-roofed hut had been going up on the other side of the stockade, but we had paid scant attention to it, thinking it was merely some additional camp store-house. Siamese workmen were on the job, and with their superior knowledge of hut-building, had completed their task by noon. Then they had disappeared and we had lost interest in them. From my elevated position I could now see over the top of the flat hut to the land beyond. The Siamese had not gone home, as we had thought, but were now busily engaged with pick and shovel levelling out a long strip of padi into what was all too evidently a runway. In my excitement I almost fell off my perch. Once more the Japanese had shown their diabolical cunning. Nakawn Patom camp was meant for us without a doubt. But we poor prisoners were to be the shield and buckler of the enemy. What could be safer than to build an aerodrome next door to a Red Cross camp? The place would be immune from attack, for no Allied plane would dare to drop its bomb-load at the risk of destroying countless British, Dutch and Australian lives. I looked again to make sure. Yes, I was right. The low-roofed hut was no store-house; it was a hangar. I slid down quickly from the roof, and fell in with the rest of my squad for the usual check-up. Immediately I had boarded the homeward-bound lorry, I broke the sad tidings to Nunn. To my surprise, he received the news calmly. "I shouldn't worry, Mac," he said at last, "On the whole, I think it's a good sign." "A good sign—of what?" I inquired shortly, "that we're going to be blown up in our beds?" "No," said Nunn, quietly, "I think it's a sign the war's coming closer. Maybe the Yanks *did* get that convoy off Bangkok after all. Nakawn Patom will be the Japs' nearest fighter 'drome. That means they're afraid of more trouble from the Yanks." I lapsed into silence, busy with my thoughts.

We arrived back in Nong Pladuk just before six o'clock. I had polished off my last grain of supper when Elkins arrived to chat with me. Elkins, or as we more commonly termed him, the Elk, was one of my Nong Pladuk circle of friends. He had been in camp all day, and was now anxious for a chinwag. "Hallo, Elk," I said, laying down my blanket for the night, "had a nice day?" "Here, Mac," he said, "before I forget, I've a message of good wishes for you from an old pal, name of Shaw." I dropped my blanket and turned to him excitedly. "Bill Shaw," I exclaimed, "I thought he was at Kanchana Buri. Is he here in Nong Pladuk?" "He was—this afternoon," replied Elkins, "but he's gone now. He came in with a party bound for Japan. He was asking for you and Nunn, and seemed very disappointed to have missed you both." I groaned inwardly. What appalling ill-luck! I had not set eyes on Bill Shaw since we had worked together at Whanpo, and now we had passed each other, like ships in the night. We had heard rumours that parties of prisoners were being transported from Bangkok to Japan, but had paid little attention to them. It was tragic that we had come so close to each other, and separated again so widely during a short afternoon.

As the days passed into weeks and the monsoon came again with all its teeming discomfort, I waited anxiously for news. One afternoon in August, I was chopping dry bamboo for the cook-house fire when I saw a small party of men arrive on foot from the direction of Ban Pong. The party was halted and fell out in the middle of the parade-square. One of the men came over to the cook-house in search of a dixie of tea. Our cook-house staff gathered round him interestedly. He had apparently a story to tell. I moved across to where the newcomer stood. He was waving his arms excitedly as he elaborated on his narrative. "Torpedoed," he said, "the whole bloody convoy. We were landed in Saigon, but God knows what's happened to the rest of the chaps." I waited no longer, but fairly pelted across the square to where the rest of the party were gathered, awaiting allocation to huts. Was Bill with them? I could not see him anywhere. Feverishly I sought backwards and forwards amongst the ranks of tired, hungry men. Then I spotted an old Changi acquaintance, Gilbert by name. He had known us all in Singapore days. He would surely have some definite news.

"Hallo, Gibbie," I cried, shaking him by the hand, "were you on this party?" "Sure thing," he said grimly, "who are you looking for?" "Bill Shaw," I replied anxiously, "you haven't seen him by any chance, have you?" "Sit down on my kitbag a minute," replied Gilbert, abruptly, "and I'll tell you." I feared the worst immediately, for his eyes were full of sadness. "Is he gone, Gibbie?" I whispered, but I knew even before the other spoke, that I would see my dear friend no more. "I'm afraid so," replied Gilbert, "he was with me right on to the end." "Tell me about it," I said firmly, "I'd like to know the details." "Well, there isn't much to tell, really," he said, solemnly, "we left Bangkok in big Jap transports, and were meaning to hug the coast right round to China, before making a dash for Japan. Bill and I were on the same ship and palled up at once. Bill was a funny guy, you know. He seemed to have some sort of, of . . ." He hesitated for the word. "Hunch?" I suggested. "Yes, hunch," continued the other, "you know, that-bullet's-got-my-number-on-it kind of thing." "I know," I replied, quietly, "Bill was always like that. Go on, please." "Well," said Gilbert, "Bill seemed to think that we were going to be bombed or torpedoed, anyway, and arranged with me that if anything happened, I was to meet him at a certain spot on deck, and then swim for it. There were plenty of rafts and things on deck, you see." I nodded and he went on. "During the day we were battened down like cattle, but at night some of the

146

hatches were left open. It was early morning when the sub. plugged us fair and square amidships. God knows if it was a British sub. or a Yank, but she made a dirty big hole in us anyway, and I legged it for deck all I could go. Men were yelling out everywhere, but I found Bill O.K. Together we shoved off one of these round rubber sausage-looking things into the sea, and I dived first. I grabbed the edge of the raft and looked up at the ship's side. The moon was shining and I could just see Bill standing by the rail, waiting for the ship to roll over so that he wouldn't have so far to drop. Then, I think, another torpedo must have hit the ship. There was one almighty crash, and a great burst of light and Bill just fell off into the sea. He was so near me that I could grab him with one hand. Men were dropping into the sea all round. I got him up with his head over the side of the raft, but he was all limp, and I knew he must have been struck by something. I had just got one arm under his shoulder when the blasted raft keeled over. I lost my hold on him and he was gone. I never saw him again, and he wasn't picked up. I'm sorry, chum, but that's the lot." He turned away quietly.

The lump in my throat had grown to the size of an egg while Gilbert told me the tragic story, and I could not speak. I walked quickly to the cook-house, where, amongst the dry bamboo in the back store, I could be comparatively alone. Nunn was out at Nakawn Patom, but I would see him later. Until that moment, I thought I had forgotten how to weep, but in the quiet of the wood-store, the hot tears rolled down my cheeks. The sergeant-major had gone, Livesley had gone and now Bill, my closest and most trusted friend, had died in this wild country, so many thousands of miles from his own land which he loved so well. Like me, Bill was an only son, but his father was dead. This would break his mother's heart. It had nearly broken mine. In the confusion of a sinking ship he had gone on before me, quietly, resolutely, unflinchingly, and all the trumpets would sound for him on the other side. For us who still struggled on in suffering from day to weary day the future was dark and un-promising. But he had reached his last haven in a happier land.

bamboo platform head-first, and lay with my hands over my head, my heart thumping like a trip-hammer.

I had no need to shout, for Nunn was beside me in an instant. We lay shoulder to shoulder, quivering with fear. Every battery round the camp seemed to have opened up, and the hut was in an uproar. Men shouted in terror and frenziedly sought cover, crashing into bamboo beams and tripping over their still half-awake comrades. Some rushed outside, where it was now as bright as day, throwing themselves into ditches and drains. There were no slit trenches in Nong Pladuk camp. Above the roar of the guns, I could hear the alert wailing out over the camp like a death-knell. "This is sheer suicide!" bawled Nunn in my ear, "the whole blasted camp will be lit up, and they'll plaster us like hell." I could not speak, for my teeth were chattering like castanets. Unless the planes dived on us, the Bofors guns would be ridiculously short in the range, and would be merely signing our death warrant besides their own. The furious shelling went on without ceasing. Tumpa, tumpa, tumpa. I thought my head was going to burst. Something fell through the roof of the hut with a crash and landed on the bamboo platform a few feet away. I closed my eyes and waited to die.

Suddenly the guns were silent and the searchlights doused. It happened in a moment and the unexpected quiet deafened me. Then I heard the drone again. It was slowly dying away in the east. The planes had circled the camp but had not attacked it. I cautiously raised my head. A piece of broken attap fluttered down from a jagged hole in the roof. I looked around. Everywhere men were peeping from below beds, and I could see their white faces in the ghostly moonlight. Of our Korean guard there was no sign whatever. He had vanished as if into thin air. He had legged it out into the padi-fields at the first shell-burst, and was now probably a good half-mile away. The Koreans were even more scared than we. At least one Japanese remained in the camp, however, for I could hear him shouting ferociously in the distance as he chased wandering prisoners back into their huts at the point of a rifle. He probably thought some of us might try to make a break for it, but he should have no worries on that score. If we had wanted to escape, we could have done so several times in the past, but we knew we had no chance whatever.

Nunn and I rose to our feet. A large piece of broken shell had fallen through the hut roof and lay on the bamboo sleeping platform. It was a mercy that no one had been directly under it. Joyce still lay on his bed, swathed in his grey blanket. "You're a cool customer," I said, "I thought you would have hit the deck like the rest of us." "So I would have," he replied with a grin, "but I was so dashed scared I couldn't move!" I crawled back into bed, but morning found me still awake.

With Nunn, Joyce and several other friends, I moved to Nakawn Patom with a sick party early in September, 1944. We were, I think, all rather sorry to say good-bye to Nong Pladuk, for we had made many new friends there, and it was a pretty good camp, as far as prisoner-of-war camps went. It had its usual quota of bugs, lice and mosquitoes, of course, but these were inevitable guests whose presence had to be tolerated. Nong Pladuk had a definite personality and community spirit which were sadly lacking in such a camp as Chungkai. We looked forward to making Nakawn Patom a second Nong Pladuk, where we might complete our term of captivity in an atmosphere of quiet, cheerful retirement. We had done our share of toil, and would now hopefully await the coming of that glorious day of liberation, which we all felt to be just round the corner somehow. The war could not possibly go on much longer, men said. Japanese wounded, returning from Burma, had brought tales of flame-throwing Americans and grim, murderous Housa trackers. The Allies were advancing slowly but surely to our relief. Every day their aircraft flew high over us, bound for the go-downs at Bangkok, or the aerodromes of Northern Malaya. We had become accustomed to the sudden warning cry of "Skawki!" * and the abrupt order to take cover. By Christmas, we thought, we might be eating plum-pudding again. The idea was most exciting. From the countenances of our guards we could see that the tidings from their far-flung

*Skawki (Jap.)—Aircraft.

battle-fronts were far from encouraging. We chuckled inwardly, revelling in their misfortune. The tables were being turned, and our little slant-eyed tormentors were getting their own deadly medicine cast back at them. Of course they vented their spitefulness on us, but we expected that. After all, we were merely prisoners, unarmed and sick, who could not fight back. We were not so sick, however, but that we could still raise a rifle and pull a trigger. We outnumbered the Japanese by roughly a hundred to one, and if we were armed overnight by friendly Siamese, the camp would speedily be ours. But, of course, that could not happen until we knew our allies were close at hand.

Try as we would, however, we could not make Nakawn Patom a really happy camp. The huts were comfortable enough, and we had little to do in the way of work. We had a greater supply of washing-water than we had enjoyed in Nong Pladuk, and the food had not deteriorated to any marked extent. But as time went by, more and more sick men arrived in Nakawn Patom from other camps, until finally the whole atmosphere of the place became irksome. There was a lack of purpose in the camp which sapped the prisoners' strength. Some men even went mad, and had to be lodged in a special hut, barricaded around like a fort. The Japanese were terrified by mental illness, although they could view physical suffering dispassionately. I often saw those poor crazed creatures with their haunted, empty eyes, and pitied them intensely. They had been sane men once, with wives and sweethearts; now something had cracked under the terrible strain, and they were no longer themselves.

The days dragged by into weeks, and I thanked God constantly for my friends. Without friends in Nakawn Patom a man must surely die. Despite its neat appearance, it was as grimly dangerous a camp for a man's morale as Chungkai. I longed to return to Nong Pladuk.

Japanese aircraft landed and took off from the nearby airstrip regularly, but the camp and the makeshift aerodrome were still left unmolested. Then, towards the end of the year, a tragedy happened. One afternoon, as the prisoners lined up at Nong Pladuk for their evening meal, their camp was bombed by

Allied planes. They were the biggest aircraft our men had ever seen, and they flew so low that their bombs could be plainly seen tumbling from the open hatches. Nong Pladuk offered little shelter from the deadly blast, and, in that lightning raid, a hundred men perished and four hundred were injured. The worst cases arrived in Nakawn Patom, and once again I gazed dumbly on stark human suffering. British, Australian and Dutch—they were all there with gaping wounds and terror-stricken eyes. My Dutch friend, De Vries, who had sat for hours trying to teach me the intricacies of chess, lay groaning in agony before me, with an arm and a leg severed from his body. The doctors said he could not live more than a few hours. Van Mellen, another Dutch acquaintance, whose left hand and arm were terribly mangled, told me haltingly about the raid. The bombs weren't big, he said, but they split into millions of needle-like fragments, which could go clean through a man. He glanced at De Vries and shook his head sadly. De Vries had been foolish. He had run out into the open, straight into a bomb. A lot of men had done that, and a lot of men had died. De Vries died that night. It was all a fearful mistake, and I knew in my heart of hearts that our airmen couldn't have known. All the same, I blamed them bitterly at the time. I called them fools and butchers.

The New Year came and went, but it brought no relief from our suffering. Leeringly the Japanese told us that the tide of war was turning again in their favour, and we almost believed them. They taunted us in our misery and said we should be prisoners for many more years. The prospect of even another year of this slow torture was intolerable. I began to doubt my own strength. Nothing short of a miracle could save us now from death. Our hopes had been shattered, and our most earnest prayers had gone unanswered. The day of our deliverance had not even begun to dawn. Nakawn Patom was getting us all down.

Early in January, 1945, another member of the section arrived in camp. Wrigley came in with a party from up-country. He was terribly emaciated, and looked much older, but he was still comparatively cheerful. He had seen Harris, Dorfman and

Bussey at various camps up the line, and said they were expecting to arrive in Nakawn Patom soon. Of Ullman he had no information, but he thought he was all right. I began to wonder whether my friends might not be better off where they were than in the unhappy confines of "Non-Combatant", as our camp had come to be nicknamed.

To make matters complete, I contracted malaria. I marvelled that I had not caught it earlier, for my faithful blanket had now become a mere wisp of transparency, in and out of which the mosquitoes flitted at will. At night they bit me mercilessly, spreading their particular germ with devilish efficiency. Three-quarters of the camp were down with fever. Nunn was still apparently unaffected, but Joyce was having a daily attack, which left him weaker every time. Quinine supplies were strictly limited to the worst cases. The Japanese were running short of the drug, for Java, its main producer, was now apparently cut off from them by sea. We wished that just a little might trickle through.

At first I hardly noticed the fever, and shook it off quickly after a two-minute rigor. But in ten days or so, it would return more severely than before. The rigors lasted fifteen, thirty, even forty-five minutes. I felt increasingly weak and ill. By the end of March I had had ten distinct attacks, and my strength was waning rapidly. I walked about with a permanant headache, and began to fear the heat of the sun. My blood turned to a pinkish water, and I was given a transfusion. I was haunted by the fear that the dread disease would reach my spine when I should most assuredly die. I had seen men die of spinal malaria already. It was far from pleasant.

On 2nd April, 1945, a day when I was for once free from fever, the Japanese announced that a light working-party was required to leave Nakawn Patom immediately for Malaya. The nature of the 'light work' was not divulged, but I knew, deep down within me, that unless I went on this party, I should die at Nakawn Patom before the month was out. I knew that I was ill-equipped for such an expedition, and might perish on the way, but I could no longer stay in that dark, unhappy place. Once before, at Chungkai, I had taken a chance and won. Perhaps I should win again. I prayed to God for strength and gave in my name to the Japanese. Nunn and Joyce did the same. We three should stick together to the end. With typical cynicism, the Japanese passed us all as fit, but I could have blessed them. We left by train for an unknown destination on 3rd April.

IV

I Walk with the Ox

ONCE AGAIN THE JAPANESE HAD TRICKED US. OF COURSE WE should have known better than to volunteer for light work. By the beginning of 1945, there was not a man amongst us but who was well acquainted with the bland cunning of our enemies. We had learned to read the day's disasters in the morning faces of our guards; we had come to watch the clenched fist or the upraised rifle-butt with open-eyed preparedness; we had even inured ourselves to withstand the shattering buffet, which was invariably the wages for ignorance or slothfulness. Our long period of comparative inactivity and Nakawn Patom, and the new exciting rumours of Allied successes in Burma and the North Pacific had apparently taken the keen edge off our memories of what had been. We had forgotten that Ukemi himself, the arch-fiend, had once called the Railway of Death a 'light operation'. We actually thought that the Japanese had shot their last vicious bolt. But once more we were all mistaken.

When the proud sad history of Far-Eastern prisoners-of-war comes to be accurately set down, the Railway of Death will loom darkly in its pages—and rightly so, for that stupendous task, which cost the world so many thousands of young and precious lives, must go down to posterity as an awful symbol of lawless tyranny and fettered suffering. The great red fire which burned on Kinsyok Hill will not be readily put out in a lifetime; and the free nations of the world would do ill to forget that, when once the tiger has tasted the blood of men he cannot easily be contained by frail chains or in an unlocked cage.

The Railway of Death was a supreme tragedy, cast on tremendous, heroic lines. The building of the Mergui Road in 1945 must always remain, in comparison, an intimate drama, presented by a small cast of tired but seasoned players. Many men have returned, seared in mind and body, to tell a horrified world of the rigours of Nikki Nikki, Kanu, Kinsyok and Chungkai. The nations have striven to console their sons. Many have stopped their ears, as if with wax, lest the tale become too bitter to bear.

Few men came back from the Mergui Road. Even as the glad hosannas of victory rang out from every city and hamlet of the free peoples, even as the streets were full of singing and the tolling of bells, the men of Mergui still looked to God for deliverance, and prepared to die. The tidings of peace reached many too late, for they had already set out on their last journey across the great river, and could not turn back.

Had we light workers of the Nakawn Patom party realised fully the true significance of the Mergui Road, we might well have undertaken the task with willing hands and rejoicing hearts. Therein lay the bitter irony of Fate. We had already helped to build a great railway from Ban Pong to Moulmein, and had seen the Japanese legions pass over it in triumph on their way to the Burma battle-line. Night and day vast supplies of war materials had poured northwards in a never-ending stream. Despite the rosy reports of Allied successes, given us stealthily by passing natives, despite the thunder of Allied warplanes over Nong Pladuk, it seemed inconceivable to most of us that the powerful Japanese thrust in Burma could be so quickly turned. The true purpose of constructing a road through the jungle from Prachuabkherikun on the Gulf of Siam to Mergui on the South Burma coast seemed to us, therefore, to enable fresh enemy attacks to be mounted, and fresh victories to be gained by the advancing Japanese forces. We had been prisoners-of-war for so long that we had almost forgotten that an advance can speedily become a retreat, and that victory can be changed to disaster. We did not know that the Mergui Road was merely intended as a back-door through which the broken forces of Imperial Japan might yet escape the relentless fury of total war and utter annihilation. It was not wise that we should be told such things.

We were ill-equipped to face the task, for our reserves were nearly gone. Three years of harsh treatment had tried us sorely;

our bodies were weak through malnutrition and disease; our minds were growing dull with the eternal misery and hopelessness. Our defences were down, and we had no longer sufficient strength to raise them anew. Day followed weary day, until some men began to pray for death as a blessed release from their intolerable suffering. Others lived on, awaiting the summons. It was not worthy to rush uninvited into Heaven.

Our worldly possessions consisted generally of the barest necessities of life—water-bottle, pack, ground-sheet, mess-tin and blanket. Some were still fortunate enough to have tattered shorts and ragged boots, but my entire wardrobe comprised a black loin-cloth of Japanese origin. I went barefooted in the jungle, through dust and mud, rocks and thorns. My blanket I used as a towel. Two rice-bags, sewn roughly together, served me as coverlet by night. At the very bottom of my pack I carried a dog-eared, mud-bespattered pocket edition of the New Testament. The little book had travelled with me from England, and had had several perilous adventures. Twice it had been confiscated, as subversive propaganda, by the Japanese, and twice it had found its way back to me by devious routes. If God willed that I should die in captivity, I should take the Message with me across the dark river, and the water would be less cold and bitter.

Surprisingly enough, Joyce, Nunn and I seemed to have found a new lease of life on the Mergui Road. We had toiled on the railway; we had suffered agony from tropical ulcers; we had all three fallen victim to recurrent malaria at Nakawn Patom. Joyce, of course, had always been immensely powerful, but neither Nunn nor I had ever displayed unusual powers of endurance. In captivity we had lost weight. Joyce had dropped from fourteen stones to just over nine. I was cadaverous. Nunn had grown rather like some wizened Egyptian mummy. Yet we laboured day after day, month after month, like men possessed, watching others die around us. Perhaps, as the saying goes, we were merely living on our nerves; but I like to think that our extraordinary vigour came from God. From April until late July of that last year of war, neither Nunn nor I suffered the slightest twinge of fever, and Joyce had had only one short attack—and this in a countryside peculiarly favourable to the spread of malaria. It was quite inexplicable.

The task of driving a narrow winding road across the Himalayan foothills from the Gulf of Siam on the east to Mergui on the west appeared at first to present no extreme hardship or difficulty. In effect, the road was little more than a sandy track through the jungle, varying in width from fifteen to twenty feet. On either side ran a narrow ditch to help drain away the monsoon waters when they came. It was the dry season, and we drove forward quickly through the soft soil. We had soon penetrated to a distance of over twelve miles. As we advanced we established small reserve camps at regular intervals of four or five miles. The first was at Maudung, which took its name from a nearby mountain-torrent, the second at Tahang, the third at Mengui. These camps accommodated small gangs of prisoners, employed as maintenance men in the immediate area. Each possessed its own store of rice and dried vegetables, replenished regularly throughout the dry season by lorry from the coast base at Prachuabkherikun. In special huts were housed our supplies of road-building materials—picks, shovels, changkols, baskets, saws, axes, coils of rope and boxes of dynamite. Picks were light and unreliable, shovels were loose in the haft and worn in the blade, axes and saws had lost their keen edge, but they were the only implements we had, and we had to be content with them. With every day's service they became more dilapidated, increasing our difficulties a thousandfold.

Our guards were, for the most part, Japanese, although they included a small group of Koreans. They were not, generally, so rigorous in their treatment of us as had been our guards on the railway, but they were never lenient. Each camp had a holding force of some twenty Japanese, under the command of an officer or gunso. Our particular camp was commanded by one, Shegara, a regular sergeant, who had the confident bearing of the seasoned campaigner. Shegara was no youngster, but a man between thirty-five and forty years of age. He had fought his way dourly through the Chinese and Malayan battlefields, and had not visited his native Osaka for over eight years. He was grimly efficient, holding absolute authority over his men.

His skin was tanned deeply by wind and weather, and his shoulders were so broad that he appeared almost dwarfish. But in the eyes of his followers, he was a giant.

As far as Mengui we had advanced simply by widening an existing path. While helping to erect the cook-house there, I made an interesting discovery. On the massive, twelve-foot high root of a teak-tree, I found that someone had carved out certain letters which had been almost obliterated through the passage of time. They would be native symbols, probably, traced by some bold adventurer, who had penetrated thus far into the dark jungle after some straying cow or wounded tiger. Then I scanned the sprawling letters more closely, and in an instant, I was down on my knees beside the tree, rubbing excitedly with the palms of both hands on the lichen-clad root in an effort to decipher the inscription. I had seen the letter 'F' and underneath it, an unmistakable '4'. These were no unintelligible native symbols, but English characters. I spat and rubbed until finally the lichen rolled off like a thin skin, and the mute, proud message was revealed. 'A.I.F. 1941.' it ran. A.I.F.! Australian Imperial Force! I felt rather as Scott must have felt when he discovered that the Norwegian had reached the Pole before him. The Australians had been here four years before. I examined the surrounding roots carefully, but no further inscriptions were to be seen. The path we had followed up from the coast had been carved out of the virgin jungle by Australian prisoners. Where had they been taken? Hong Kong? Indo-China? Siam? They could not have come from Malaya anyway, for Malaya had not fallen in 1941. It was a complete mystery. The path stopped just beyond the tree. What grim tale could this tree tell? Why had the path been carried no farther? Perhaps the Japanese had originally intended that the railway should be driven through this jungle, but had given up in face of insuperable difficulties. If such were the case, then we should meet those same difficulties ere long. This was evidently 'bad country', for our Australian comrades did not appear to have sojourned in this place. Not even the ruined remains of huts were visible.

From Mengui we pushed steadily forward. Progress was

exceptionally slow, for at every step we encountered great trees and clumps of intertwined bamboo which had to be blasted clear. The heat was stifling, and the perspiration dried on our bodies in a fine layer of salt. By mid-June we had established yet another camp, which, for want of a name, was merely called Number 4. The ground had already begun to rise steeply under our feet, and through an occasional break in the leafy canopy above us, we could glimpse sheer, rock-bestrewn mountain-slopes. The task of climbing those heights would be considerable, let alone of driving a road over them. But still we toiled onwards under Shegara's eagle eyes and iron discipline. Many men fell sick daily, but were returned to Mengui and Maudung, and reserves were brought forward.

By the beginning of July we had erected Number 5 camp by the shores of a rushing stream which cascaded down in a series of wild waterfalls from the summit of the mountains. Here we received the cheering news from Shegara that a strong team of natives were advancing to meet us from Tenasserim, on the other side of the hills. I could not help thinking of that other team of white men who had fought their way southwards from Moulmein two years before to effect such a meeting on the railway. Then the British and Dutch had been caught by the monsoon at Kinsyok, and had perished in their thousands. It would soon be time for the monsoon to break once again. Day after day we scanned the skies anxiously, watching for darkening clouds and warm breezes, but the dry weather held and we hacked and blasted our way upward with frantic effort. Every morning we padded over three miles along our narrow stony road to the roof of the world, where we toppled great teaks over mighty precipices, and carried loaded baskets of rubble till our arms ached and our backs nearly broke with the strain. It was gruelling, heart-breaking work, but we dared not stop, lest we collapsed from sheer exhaustion.

By the end of the first week in July, the accursed road had been completed, and a Japanese lorry drove over it from Mergui to the Siamese coast. The driver took his life in his hands at every tortuous bend and zigzag incline, but with luck rather than skilful management, he brought himself and his heavy vehicle through unscathed. Our road had passed the test satisfactorily. Shegara was well pleased. We were ordered back to Number 5 camp to rest. Our work was done. Before the monsoon broke we should pull out and return to dry billets on the coast. Such was our belief, but Fate had decided otherwise. One evening in the middle of July, on the very eve of the monsoon, Shegara informed us that none of us was going back. We were to stay on as maintenance men, ensuring that the road we had made would not fall into disrepair during the forthcoming wet season. We received the news in shocked silence, for each man knew in his heart of hearts that the end could not now be long delayed. In our utterly exhausted condition we could not but go down before the rending fury of the elements. The dice were loaded against us, and there would be no returning, after all, to England's green and pleasant land. I looked with a new interest on the grim, emaciated faces of my comrades—my fellow-Scots, Anderson and McPherson, the Englishmen, Stanton, Mayhew, Joyce and Nunn, the New Zealander, Fairbairn, the Dutchman, Van Groet. They were an honourable company who bore their scars nobly, who would not flinch when they gazed in Death's dark visage. I felt strangely comforted, for, if it was my lot to die, these men would journey with me into Paradise. I could ask for no better, braver friends.

All day long a hot breeze had been blowing through the jungle. No birds sang, and even the ceaseless high-pitched chatter of the monkeys was stilled. Only the dry rustle of the wind in the tall elephant grasses broke the hushed silence of the great forest. It was zero hour. As we lay sweating as if in some giant oven, we waited for the coming of the monsoon. In England it would be a quiet summer morning, and the cattle would be standing knee-deep in the lush meadows, blinking dreamily in the bright sunshine. The bumble-bee would be droning busily from flower to flower, while the dragon-fly flitted past on waxen wings.

I sat upright on my bamboo bed, straining my ears. In the distance I seemed to hear the rushing of a great wind, and in a moment a scurry of raindrops pattered across the attap roof.

The patter rose to a drumming, the drumming to a surging roar. A piece of attap fell across my hot face. It was wet and clammy to the touch. The air became suddenly cold and I shivered, drawing my rough sleeping-bag more tightly round my shoulders. A steady stream of water coursed down on my forehead. I rolled over quickly to a drier position, but there was no escape. The roof was leaking like a sieve, and everywhere men were hurriedly covering their meagre possessions with their ground-sheets. I pulled in my pack and cast my ground-sheet over me with the rubber side uppermost. I heard a man groan in the darkness and another swear. "Hell!" said a deep voice near me, "the floor's flooded." It was Larry Fairbairn. I heard Van Groet's merry laugh. "Women and children first!" cried Stanton, "my bed's dry." "You're a lucky devil, Stanton!" said Nunn, "I'll swop with you." "Oh go to sleep," said Mayhew angrily, "you fellows talk too much." "All right, son," retorted Nunn, "but tomorrow, you can have the shovel and I'll take the pick." "Perhaps the monsoon will wash them all away," I suggested. "Oh shut up, Mac," said Joyce dreamily. The rain was gurgling in the ditch outside the hut. "I hope Shegara's bed's wet, anyway," came a voice. Then all was quiet, and we lay listening to the monsoon. There was something utterly merciless about this incessant downpour. It was the life's-blood of the jungle, but for us it meant nothing but desolation and misery. In the morning, our road would be washed away completely, and in its place would lie a great quagmire of liquid mud. The Japanese would not trust their lorries in such hazardous conditions, so we should have to fall back on the buffalo-carts. It would be a tricky business getting through to Number 4 camp for rations, but some of us would have to go, if we were not to starve. In this weather it would be all men to the wheels of the heavy carts, straining, slipping, cursing as we turned the thick wooden spokes. The fittest would have to go. But who were the fittest? Anderson and McPherson were still in fairly good shape. Stanton couldn't make it for he had fever. Fairbairn was hobbling along with an ulcer on his leg, but he wouldn't wish to be left out. Larry was always like that. So was Van Groet. Joyce would be chosen whether he could make it or not. There were sometimes distinct disadvantages in looking so powerful. The Japanese rarely passed him by. Mayhew was a sticker who would see anything through. These Lancashire lads were made of the right, dogged stuff. Jack Nunn and I would not be left behind. Neither of us could lend a great deal of weight, but we could always help to turn a spoke. Shegara would finally decide who was to go, but no matter whom he chose, the trip would certainly be no picnic. It was over four miles back to Number 4, and the road was far from level, even in the dry season. Now, in this teeming monsoon, it would be as slippery as a skating-rink, and as humpy as a whole army of camels. Still, I had been advised more than once before not to go half-way to meet disaster. Let the morrow bring its own difficulties. I turned over and fell asleep.

The buffalo has a definite mind of his own. Even when broken in by the will of man, he will follow his own intention, be he pushed, pulled, goaded or cajoled. The tangled jungle is his home. For defence Nature has provided him with a thick, hairy hide and a pair of immense horns, so keen that even the angry tiger will hesitate to attack. He recognises no highway code, following a man-made path only because it is more convenient to do so. When harnessed to a high-wheeled wooden cart, he will sway forward from left to right across the road, carefully avoiding ruts and potholes.

When we first arrived at Number 5, we had possessed six carts and twelve buffaloes, but ten beasts had been withdrawn for service at Tahang and Maudung, leaving us with only two. These gallant survivors were almost as exhausted as the prisoners who drove them, for they had been worked pitilessly by the Japanese. They were yoked together to the long central pole of one of the six carts, the remaining five being manned entirely by prisoners. Every day during the dry season the carts had made the journey to Number 4 for rations, returning just before nightfall, loaded high with rice, fresh water-melons and an occasional side of pork.

As I ventured outside the hut on the first morning after the monsoon broke, I found our road in an even sorrier state than I had feared. Overnight it had become an ankle-deep morass of gleaming black mud, slimy and treacherous. The skies were a misty grey, and the tropical rain sluiced down on my bare flesh, chilling me to the very marrow. Our cooks had wisely laid in a fair store of dry firewood under cover, and breakfast was on the boil. I waded through the mud as far as the little stream which ran by our camp. It was now no longer a stream, but an all-devouring chocolate-brown torrent, sweeping dead bamboos and brushwood before it like chaff. The road was already flooded to a depth of two feet in places. As I returned, wet and shivering, to camp, I passed the spot where the six carts stood. They were black and greasy and would need careful handling. The two buffaloes stood patiently under the doubtful shelter of a bamboo-clump, awaiting the will of their masters. Suddenly one of them groaned deeply, and turned his great head in my direction, as if dumbly appealing for help. I moved over beside the beast and minutely examined his hairy body for a possible laceration in the flesh. The buffalo eyed me mildly, sensing that I was a friend. Another groan burst from him. Some internal trouble, I judged—a chill, perhaps, or a weakened heart. I prodded him suddenly just behind the massive shoulder, and he shied back violently, lurching against the other animal. It might be nothing more serious than a torn muscle after all. The trip to Number 4 would bring out the trouble, whatever it was. I patted the poor brute and went back to the hut.

Immediately after breakfast we paraded in the lashing rain before Shegara. He wore a light oilskin cape and hood, under the edge of which his eyes gleamed like those of a wild-cat. He had been washed out in the night, and was in an evil temper. Coldly he selected us for the ration-party. Only three carts were to travel that day, apparently, and we thanked God for small mercies. Anderson, Fairbairn, Nunn and I were picked for the same party. McPherson and Joyce were ordered to the cook-house, where two men had gone down with malaria. Mayhew and Van Groet were evidently to be kept back for maintenance duties. Stanton, who had struggled out on parade with the rest of us, narrowly missed being sent along with us, but he collapsed face downwards in the very nick of time, and was sent back to bed. He had a temperature of 103 degrees.

We were to travel on the first cart, using the buffaloes, while six men were allotted to each of the other two carts. The two lumbering beasts were harnessed by their necks to the centre-pole. I was certain now that one of them was ailing seriously, and drew Shegara's attention to the fact. The buffalo was groaning like a wounded man, but Shegara had never heard of kindness to animals. He cuffed me furiously with his open hand, indicating that the buffalo would stay where he was until death delivered him from his suffering. We started off cautiously along the slippery road, back to Number 4. The other two carts fell in behind us, two men hanging on to each centre-pole.

As we had anticipated the going was hard from the very beginning. In a very short time we were bespattered with mud from head to foot, and the rain washed our hair down into our eyes, blinding us. Sometimes the cart moved away from us altogether, and we were left to drag our feet clear of the clogging mud. By the time we caught up again we were exhausted and gasping. Over bends and down valleys we went, finding sharp stones at every step, and knee-deep water at every hollow. Behind us the voice of Shegara sounded hoarsely, spurring us on to even greater effort, cursing us for every delay. I turned the spokes of the great wheel till I thought my arms must break with the strain. Fairbairn was at the other side, gasping and panting like an exhausted swimmer. That ulcer in his leg was giving him plenty of bother, but he had a great heart, and would not give in till he collapsed utterly. He was magnificent, that New Zealander. It would not be his fault if the men of Number 5 failed to get their usual rations.

We reached Number 4 at noon, and quickly loaded up, for we knew the return journey would take longer. The sick buffalo was now groaning and wheezing horribly, and every moment I thought the beast's last hour had come. We had dinner at Number 4, but the camp was almost deserted. They too had to brave the elements to secure rice from Mengui. We learned one interesting piece of news. During the night an elephant had crossed from Tenasserim, and its Burmese mahout had brought an exciting, though garbled tale of war-weary Japanese, fleeing in confusion before the hammer-blow attacks of seasoned British and Indian troops. I prayed to God that the report might be true, for none of us could possibly last much longer. Number 4 was in as perilous a state as Number 5. Farther back, we were told, things were even worse. Hundreds of men had perished of dysentery and spinal malaria, and Maudung was now called "Death Valley". At Tahang, an epidemic of typhus had broken out, and men's lives were flowing away like water. We set our teeth grimly and made off hurriedly on our return journey.

In two hours we covered only two miles. We had reached a point where the road dipped down sharply into a flooded hollow to rise again on the other side in a series of heart-breaking zigzag curves. We halted our cart for a moment on the summit of the hill to ensure that our rough wooden brake was set in position before we tackled the treacherous downward slope. Behind us the other two carts were drawn up, but their teams were impatient at our snail-like progress, and shouted to us to draw our buffaloes clear so that they could take the hill at a run. Quietly we drew in our vehicle to the side of the road, and watched the other two carts go down the slope at a breakneck gallop. They hit the water belt with a mighty splash and in a moment were through and half-way up the opposite slope, with men hanging on the shaft and wheels like limpets. It was a most dangerous manœuvre, but it had brought its reward. One of the carts was almost at the top of the zigzag incline already. The other was close behind it. We began the slippery descent into the valley.

The two buffaloes picked their way gingerly and we practically sat on the hand-brake as the cart skidded downwards with locked wheels. We reached the hollow safely and waded through the miniature lake where the surface had been churned to a flecked foam by the sudden passage of the other two carts. Laboriously, with heads bowed almost to our knees, we started off on the hard upward climb. It was push all the way with every man exerting every ounce of his flagging strength. I raised my head cautiously to see how our sick buffalo was going to take the climb. The great beast was now gasping desperately, and its whole body was trembling with the strain. I felt a great wave of pity sweep over me. The buffalo was most surely dying on

M

his feet. Something had to be done quickly to relieve him from his agony.

"Pull up a minute, lads." I barely recognised the voice as my own, it was so hoarse and crackling. The cart came to a sudden standstill on the face of the slope, and Nunn hurriedly sat on the brake to prevent it sliding backwards down again. Fairbairn straightened his aching back and looked across at me quickly. "What's up, Mac?" he inquired kindly, "Got fever again?" "The buffalo," I replied, pointing with shaking finger at the ailing beast, "Larry, untie that poor brute for heaven's sake, or it'll collapse." There was a sympathetic grunt from Anderson. "Yes, do that," he said, "I can't stand to see a sick beast suffering like that." Larry pulled his feet clear of the slime and turned towards the centre-pole.

Suddenly I felt a tremendous blow across my bare back and fell headlong in the mud. For a minute everything seemed to go black before my eyes and then I gradually recovered, giddy and sick. I looked up to find Shegara standing over me, his dark face livid with anger. In his right hand he held a thick bamboo pole, with which he was preparing to strike me a second time. "Curra, bagero," he screamed, his angry countenance only a few feet from mine, "curra!" I scrambled to my feet and stood to attention quickly. "Buffalo no goodterna," I said, pointing to the animal. "Buffalo O.K.," shouted Shegara, "oro men PUSH!" As we bent our backs once again, Shegara strode forward and poked the wounded buffalo on the flank. "Buffalo," he shouted, "speedo." The beast did not respond to his little tormentor. With a great, heart-rending groan he sank on his knees, dragging the other animal down with him. The centre-pole creaked, but bore the strain. Suddenly the leather neck-band parted, and the dying beast rolled clear of the cart. For a moment his great legs twitched in agony and a flurry of red spume burst from his gaping jaws. Then he lay still. He was dead. I stepped aside and patted the hairy carcase.

This was more than Shegara could stand. To him I appeared the ringleader of a group of muddied mutineers, and I had to be taught a lesson. He shouted to me and pointed to the centre-pole. For a moment I did not comprehend his intention, but moved forward towards him. My comrades were standing in silence, wondering what new wickedness was to take place.

Then, in a flash, I saw it all. I was to be the new buffalo, taking my place beside the remaining animal! No one but Shegara could have invented such humiliation. I glanced round at my three comrades. I saw Fairbairn's jaw harden and the muscles of his neck stand out like whipcord. Anderson had clenched his fists and was evidently preparing for sudden action. Nunn was standing with a look in his eyes which I had never seen there before. It held nothing but murder. "Hold it, lads," I said as quietly as I could, "I'll go in the shafts."

Under Shegara's baleful eye, I grasped the wooden cross-bar firmly and raised it. The other buffalo gazed at me suspiciously and shook his head. Then he started off so suddenly that I was swept off my feet. I hung on grimly, not daring to let go, lest I fell under one of the wheels of the cart. My arms were nearly jerked from their sockets, and I felt sick with the beast's nauseating breath in my lungs, but, after what seemed an eternity, we reached the top of the hill. The other two teams had gone careering home, of course, for they also hated Shegara's grim supervision, and had been quick to avail themselves of the heaven-sent opportunity to get clear away.

As we jogged forward over more level ground, I studied the pace of the buffalo carefully and gradually attuned my step to his. That made the going easier. When he swayed over to the right, I swayed with him, when he lurched back to the left, I drew my feet clear of his heavy lumbering hoofs. By the time we sighted Number 5 I felt as though I had walked with the ox all my life. I had reached the very nadir of bitter experience, but I had survived. Fuku had been right. He had said he would lower the British soldier to the level of the coolie. Shegara had gone still further. He had brought him to the level of the beasts of the field.

Every day brought fresh disasters. During the third week of July, an event occurred which was destined to have tragic consequences for the men of the Mergui Road. A lightning attack was launched by Allied warplanes on the coast base of

Prachuabkherikun. The hastily-camouflaged store-sheds and petrol-dumps suffered severe damage. It was the bitter irony of Fate that those store-sheds had contained vital food and medical supplies, earmarked for delivery to the five prisoner-of-war camps on the new road. By the end of the third week of July, the driving monsoon had eased sufficiently to allow lorries to travel as far into the jungle as Maudung at least, although, beyond that camp, the road was still impassable. But no lorries could come, because there was no fuel left to drive them. Buffalo after buffalo had been slaughtered to provide food, and now the heavy wooden carts were almost useless, for men had no longer the strength to push them. Even our Japanese guards were on starvation rations. Every day, bands of heroic prisoners, British, Australian Dutch and American, fought their way grimly from camp to camp in a desperate effort to secure meagre supplies of rice and medical equipment for their fellows. Every day fewer men were on their feet. Every day more men died.

Number 5 camp presented a particularly sombre scene. During the dry season we had built a crude hospital across the little stream on a strip of scrubby rising ground. While the sun shone, the numbers of our sick had been comparatively few, for all really serious cases had been removed to Maudung. When the rains came, our sick had to remain with us, for no transport was available. As our daily rice-ration diminished, our hospital cases increased alarmingly. Only a handful of men appeared on parade each morning. The common malady was malaria. Without an adequate supply of quinine, men strove desperately to shake off the vile fever which racked their limbs and befuddled their minds. It was of no avail. As attack followed attack with inexorable rapidity, they became weaker and weaker, losing all desire for food, existing only on water. No man could long survive such fearful suffering. Day after day we saw our dearest comrades succumb to the ravages of the dread disease. We were powerless to help them, and could only pray that their passing would be swift.

Of our intimate little circle, Van Groet was the first to die. One morning in late July, I went to rouse him from his sleep and found that he was gone. He had not waited to say farewell, but had set off bravely, with a smile on his lips, to prepare for our coming. We buried him in the lonely jungle, where others would not tread upon his grave. The same day, as the first shades of darkness gathered in the lofty tree-tops, Larry Fairbairn, that very gallant gentleman, quietly slipped away. I went out into the dark jungle and wept bitterly. The following morning Anderson and Stanton were removed to hospital. Nunn and I had been out all day in the drenching rain, chopping down saplings with which to log the greasy road. At first Shegara had demanded that each man who could drag himself out to work should fell ten trees in a day, but, as our numbers dwindled, the daily quota was raised to eighteen. To a man in a normally fit state, the task would have presented little difficulty, for these saplings were soft and easily chopped. But we were not fit men and our tools were blunt and heavy. It took every ounce of our flagging strength to shear through one tree, let alone eighteen. Many saplings had to be discarded in the end, as their bushy tops were so intertwined with jungle creepers that we could not drag them clear. As we strode barefooted from glade to glade, over a glistening wet carpet of fallen leaves, leeches fastened themselves firmly in the spaces between our toes. More often than not we remained unaware of their presence until it was too late and they had rolled off, loathsomely distended with their feast of blood. This also weakened us steadily.

In the evening we returned to camp, dragging our legs as if they were weighted with lead. As we entered the hut, Joyce met us with the bitter tidings that Anderson had died at noon, and that Stanton was expected to go at any moment. It was a cruel blow, and we hastened across to the hospital at once. We arrived ten minutes too late. He had gone.

Van Groet, Fairbairn, Anderson, Stanton. We had lost four of our most trusted friends and brothers-in-arms. I had no stomach for my supper that night, but sat staring dully at four empty bed-spaces, until Nunn implored me to eat if I wanted to live. Mechanically I turned the tasteless rice over in my mouth. Did I want to live? What earthly good did it serve to prolong this hideous agony from day to day? Our medical supplies were gone, our food-stores were sadly depleted, our hope of deliverance was withering with every day that dawned. It was so easy, so delightfully easy to die. Van Groet had gone in his sleep so peacefully that not even the folds of his blanket had been ruffled. It must be glorious to escape from it all like that—no fuss, no anxiety, no awakening. Nunn laid a hand on my shoulder kindly, sensing my thoughts. "No, Mac," he said quietly, "eat your rice like a good lad. We must not go before we are called." "Why not?" I asked, without raising my eyes to his face, "don't you think it's easy to die, Jack?" "Certainly it is," he said, "but it's much more difficult to live, and we must always take the hard way. Life was never really meant to be easy for any of us, otherwise there would be no point in striving at all." "Is there anything left to strive for now?" I asked, "you know as well as I do that we're dying on our feet—all of us. What's the use in hanging on, just to sit by and see the others go? Wouldn't it be wiser just to cut things now before it's too late?" Nunn shook his head slowly, gazing straight into my troubled eyes. "I'm surprised at you, Mac," he said reprovingly, "I always thought you had a faith that would move mountains, and now you're talking about going before it's too late. Don't lose that faith now, for God's sake, for it's being tested sorely and you're being tested with it. How do you think you've come through so much already? By your own strength of body?" He laughed bitterly. "Not on your life, son. You've said your prayers and that's worth more to a man than big muscles, take it from me." I looked at him in surprise, for I had never regarded Nunn as a very religious man. "Yes, Mac," he continued, reading my thoughts, "I can pray too, you know, though maybe not exactly in the same way as you do. I reckon our prayers all get to the right place in the end, provided we pray for the right things. You can't just ask for things on a plate without making some definite move to get them for yourself, you know. We've got to fight hard and long, but God helps us in the end. That's just a little way He has, and a lot of folks in this world don't fight long enough to discover it." I regarded my friend in amazement. Here was a man who spoke with authority, whose personal faith was greater than mine. Somehow I felt thoroughly ashamed of myself. I determined to make amends for my indecision. Nunn glanced sideways at my serious countenance and laughed. "Mac," he said, "we're a couple of earnest old owls. I think I've still got a couple of rolls of tobacco left, so let's have a smoke and relax."

I awoke next morning to find myself once more in the grip of malaria. Nunn collected my slender morning ration of rice and tea for me, and sat anxiously on my bed, as I struggled hard to swallow the unappetising meal. My teeth chattered violently, and my hand shook so much that I spilled badly at every mouthful. My whole body ached as if I had been beaten with iron bars. Dourly I persisted, however, until my ration was gone. I lay back on my bed, utterly exhausted, and looked at Nunn.

He did not look very well, I thought. There was a strange pallor on his cheeks which had not been there the day before. His whole frame seemed to droop listlessly, and his eyes were deeply sunken. Suddenly he coughed. It was a racking cough which came from his very feet, and he turned his face away quickly. "You're not well, Jack. You'd better go sick this morning." Nunn gave a crooked smile, and shook his head. "What—with peace maybe just round the corner?" he said, "not on your life. I'm not going over to that mortuary of a hospital, thank you. I'll be all right when the sun comes out, you'll see." I gripped my hands together tightly in an effort to stay my trembling arms. "You're the one who'll have to go sick. You've got a lovely fever this morning." "Ye-e-es," I chattered, my teeth clicking like castanets, "but I'm not going to the hospital either. They ran out of quinine ages ago, and I'm as well off where I am." "I think I've got the beginnings of malaria too," said Nunn, stretching out his legs painfully, "but I dare not lie down in case my legs seize up on me. I think I'll go out to work just as usual. The movement may loosen me up a bit." "Maybe there won't be any work today," I suggested hopefully. "Don't you believe it," replied Nunn grimly, "Shegara's wanting a party of twelve men for tree-chopping, but I don't think he's going to get them. I don't think there are twelve fit men left." "You're not one of them, anyway," I said with a smile. "And neither are you," he retorted, "I'm going out." He turned to collect his water-bottle from his bed. "Don't be a fool, man," I implored, "you'll fall down the first time you swing an axe." "I'll take that chance," he replied, "you stay where you are and look after yourself. Use my blanket if you want to. It's a bit warmer than that ground-sheet. What's up with your rice-bag?" "Lice," I replied, "the thing's alive with the brutes." He made a quick grimace, and turned to go. "See you at lunch-time," he said, "you'll have a head like a bear by then, I bet." I lay watching him as he walked unsteadily out of the hut. The man was definitely ill. As he reached the door, I saw him pull up for a minute and cough painfully. His thin shoulder-blades stuck out sharply.

"Ju-ni men." I heard Shegara's deep voice through the attap wall. "Ju-ni men—speedo." Speedo. These vile little butchers knew no other term. It had been speedo at Changi, speedo all the way from Ban Pong to Moulmein, speedo on the Mergui Road. It would be speedo till we all died. I turned my head wearily and looked along the dark hut.

There was no comfort there. Men lay almost motionless under their rags of coverlets, too ill to speak, too tired to struggle. Starvation and disease had stripped the flesh from their bodies and left them mere skeletons, like the blackened hulks of ships, cast up on the shore by a cruel, hungry sea. Some groaned in their sleep, others gazed unseeingly into space. Some plucked nervously with bony fingers at their straggling beards, others clasped and unclasped their hands as if in prayer. This was the breakdown of humanity, the final, demoralising collapse of civilisation itself. I closed my eyes to shut out the dreadful scene. The rigor which had racked my limbs was gradually giving place to a sensation of warmth and increasing drowsiness. The back of my head ached and I was parched with thirst. I drank greedily from my water-bottle. Then I fell asleep.

When I awoke again, it was almost noon, and I felt much better. As Nunn had prophesied, I had a blinding headache, but the fever had almost gone. Above me, through a hole in the roof, I could see blue sky and white fleecy clouds. The sun was shining and the hut was becoming stiflingly hot and foul. I decided to get up.

The workers were just returning for lunch. I sat on the edge of my bed-space, waiting for Nunn to come back. I saw him stand for a moment at the door, shading his eyes with his hand. Then he came forward along the centre passage towards his bed.

I saw him stagger like a drunk man and almost fall. His thin legs tottered beneath him, and I moved forward to put my arm around his frail body. His face was a chalky white, but two angry red spots burned on his cheeks. His breath came in choking gasps. He was all in.

With difficulty I managed to get him into bed, tucking his blanket tightly in at his feet and sides. His eyes were closed. I put his water-bottle to his lips and, without opening his eyes, he grasped at it eagerly and would have choked, had I not drawn it quickly away. "Easy does it, Jack," I whispered, "get your breath back first." After a few moments, a little colour began to flow back into his wan cheeks. He opened his eyes and looked at me wearily. "Don't speak now," I said, "I'll get your dinner for you." I drew his ration and my own, and went back to him at once. I found him lying on his back, his legs drawn up, his hands gripping the blanket.

At first he would not touch a morsel of rice, turning his head away impatiently. I coaxed him to eat, poising a spoonful in front of his mouth. Finally he swallowed a little and drank his ration of tea. I kept him company, although the rice-grains tasted like sawdust.

I thought I would try a little feeble humour. "You were quite right, Jack. I have a head like a bear, just as you said." There was only a faint, answering smile. Then his face clouded over quickly and he grasped my hand. There was an insistence in his eyes, as if he wished to give me a message and was fearful lest he might be too late. I bent my head nearer. He began to speak hurriedly, in a voice which scarcely rose above a whisper.

"I've had it, Mac." I made to speak, but the look in his eyes silenced me at once. "I'm going any time now and I know it. I have no pain, but I just feel tired and want to sleep." "Well, sleep, then," I replied, "it'll do you a world of good." He shook his head abruptly. "No, no," he said, "it's too late for that. Look, there's something I want you to do for me." "Anything you like, Jack. What is it?" He summoned his strength in a great effort. "Take my wristlet-watch back to my wife," he whispered, "and use my pillow yourself." "Your pillow?" I inquired puzzled, looking at the little square piece of folded canvas which lay behind his head, "You want me to have your pillow?" "Yes," he replied, "you'll find over a hundred dollars sewn up inside it. Use the money to—to——" His voice weakened so much that I could not catch his words. "Yes, Jack, to—what?" "To get away," he said, and closed his eyes. I sat watching him anxiously, but he had fallen into a deep sleep.

"Ju-ni men—starto!" Shegara was calling his twelve men together for the afternoon shift. In a very short time it would be noticed by the watchful gunso that Nunn was missing from the parade, and someone would be sent post haste to recall him to the ranks. Perhaps Shegara himself might come to lend weight to the proceedings. This must not be allowed to happen, for a sudden blow might well kill Nunn in his perilously sick condition. In an instant I had gathered up my water-bottle, and joined the little group outside the hut. My head still throbbed agonisingly, but I was steadier on my legs.

Since the unfortunate episode of the buffalo-cart, Shegara had shown a marked dislike for my company. Perhaps he still regarded me as a potential mutineer, who carried a permanent chip on his shoulder against him in particular and his slant-eyed brethren in general. Besides, my eyesight was evidently so bad that I did not see him if he beckoned to me with an imperious uplift of his outstretched hand. That failure of vision had already brought me more than one angry buffet. The burly gunso eyed me balefully.

"Tomadachi very sick. Me worko." Shegara was not impressed. He glowered at me for a moment and then shouted "Tomadachi worko speedo." I faced him quite firmly. "Tomadachi worko nye," I repeated. He looked me straight in the eyes, and I saw him clench his fist, but he did not strike me. I stared back as boldly as I dared. The gunso's eyes flickered for a moment, and then he gave the ghost of a smile. "O.K.," he said, "you worko. Tomadachi worko nye." He turned on his heel and I sighed with relief. The next instant we were off, armed with axes and cross-cut saws.

As I padded quietly forward, an axe slung over my shoulder, I thought anxiously of Nunn. There was something mysterious about this sudden illness which he appeared to have contracted overnight. I felt sure that it was not malaria. Once again I saw those insistent eyes and felt that quick grasp of his hand as he whispered his message. "I'm going any time now and I know it," he had said. He was so certain that he was going to die. I had sat beside a dying lad at Nong Pladuk, and he had known too that he was nearing the end. He had raised himself on his bed, his eyes shining, his arms outstretched as if in welcome. Soldiers stood around his bed, he told me, but I had looked and had seen no one. After that, the lad was impatient to be gone. Had Nunn also caught a glimpse of those ghostly legions as he swung his axe in the leafy jungle glade? Strange things could happen in the jungle. Instinctively I glanced around me, but the great forest was empty of men. Only the monkeys chattered as they swung from tree to tree.

Shegara strode along at the head of the party, his shoulders slumped forward, his arms swinging loosely by his sides. Every now and then he stumbled ever so slightly as he went. I watched him curiously. I had seen men walking like that before on the Mergui Road when their strength was almost exhausted. Could it be that even his immense frame was beginning to break down at last? For weeks past, the Japanese had been living on the same meagre rations as we. Several had contracted malaria. Once, while chopping wood for the cook-house fire, I had turned to find Shegara looking at me with a strange, almost frightened gaze. Then he had shivered as if with fever. I could not imagine this burly gunso going down without a dour inch-by-inch fight. Yet that sudden stumble on the road told its own story.

We struck off into a little clearing by the wayside and halted. From here we were to branch out at will into the dense under-growth, seeking straight saplings, which could be chopped through and dragged free from their creeper entanglement. In the centre of the clearing stood a pile of freshly-cut trees which the party had brought together during the morning. Shegara seated himself suddenly on a log, took off his cap and began to mop his forehead. The man was perspiring heavily. At the verge of the clearing I stopped for a moment and looked back. Shegara had grasped his knees with his hands and his head was bowed. A shudder shook his whole frame. As I turned alone into the deep jungle, I wondered how long the man could stay on his feet.

I went along, carefully blazing my trail by hacking pieces out of the trunks of nearby trees. It was so easy to lose one's sense of direction in the jungle. One of our men had been lost for over twelve hours one day, and had found his way back to the road only by the mercy of God. These long glades gave one a sense of false security. They were open, grassy tracks which seemed to the careless passer-by to have been fashioned by the hand of man. They ran on for several hundred yards, only to merge into another glade, running cross-wise. In the twinkling of an eye a man could take a wrong turning and then heaven alone could help him. Parched with thirst and plagued by insects, he would struggle on and on, trying desperately to escape from the hopeless maze into which he had fallen. Finally, overcome by fatigue and weakened by countless leeches, he would collapse and die with perhaps only a few yards between himself and freedom.

The throbbing in my head had died down to a dull ache. As I steadied myself with my legs wide apart and made a few trial swings of my axe to test its weight, I could not help seeing my emaciated frame. My thigh-bones stood out like saucers, there was a hollowness round my shoulders, my arms were bone and muscle only. I marvelled that I could still go on in such a condition. I must have lost several stones in weight. Yet I took a long, deep breath and felt no pain. My heart-beat was only slightly increased. I selected a suitable sapling and swung at it with the axe. With a few quick cuts I had shorn my way through its soft trunk. I stood clear, expecting it to fall, but its top was entangled and it hung suspended. I laid down the axe and began to drag the trunk from side to side in an effort to bring it down.

I was so occupied with what I was doing that I did not see
Shegara approach. I turned quickly at the sound of his voice.
"Sojo," he said, "you yasume." I certainly did not expect to
be told to rest so early in the afternoon, but I was the last to
quarrel with the gunso's decision. I let the tree-trunk go, and
sat down quickly on the damp earth. Shegara seated himself on
an old stump, only a yard away. He looked at me intently for
a moment. "You malaria-ka?" I nodded my head. "Malaria
no goodterna," he said, clasping his shaking hands together,
"me malaria." So I had been right after all. Shegara had fever.
I saw that he had no water-bottle with him, so I offered him mine.
He took it and drank greedily. Then he thanked me and handed
it back.

"Tomadachi worko nye," he said, "tomadachi mato-ka?"
He was inquiring whether Nunn was dead. "Tomadachi mato
nye," I replied, "tomadachi very sick." The Japanese nodded
his head. "Tomadachi mato—sleepo." He was trying to tell
me that Nunn would die in the night. I shook my head. "No,
tomadachi mato nye." But Shegara merely coughed deeply
several times, indicating that he had heard Nunn cough that day.
"Oro men mato," he went on, "me mato, you mato—oro men
mato." He seemed to be very sure that we were all going to
die. I thought I would try a new line, for the conversation was
becoming rather grisly. "War finish soon?" I suggested,
looking straight into his eyes. He gave a crooked smile. Then
he nodded his head. "War fineesh O.K.," he said, "oro men
campo mato." So that was it. He knew that his nation was
on the losing side, but he did not think any of us in Number 5
would come out alive. For the first time in my life I suddenly
realised that Shegara was lonely. The thought that he had come
to me for comfort and companionship almost made me laugh
outright. These Japanese were like children. This hairy ape
had beaten me to my knees in the buffalo-cart, yet he was beside
me now, imploring my sympathy in a bout of fever. If ever
clear proof was needed of the utter stupidity of war, here it was
surely in this lost corner of the jungle. Shegara's iron nature
was definitely breaking down, but the change was coming too
late. Already he had earned himself the undying hatred of the

men of Number 5 whom he had driven so brutally. No one would have pity on him now. No one? Did I really hate this man? I looked again on the drawn face of the gunso, and began to wonder. Through weakness I must be slipping badly. Then, with a sudden shock, I realised that I was genuinely sorry for him. It was a dreadful admission, tantamount to treachery. I turned my head away.

"Sojo." The voice was almost beseeching. He had sunk forward on the tree-stump. "You brozzer-ka?" I replied that I had no brothers or sisters. "Me brozzer," he said slowly. I gave him a quick glance. Was this man trying to tell me that I was his brother in a larger, world-wide family? I had heard before that there was more than one Communist in the army of Imperial Japan. If Shegara were one, then I should return speedily to my tree-felling, for I found such doctrines unpalatable. I began to get on my feet, but Shegara gestured impatiently with his hand. I had misunderstood him. "Me brozzer Nippon submarino," he said in a strange broken voice, "brozzer mato Pacific. Americans boom-boom." He stretched out his arms wildly, and flung his head back in an effort to explain how his brother had died. Once again I felt this sudden inexplicable surge of pity. The revelation startled and confused me. Deliberately I kept my gaze fixed on the ground, not daring to betray my feelings, but Shegara had sensed them with that quick intuition which tells a man whom he may or may not trust. He laid a hand on my shoulder, and when I looked up I saw he was offering me a cigarette. I had never seen him do that before to any man, not even to his fellow Japanese. I accepted the offer gratefully, for I had been without tobacco for several days, and its absence was beginning to tell on my temper. Shegara silently handed me a small magnifying-glass which he carried in his pocket, and watched as I carefully centred the sun's rays on the tip of the cigarette. A moment later I was giving Shegara a light also. His hand shook slightly as he bent forward, but I could see by his face that his rigor had passed. For a few minutes we sat together quietly smoking, each busy with his own thoughts. Then I stubbed out the cigarette so that I might use it again when I returned to camp. Shegara saw the movement and smiled.

It was the first time I had ever seen his teeth bared except in anger. Quickly he handed me another cigarette, and rose abruptly to his feet. The interview was over. As I turned again to grasp the young tree, I watched the gunso depart through the green curtain of leafy bamboo. I could almost imagine that he walked with a firmer, lighter step, as one who had sought comfort from a fellow-man and had not been disappointed.

By late afternoon I had felled and piled ten trees. I had halted only to dislodge tenacious leeches from between my toes. My head felt much easier, but my limbs ached with sheer fatigue. As I sank my axe into yet another sapling, I heard Shegara's deep voice calling us in. By the time we reached the camp, darkness was falling.

The hut was gloomy and cheerless. As I reached my bed-space, I saw that Nunn was no longer there. Only the empty laths leered at me mockingly. A sudden cold fear laid hold on my heart. Someone lying on the other side of the passage told me he had been removed to hospital—that mortuary of a place across the stream which he had vowed he would never visit. As fast as my tired legs would bear me I hurried past the cook-house and waded across the stream.

He had been taken to Number 3 sick hut. As I entered, I met a friend on the threshold. "Is it Jack Nunn?" he asked. I nodded my head impatiently. "Sorry, Mac, but you're too late," he said quietly, looking out into the jungle, "he just flicked out a short time ago." For a moment I stood quite still, my eyes closed, fighting against the shock. "What happened?" I whispered, "tell me quickly." "Pneumonia," he replied, "he went in his sleep."

Nunn lay at the very end of the hut, completely enveloped in his blanket. An orderly stood by. "Do you want to see him?" he asked me in a bored, matter-of-fact sort of voice. I hesitated. "No," I replied, "I don't want to see him. He asked me to look after his wristlet-watch and pillow for him. Can I have them, please?" The orderly glanced at me. "He had nothing but his blanket when they brought him in," he said. "I should try his hut if I were you."

Slowly and wearily I returned across the stream. Something

vital had gone from my life, and I felt alone. Nunn had not waited for me after all, but had gone on to join the others. I would not look again on his face, but would remember him as he had been. I stumbled back to my bed-space. Then, by the light of a flare, I examined the place where he had lain.

There was nothing there. Only a tiny piece of broken attap lay across the bamboo laths. Someone had robbed a dying man. After three years of captivity, some prisoners had forgotten that even a dying man had a right to his possessions. I lay back on my bed quietly. I would not take the watch back to England after all, and I would not have the means to escape. Nunn had departed, naked and poor in the things of this world, but he had left with me riches which no man could ever steal. I would treasure them for his sake. They were the bright, sparkling jewels of the heart, beyond price and beyond compare. No man could gain a more precious inheritance.

As nearly as we could reckon, it was 8th August when I entered hospital. For two days I had suffered incessantly from malaria. There was no quinine in the camp, but we drank large quantities of a brownish mixture called "warta wari", which was brewed daily from leaves gathered in the jungle. I must have been a difficult case, for the medicine had no apparent effect on my shivering limbs and chattering jaws.

For a day and a night I lay befuddled in that second Chungkai. I awoke on the morning of the 9th to find my neighbour dead. Long before the sun had climbed high in the heavens, three more men lay dead in the hut. As I staggered out into the sunshine, I passed a lad from Newcastle. He lay on his stomach with a hideous ulcer gaping like a bloody shell-hole in his buttocks. My heart chilled as I thought of the agony which this poor creature must have endured. The orderly came round to dress the wound. The flies buzzed greedily round the bed. The foul air made me feel sick. I hurried out, gasping for breath.

Near the road a party of prisoners stood in a gaunt little group. As I moved slowly towards them, Joyce came over to meet me. Since Nunn's death I had not seen much of the tall Londoner, for he had been allotted to cook-house duties. I greeted him with as much cheerfulness as I could muster. "Wot cher, old cock," I said with a smile, "this is a rum do, ain't it?" I noticed that Joyce carried his water-bottle. "You're not off to work, are you?" I asked. "No, Mac," he said, and his eyes were very serious, "I was just coming over to collect you. How would you feel about walking back to Number 4?" I gazed at him as if he had suddenly taken leave of his senses. "Do you mean to tell me that you're taking a cart back to Number 4?" I stammered. "No mate," said my friend with a faint grin, "I don't think that even I could do that now. The truth is—believe it or not—that the Japs have said that any man who feels he can make Number 4 under his own steam can have a go at it. I gaped at the news. "How about you? Can you make it?" I stood in silence, thinking of that long, muddy road which led over four miles of steeps and hollows. It was a road which might lead to freedom, but could I make it? I was horribly weak and unsteady on my feet. "Afraid I can't carry you this time, old chap," said Joyce with a worried look. "I'd like to, you know, but I think it would just about kill both of us." I nodded. "You go on," I said, "I'll try to come along later." "O.K.," said Joyce, "take it easy and I'll have a place ready for you at the other end." "Yes, do that," I said grimly, "I'll be needing it by then."

I stood watching the party go. Joyce staggered from side to side as he walked, and I doubted whether even he, with his superior strength could reach Number 4 alive. As always, he led the party forward. Those men would follow him to the end. I turned back to my hut, wishing them all a silent God speed on a most perilous journey. On the way I passed Shegara. The gunso looked bent and old, but his eyes had not changed. He regarded me now questioningly, searchingly, as if testing my courage. "Oro men starto," he said quietly, "you sleepo tomadachi-ka?" Would I sleep with Nunn in this desolate camp? Would I risk my life on the road? "Me starto nye," I replied, and passed him by, my eyes averted. I did not wish this man to see how much of a craven I was. I returned to my bed, unhappy and ashamed

I must have fallen asleep, for when I awoke, it was just after noon   Somewhere outside the hut I heard the distant clink of mess-tins.   Although I did not in the least feel able to eat any rice, I thought I had better try, if it did nothing more than break the monotony of this soul-destroying sick hut.   I should fill up my water-bottle too in case my fever returned during the afternoon.   Giddily I made my way through the hut.

As I came to the door I had to pass the lad with the ulcer.   He was lying on his side and met my gaze with a smile.   I smiled back mechanically, racking my brains furiously to think of some word of comfort to offer him in his distress.   "It won't be long now, chum," I managed at last, though my tongue was dry, "you'll be between cool hospital sheets before you know where you are."   The young Geordie beckoned to me to come closer. I bent down to catch his low voice.   "They say we're pulling out," he whispered, "a party set off for Number 4 this morning." "I know," I replied, "I saw them off."   "And you didn't go yourself?"   His voice seemed to hold a note of reproach.   I shook my head.   "Didn't feel up to it," I said, my eyes averted from his face.   He grasped my hand suddenly, just as Nunn had done several days before.   "By God, lad, you don't know your luck," he said chokingly, "I'd be off if it wasn't for this hole in my back, I can tell you.   Go on, have a crack at it.   You'll only die here, you know."   I hardly heard him for my mind was back with Nunn.   He had said something like this too.   What were his words again?   "It's more difficult to live, and we must always take the hard way.   Life was never meant to be easy for any of us, otherwise there would be no point in striving at all."   I looked at the lad again.   He was still holding my hand and gazing earnestly into my face.   Suddenly I made up my mind, coolly, almost dispassionately.   "I'm going," I said, "immediately after I draw my rations."   "Good luck," he whispered, and closed his eyes.

I made my preparations carefully, for I knew that I should require every atom of strength for the task which lay ahead. First I drew an extra large ration of rice and fought my way through it resolutely.   Then I filled my water-bottle to the very brim.   I washed my body in the stream and shivered at the coldness of its water.   One by one, I stowed away my few possessions in my pack, tightening its webbing so that it would sit high on my shoulders. Finally I went out and selected a thick bamboo to serve me as a staff. My pack on my back, my stick grasped firmly in my hand, I was ready to march. Without as much as a backward glance I set off alone along the familiar road leading back to Number 4. Shegara was not there to see me go, but I felt that Nunn walked once more by my side.

I lowered my head so that I might not see the vast distance which I had to go. The sun shone brilliantly and the jungle was asleep. It was the first time since being taken prisoner that I had ever been permitted to venture out, unaccompanied by other men, unguarded by a Japanese sentry. I felt almost a free man again. Perhaps I would be free soon. If only I had not contracted those shattering attacks of malaria, I would have been strong enough to walk all the way to the coast at Prachuabkheri-kun. How far was it exactly? I stopped for a moment to calculate. Four miles to Number 4, five more to Mengui, four to Tahang, four to Maudung and five to the sea. Twenty-two miles altogether. If I covered a mile every thirty minutes for twelve hours, I could make it comfortably. A mile every thirty minutes! I smiled grimly to myself. During the twenty minutes I had already taken since leaving the sick hut, I had gone little more than two hundred and fifty yards. Yet I seemed to have been marching at full speed. I should have to do better if I were to reach Number 4 by nightfall. I set my teeth and plodded forward.

In many ways, I considered I was lucky. The road had dried up a lot since the monsoon, and I did not slither from side to side in a sea of mud, as I had done when I travelled with the buffalo-cart. My arms and legs swung freely, for all my worldly posses-sions were in my pack, piled on the nape of my neck in a manner favoured by the natives. The sun was hot on my naked flesh, but not burning. I had a full water-bottle and I would not use it unless I had to.

I struggled breathlessly up the first slope, and left Number 5 for ever behind me. I felt suddenly that I had escaped from something evil, and a new hope began to arise in my heart. I leant heavily on my bamboo staff, but it seemed that my stride had grown a few inches longer. Frequently I paused to fill my lungs, but I did not look up, for dread that I should find myself back in that accursed camp. The memory of those sick huts and dying men haunted me horribly. I had travelled little more than half-way to Number 4, when I became aware of a most curious sensation. It was as if the road upon which I trod had suddenly begun to incline sharply. I stopped, closed my eyes and looked again. No, the road was quite level. Once more I started off, only to find the same extraordinary mirage taking place. I ground my teeth together and determined to beat the hallucination by marching steadily towards it. I had taken only a few steps forward when the road seemed to rise like a solid wall before me, and all at once I banged my head against the wall. I came to to find myself lying full-length in the soft mud. I had fainted.

This sort of behaviour would never get me to Number 4. I raised myself cautiously on my knees and drank a mouthful of water from my bottle. The liquid was lukewarm, but it revived me greatly. I got on my feet once more, eyeing the road suspiciously. For the next hundred yards or so, it behaved itself very well, and I made progress. Then I felt the mirage coming back. This time, however, I knew that it was no mirage, but merely my own terrible physical weakness. The road rose again like a wall, but now I put out my hands cautiously in front of me, and came to on all fours. I was doing better. The next time I would halt the very instant the road began to rise, and wait till it subsided to natural dimensions. I started off more cheerfully. Suddenly there was a throbbing in my ears and the whole sunny world went black before me.

This time I took longer to recover. I felt giddy and my skin was pallid under the tan and clammy to the touch. Once more I drank from my water-bottle. I would not venture on my feet again for another ten minutes. The rest would do me good. I rolled over to a shady patch, and propped my back against a tree. For a blessed half-hour I slept deeply.

I awoke to find the shadows lengthening around me. The thought of spending a possible night under the open sky did not disturb me unduly, for I was rapidly reaching a stage where the jungle held no further terrors for me. I had sufficient water left in my bottle to carry me through the night, and by morning other men might have decided to risk the journey from Number 5, and would help me along. I had, of course, been most foolish in setting off alone, but then, I reflected, I might have died at Number 5 unless I had taken the decision. It was better to die here on the open road than in that foul hut anyway.

To die? But I must not die. I had a life to live. So much was waiting for me beyond that leafy curtain. I must not allow myself to sink to my knees and perish in this lonely place. That was what the buffalo had done. I was surely higher than the buffalo. There was no pressing hurry to reach Number 4. The camp would not run away in the night. I could make two miles on my hands and knees surely, even if it took me an eternity.

On my hands and knees I started off again. I had gone little more than twenty feet when I became startlingly aware of a new strength pulsating through my entire frame. I stopped, completely mystified. This was ludicrous. Here was I moving slowly forward as if I were playing a childish game of tigers, and all the time I felt as fit as a fiddle. "Get off your knees, Mac," I seemed to hear Nunn's faintly mocking voice, "you're not done yet—by a long chalk." I stood upright. The road ahead was as steady as a rock. I moved forward lightly, almost joyously. The next few yards would tell whether my new-found strength was real or imaginary. I waited for the wall to rise up again, but it did not come. The mirage had gone.

From that point onwards it became a triumphant march. I cast away my bamboo staff, for I had no further need of it. I tucked my thumbs into the shoulder-straps of my pack and strode forward erect, as I had done so often on route-marches through the smiling Kentish countryside. Only the monkeys and the macaws cheered me on my way. Up and down slopes I travelled, never feeling the sharp stones beneath my naked feet.

As the sun was dipping below the distant tree-tops, I marched into Number 4, far fresher in mind and body than I had been when I left Number 5. Had it been earlier in the day, I could have gone on without difficulty to Mengui or even to Tahang, but I would not imperil my chances so ungratefully. I saw a Japanese sentry gazing at me open-eyed with astonishment, as I passed him by. Then I entered the camp and was, once more, among friends.

By 13th August, I had reached Maudung, the first of our jungle camps. From Number 4 I had come by easy stages with straggling parties of walking sick. There was still no indication whatever that the war was nearly over. It was the general belief that we were being evacuated to the coast, merely to be reformed for yet another task. At the very thought of having to undertake further arduous duties for the Japanese, many men died. It was so hard to maintain hope when the situation appeared so hopeless.

Maudung had come to be called Death Valley. The name was well deserved. More men had died at Maudung than at any other camp on the Mergui Road. Death struck every hour of the day and night. Prisoners perished not so much from any single definite disease, but from the crushing combination of many diseases—dysentery, beri-beri, septicæmia and spinal malaria. It was a camp of the walking dead.

The camp stood on a little wooded promontory, from which a flight of broad earthen steps led down to the edge of the river. As at Chungkai, the huts had once been lofty, but through wind, weather and general neglect, they had become sadly dilapidated. In many places the bamboo sleeping platform had entirely collapsed, and men lay on the ground on a tangled bed of dusty laths and withered attap. One of the huts had become so infested with bugs and lice that it stood empty, its inhabitants preferring to lie in the open, under the shade of an adjacent banana-grove. A few men were still able to move slowly as far as the cook-house and back, but the majority lay inert, staring stupidly into space with eyes which had lost both lustre and interest. It was more than a man could stand to look at those human skeletons overlong.

I had done little more than find myself a bed-space in Maudung when I once more went down with malaria. The attack raged off and on until the early morning of the 18th August. I lived in a strange half-world of my own, hardly aware of the change of day into night or of night into day, accepting a mouthful of rice or a draught of water only when some kind friend gave them to me. As often as I tried to sit up or crawl out of the hut, dark seas rolled over me and I sank back unconscious on my ground-sheet. Through the oblivion of my mind one thought hammered constantly. I must not give way. I must not sink deeper. I must not die.

I awoke on the morning of the 18th to find that the world had apparently righted itself again around me. Through dreamy, half-closed eyes I lay gazing up at the tattered roof. A small monkey had alighted on the thick centre beam of the roof, and was gleefully engaged in ripping off pieces of loose attap which he dropped with unerring aim on the heads of all who lay beneath. Involuntarily I smiled. The little fellow was enjoying himself immensely. In a short time he would have denuded the entire roof of its leaves, and then we should all be sleeping in the open whether we liked it or not. He aimed a piece of attap at my head. Then his anxious, chattering mother swept down from a nearby tree and whisked her mischievous child away by his tail. I cautiously sat up.

The clouds of delirium were slowly clearing from my mind. I felt desperately weary, and my head throbbed with every movement I made. There was a curious time-lag in the co-ordination of mind and body, but that gradually passed away. To make sure that my memory was unimpaired, I repeated several times under my breath my army number, following it with my rank, name and the numbers from one to twenty in English, French, German and Japanese. I was relieved to find there was nothing amiss in that quarter. The quick mental exercise woke me up completely and I carefully began to test my physical reactions. My lungs were functioning normally. My heart-beat was too fast, but that was the effect of the fever. My arms and legs responded well. I decided to try to get up for a wash.

By now I had learned the wisdom of making no sudden abrupt movements which might endanger the weakened control which my mind had over my body. On hands and knees I crept quietly out of the hut and across an open patch of ground as far as the top of the steps leading down to the river. The water sparkled invitingly in the sunshine. I cautiously sat on the top step and began to lower myself downwards with infinite patience from step to step. Other men were adopting the same somewhat childish method of progress. Within half an hour I had arrived at the bottom of the rough, hewn staircase. On hands and knees again, I finally reached the cool river.

It was only after I had dried out completely on the pebbly shore that I fell to wondering how I should return to the hut. From the bottom, the staircase seemed to stretch up into the very clouds. If it had taken me half an hour to descend, it would take me two hours at least to climb up again. I should attempt it in the same method as before, but backwards this time.

After reaching the third step, I had to stop to ease the furious palpitation of my heart. I refused to be panicked into sudden movements. I would take a step every hour, if necessary. What did it matter if I did not gain the top till nightfall? I was in no hurry. Grimly I started off again. Four steps. Five steps. Six steps. There were still fourteen more, for I had counted them on the way down. On the seventh step I pulled up again. This palpitation was most alarming, for it seemed as if a little hammer were beating a tattoo on the back of my throat, while my head swam with giddiness. Eight steps. Nine steps. Ten steps. I had gone half-way. For a change I turned to my hands and knees. With my nose almost brushing the ground I clawed my way, with frequent pauses, as far as the seventeenth step. There I lay gasping for full ten minutes. Twenty minutes later I had reached the top.

Back on level ground I ventured to stand on my feet. The effort was severe and I had to cling to a tree for support, but at last I found I could move slowly forward if I fixed my eyes steadily on a distant object, like a tight-rope walker. My wash in the river had really done me little good, for I was grubbier than I had been before. Nevertheless, I felt fresher. I returned to my bed.

I had just lain down when I noticed that something unusual was going on at the far end of the hut. I could hear excited voices and a feeble cheer. There was nothing to cheer about in Maudung. What could be happening? Several men had raised their heads near me and were listening intently. I was on the point of getting up again to find what the commotion was about when I saw a young man coming slowly down the hut towards me. He had the appearance of a native, but he wore an immaculate British drill uniform. I caught the bright sparkle of his white teeth as he halted for a moment to speak to a man who lay a short distance away from me. This newcomer was no prisoner-of-war, for he looked well-fed and moved with a vigorous, springing step. I scrambled forward to meet him, and he laid a kindly hand on my shoulder. I looked up into his face and knew at once that he was the bearer of good tidings.

"Is the war over?" My voice was little more than a whisper. To deceive us now would be the cruellest cut any man could give to those poor, stricken creatures of Maudung. The stranger nodded his head. "Yes," he replied in English, "Japan surrendered three days ago. You are free men once again." He handed me a cigarette, but my lips trembled so much that it fell on the ground. I did not realise what this man was telling me. The war was over. We were free. A great wave of thankfulness swept over me, smothering my heart. My eyes were hot and smarting, and at last a sob burst from my lips. "Take it easy, old chap," said the stranger, "don't let yourself go now." But it was too late. Strive as I would, I could not now halt the flow of those pent-up tears. They ran down my thin cheeks in a steady stream until at last I had to put my hands over my face to hide the nakedness of my soul. Most of the other men in the hut seemed to have taken the news composedly enough, but I was not built that way. I had always been keenly sensitive, and this sudden change in my fortunes had a revolutionary effect on my whole being. For weeks past I had schooled myself to withstand the agonising mental strain of life on the Mergui Road; I had seen myself survive while many of my closest friends had succumbed; I had exposed myself to abnormal physical hardship; I had lived and moved in a world of grotesque fears and unheard-of human suffering. The sudden easing of the strain had brought me to the verge of collapse. For most men this moment was one of relief and great thankfulness; for me it meant a tragic conflict between my memory of what had been and what had yet to be. On one side lay the horrors of Selerang, the long drawn-out cruelty of the Railway, the untimely deaths of Shaw and Nunn, the barbarous torture of the Mergui Road. On the other stretched a glittering vista of fresh hope and new achievement, of high ideals and glorious purpose. I felt as one who had awakened, trembling with fear, from some hideous nightmare, only to find myself in a sunlit, homely room.

It took me several minutes to recover from the shock. The stranger had passed on, but I managed to scramble off my bed and stagger drunkenly after him. He was standing just outside the doorway, and caught me as I swayed towards him. "Hallo," he said with a cheerful smile, "it's you again. Feeling better?" "Much," I replied, "the news is wonderful. Tell me, what's happened exactly? Have the Japanese surrendered in Burma?" "They've surrendered all over the place," he said with a laugh, "but mostly in Japan. The Americans dropped a special, new kind of bomb, you know, and it blasted a whole city. They call it an atom bomb." "An atom bomb?" I said, puzzled, "what on earth is that?" "Well," replied the stranger, "it's a bit hard to explain really, but the main part of it is an explosive so powerful that it splits atoms." I shivered at the very thought of this terrible weapon. "It's saved your bacon, anyway," said the stranger, and moved quickly away towards the cook-house. In a few moments he emerged and strode unconcernedly past the sentries at the main gate. The Japanese rose and bowed, and I noticed that they no longer carried arms. One of them came slowly over to where I stood. His bland face was wreathed in smiles, but his eyes were watchful and, I thought, a little afraid. He held out his hand. "Oro men tomadachis," he said loudly, "war finish O.K. Englando, Nippon tomadachis." I stared at him and then turned my back abruptly. This man's hands were still red with the blood of my friends. He was still mine enemy.

It was three days before the lorries came to take us out. The most seriously ill cases had to go first, and I was considered to be comparatively fit, for I could still stumble along on my feet. I did not leave till the third day. Our rations had improved from the hour of our deliverance, but they were still meagre, for rice was in perilously short supply. During those three days of waiting, several men died in Maudung. It was one of the cruellest tricks of Fate.

Once more my fever had left me and, with increased rations, I felt a little stronger. From head to foot, however, I was covered with scabies and louse-bites. My flesh tingled as if pricked by a thousand needles. I lay on my ground-sheet in the open, but could not sleep for cold and discomfort.

At last it was my turn to go. Helped by willing hands, I clambered aboard a crowded lorry, and had covered two miles before my head ceased to swim. There was barely room for another man, so tightly were we wedged together. I knelt at the back, with one hand on the tail-board, taking my last long look at a road which had cost so much in human suffering and sacrifice. I suddenly realised how much I hated the jungle. It was a hard, merciless place, where Terror lurked in the lush grass and Death peeped from behind every tree and thicket. It was the fountain-head of grief, the dwelling-place of evil.

The lorry ground to a halt, and I almost fell out headlong. A man lay gasping by the wayside, his eyes closed, his chest heaving painfully. He had set off alone from Maudung, but his feeble strength had given out, while he was within sight of the coast. Unless one of us left the lorry, there would be no room for this poor, broken creature. I hesitated. Should I go? It would mean a walk of almost a mile. Could I dare to take the risk? Then, all at once, I was back alone on the road between Number 5 and Number 4. I must have lain exhausted just like this man. He had taken the same risk as I in setting out unaccompanied. I had survived. This man must survive also. Too many men had already died.

The driver let down the tail-board with a crash. He looked at me inquiringly. "You getting out, mate?" I nodded and he stretched out his arm to assist me. Several other men clambered out and the prostrate figure was lifted gently aboard. The tail-board went up, and the lorry moved on again. I was left standing alone in a cloud of swirling dust. I carried no belongings, as I had left my pack on the lorry.

As the dust slowly subsided, I caught my first glimpse of the sea for nearly five months. It sparkled in the distance and seemed to be welcoming me back from the dead. I began to walk stumblingly towards it. After little more than a dozen paces, my legs turned to water below me and I rolled down into the sandy ditch.

I felt giddy and badly shaken, but I had not fainted. This was wonderful. I had not fainted. I was stronger than I had believed. I would master the weakness in my legs and reach the coast somehow. I put out my hands to steady myself and suddenly found that I was not alone in the ditch.

Not more than ten feet away from where I lay, with his back towards me, knelt a Japanese. I had seen that bullet head before. I had seen it from the buffalo-cart, I had seen it in the quiet solitude of a jungle glade. It was Shegara. "Tomadachi," I croaked, and the gunso slowly turned his head and looked at me. His face was drawn and thin, but I saw by his sudden smile that he had not forgotten me. "Tomadachi," he murmured, in a queer, high-pitched voice, "Tomadachi mato nye." He turned and moved forward towards me on his knees. "Shegara mato nye," I replied, "oro men starto."

Together we struggled to our feet somehow, the gunso and I. I gave him my outstretched hand to help him up, and then he steadied me until I regained my breath. No word was spoken, for we understood each other. Nature had dealt too harshly with both of us for our little three-year old dispute to matter any more. In her eyes, we were less than dust.

Together we resumed our broken journey. Together, as the shadows were lengthening, we marched into the air-base at Prachuabkherikun. The guard at the entrance motioned me to the right, Shegara to the left. Our ways had parted. The curtain had fallen. Shegara walked out of my life for ever.

V

The Last Battle

THE DAKOTA SWUNG ROUND SLOWLY INTO THE WIND, AND began to taxi forward to the take-off. From my position at one of the port windows, I saw the jungle rush towards us at bewildering speed, threatening even still to destroy us. Then the aircraft rose steeply and we climbed clear into a brilliant noon sky. At two thousand feet we levelled out on a northerly course. We had left the airport behind us. We were going home. It was a wonderful, breath-taking thought.

Four hours to Rangoon. I glanced round at my fellow-travellers. They were a motley assembly, still clad in the rags which they had worn in the jungle. They sat close together on two long, narrow benches, their backs pressed against the wall of the fuselage. Some had their heads bowed and took but scant interest in what was happening around them; others were more attentive, gazing down at the passing landscape, trying to distinguish familiar roads and places. Their bodies, though deeply tanned, were shockingly emaciated, and their faces were shrunken and lined with suffering. Every man carried his own heavy burden of grief. Some had their heads closely shaven in Japanese style; others were bearded and shaggy. These were some of the shattered remnants of the Mergui company. From all walks of life they had come to be broken on the jungle road. Now they were going home to those who had waited three long years for their return.

We had been treated kindly at Prachuabkherikun—too kindly, perhaps, for men who had just come back from the dead. They had made light of our suffering in the hope that we might forget more quickly the things that were so fresh in our minds. They were not to blame, for they had not been on the Mergui Road.

195

They could not be expected to understand how a man's soul could be laid bare and bleeding, so that every word of comfort, however well intended, was as salt on a naked, gaping wound. "Never mind, chum, you'll soon forget about the jungle," they had told us. Forget? Who could forget those lonely, make-shift graves under the clustered bamboos, those desolate, dreary camps, that tragic ribbon of a road that led only to despair and death? Some day, perhaps, a thin curtain of forgetfulness might draw over our memory of these things, and we would view them all from our place of freedom in a softer, kinder light. But that day had not begun to dawn for the men of the Mergui Road. They yearned for sympathy and understanding, but when these were offered they shrank from them fearfully. They had been shackled too long to regain their confidence easily, either in themselves or in their fellow-men. They had to be carefully weaned from captivity.

The airport had no claims to being anything other than a last-minute evacuation centre for wrecks of men who, if rushed to hospital in time, might still have a slender chance of survival. From the moment of our arrival, we were fed with dangerously large quantities of rice, yams and fresh fruit, but everyone knew this diet was little more than a stopgap until more nourishing food could be secured. The overworked airport staff toiled grimly to ensure that we got away with all possible speed; the boys of the Dakota airlift cheerfully risked their lives by flying us over perilous jungle regions in planes which had been strained to the utmost through constant war service. The men who had been prisoners, though desperately ill most of them, were not unmindful of such efficiency and heroism. They too played their part by submitting unquestioningly to every order they were given. They knew their lives hung by a thread.

Inside the plane, the noise of the engines was so loud that we had to shout to make ourselves heard. On my left sat a man whom I dimly remembered having seen at Nong Pladuk and again at Maudung. I tried hard to recall his name, but found it had escaped me. He was gazing down fixedly at the changing scene below us, and suddenly he plucked at my arm with thin, bony fingers. His eyes were excited, and, I imagined, almost wistful.

I turned and looked down. To my dim eyes the carpet of green jungle seemed to have opened out into patches of brown and grey, giving the whole countryside a strangely mottled appearance. Across the panorama ran diagonally a thin silver thread which glittered in the bright sunshine. I regarded my companion inquiringly. "The railway!" he shouted in my ear, "don't you see it?" I looked again and nodded my head. From the air it looked so insignificant, somehow. It was hard to believe that it represented a world's sacrifice. My companion's jaw was tight with emotion, and I saw him swallow quickly several times. "Chungkai," he shouted, "remember it?" I remembered Chungkai, the place where the Englishmen came to die. There had been other Chungkais later on. Once again I saw that sad camp before my eyes as I had seen it two years previously, dilapidated, dispirited, dying. The Dakota, as if in answer to a silent appeal by its passengers, suddenly dropped to little over a thousand feet, and once again I saw the Menam and the white cliff-face at Whanpo. It was there that I had parted company with the section. It was there that Ukemi had been destroyed by the hand of God. Such a short time ago, really, and yet such an eternity in the life of a man. "Kinsyok." I peered down curiously, shading my eyes with my cupped hands. I had never been at Kinsyok, but I had heard so much about its bitterness and tragedy. I saw a bald hilltop which stood out clearly from the encircling jungle. "They've burned the huts down," cried my companion, whose eyesight was unimpaired, "Look, they're in ashes." There was a note of real sadness in his voice, as if something precious and irreplaceable had been destroyed. I put my hand on his thin shoulder. "It was the best way," I said, my lips close to his ear, "In a short time the jungle will have swallowed it all up again." The poor haunted creature looked at me wildly. "But my pals are all down there," he said, with tears in his eyes. I turned my face away. It was not good to look overlong on the nakedness of a man's soul.

The aircraft began to climb steadily and soon we were above the clouds. Around us the fleecy blanket closed in, and I rested my eyes almost thankfully on its white moving folds. My companion sat huddled beside me, his body pressing against mine as the plane rose ever higher. Once more we levelled out, still heading north. The little door leading to the cockpit opened suddenly, and a boyish, merry-eyed airman asked whether we were all right. We assured him that we had no complaints. Some of us had a touch of air-sickness, but, on the whole, we were standing up well to the flight. I smiled at the young airman, and he crossed to where I sat. "You O.K., chum?" he asked. I nodded my head. "We've had to climb a bit above our limit for you chaps," he said apologetically, "there was cloud on the hills, you see, and if we hadn't gone above it, we'd have had to turn back." "Don't worry," I replied, "we've stood worse many a time." He grinned and nodded his head quickly. "Ever been up before?" he asked. "Never," I said with a smile. "We'll be going down again soon, and you'll maybe feel deaf, but just hold your nose and blow hard." I promised to do as I was bid. The airman returned to his cabin.

Gently we dropped out of the cloud-bank, and I saw the sea rippling far below us. There was a curious thudding in my ears, but I held my nose and blew vigorously several times. The deafness wore off quickly. Near me a man was being violently sick. Although our progress had begun to become rather bumpy, I felt no unpleasant sensations. For a time we seemed to be following the contours of the coast and then we were once more over land. From the air it looked flat and muddy. Suddenly we were over a large town, and, as we began to circle, I knew that we had almost reached our journey's end.

The Dakota's nose dipped sharply, and I saw what looked like a green pocket-handkerchief racing upwards to meet us. It was Rangoon airport. Before landing we roared across the narrow concrete airstrip, and I caught a brief glimpse of blurred hangars. Then we came in with hardly a jolt, and pulled up gently on the white runway. The doors of the plane were opened. I hastily shook hands with the pilot. Then I stepped out to join the others. We had arrived safely.

A young Indian greeted us with a flash of gleaming teeth and a hand upraised at the salute. He led us slowly across to the nearest hangar, where tables had been laid and food prepared for us. As in a dream, I seated myself in a chair for the first time for over three years. Had I been alone, I should have felt acutely aware of my nakedness, but we were all together and unashamed. Several white women were moving to and fro amidst the throng, bearing trays of teacups and plates of freshly-cut sandwiches. They appeared quite undismayed by our skeleton-like bodies and lined countenances. One of them approached my table. Instinctively I turned my head aside and lowered my eyes. I was terrified lest she should speak to me, for my mind was empty, and I could think of nothing to say. When I raised my eyes again, the girl had gone. Before me stood a brimming mug of tea and a plate piled high with sandwiches. Bread, real bread! I had not tasted bread for longer than I could recall. Without more ado I fell to voraciously, looking neither to right nor left. The sandwiches were delicious. It was not until I had eaten my sixteenth that a little voice within me warned me to stop. I sat back, feeling rather like some giant python which had just consumed an ox. I closed my eyes for a moment and felt giddy. My table-companion, a dark bearded man, grinned at me with a crust hanging loosely from his mouth. He had passed my sandwich-eating record quite comfortably, and was just on the point of removing the last piece of bread from the plate when the girl returned. She lifted the plate, but the bearded man clung to it tenaciously. "Just a minute, miss," he mumbled through a full mouth, "we've not finished with the sandwiches yet." The girl shrugged her shoulders and I looked up into her eyes for the first time. They were blue eyes, but they were not friendly eyes. Her lips had a permanent, discontented, downward curl. She let the plate fall on the table with a clatter. "Oh well," she said resignedly, "I suppose we've got to feed the wolves."

The bearded man and I gazed at each other as if unable to believe our ears. Then he turned to face the girl. His body was scarred and shrunken, but his eyes were blazing with anger. "Look, my dear," he said at last, and his words came out like a whiplash, "I may not be very pretty to look at, and I've lost a lot of strength, I know, but I reckon I'm still strong enough to lay you across my knee and give you a darned good spanking, you callous little baggage!" The girl flushed to a deep crimson.

"You think you're having the very devil of a rough time out here in Rangoon, don't you?" continued the bearded man, "you're missing the fun you had in Blighty, and all the boys you used to run around with. Well, my girl, I'll tell you something." He pointed at me across the table. "My mate and I haven't seen Blighty for nearly four years. We haven't seen bread for nearly four years either. And you, a kid just out of school, dare to call us wolves?" The girl fled, leaving the plate on the table. Silently the bearded man finished the last sandwich. I sipped my tea thoughtfully. The girl had acted in a most deplorable manner, it was true, but did she really deserve the furious tirade which had descended upon her unsuspecting person? After all, two men who could between them calmly polish off forty sand-wiches were not much above the level of the beasts. I determined in future to restrain my appetite, and, if possible, to bring it down to more normal dimensions. I would not forget those cold unfriendly blue eyes in a hurry though. Whatever else hap-pened, that girl certainly did not welcome us in Rangoon. She probably had not even tried to understand. But if she took up this attitude of obvious hostility, what guarantee was there that others did not feel likewise? Had we rejoined our own kith and kin after many days, only to find that they had forgotten us? It was a bitter, sobering thought. We were the Rip Van Winkles of a new era. We had been prepared to find that things had changed in our absence, but we had not been prepared for further indifference or humiliation.

From the airport we were removed in open trucks to hurriedly improvised hospitals nearer the centre of the city. As we went along I saw many signs of the devastation of war, although none of the buildings seemed to have been so badly shattered as those I remembered seeing in Singapore. Until our driver told us that the Gurkhas had been in action only the night before against Japanese guerillas on the outskirts of the airport, I did not realise that we were still so close to the beaten but unsurrendering forces of Dai Nippon. The scattered pockets of resistance would be mopped up, but it would take time, and still more men would have to die.

We halted by a tall, gaunt two-storeyed building which served as a temporary reception centre. It had once been a school, but its walls were pitted with shrapnel-holes, and its windows were blackened by fire. Inside, in a long dusty hall, several girls were seated at trestle-tables, their heads bent over sheaves of official forms. Men moved from table to table in a seemingly endless queue of broken humanity, giving what details they could still remember about themselves, their homes and their next-of-kin. Some gave the necessary information glibly, and had soon passed on to the last table; others stood, fingering their beards in nervous indecision, not sure of anything any longer. Their minds had grown rusty in captivity. At last it was my turn to go up. I was almost surprised to discover that I had forgotten nothing. "1608138 Lance-Corporal Smith, James D., formerly of the 15th Field Security Section, The Intelligence Corps, taken prisoner-of-war on 15th February, 1942, with the 18th British Division in Singapore. Next of kin—Parents, residing at——" The details came trippingly from my tongue. I smiled grimly. "Just eaten sixteen sandwiches," I added. The girl looked up quickly and smiled in a friendly sort of way. "Have you indeed?" she said with a giggle, "congratulations—but I don't think we'll put that down." "No," I said, "you'd better not, or the War Office might get to hear about it." This time the girl laughed outright. "Do you think we look like wolves?" I inquired, "because that's what the girl at the airport called us." "Then she wasn't a nice girl. You look just like men who have had a heck of a rough time." "Thank you," I murmured, and moved on to the next table.

Finally I reached the last girl. She read aloud a telegram which was to be sent to my parents at once. It assured them that I was safe and as well as could be hoped for. It was eminently satisfactory. I gave the necessary address and stood by watching her as she wrote it down. It was imperative that this particular wire should not go astray. Its arrival would mean the sudden changing of night into day, of heart-breaking anxiety into glorious thankfulness. The boy was coming home again. The soldier had reported back safely from a four-year mission.

From the reception centre I was taken to an Indian base general hospital. Dark-skinned orderlies moved quickly to and fro, seeing to our immediate needs. We were given a small meal of bread, bully-beef stew and tinned peaches. We were shepherded to wards, each containing eight beds, with snowy sheets and sparkling mosquito nets. For the first time for years I stood under a hot shower, letting the water wash the soap-flakes out of my tousled hair. It was a delicious, never-to-be-forgotten moment, one that I had looked forward to for longer than I could remember. On my way back to the ward, I passed the open door of the medical inspection room. I looked inside. There was no one there. On the floor near the door stood a set of foot-scales. I stepped on curiously, shut my eyes for a moment, and then looked at the scale. It registered exactly six stones.

The Indian orderly surveyed me coolly, almost distastefully. "You another of these Jap prisoners?" I nodded my head. "You *are* a wreck, aren't you?" he said, with a contemptuous look at my thin frame, "step on the scales." "Six stones," I replied, "I weighed myself last night." The Indian regarded me suspiciously. "You had no right to come into this room alone," he snapped. "You had no right to leave the door open," I retorted. I had already decided that I did not like this man. I had seen hundreds of faces just like his during my years of captivity. I had seen them leering at me over an upraised rifle in Changi; I had watched them smile at our sufferings in the grim barracks of Selerang. "What's that you've got all over your body—scabies?" "Yes," I answered shortly, "haven't you seen scabies before?" The Indian produced a jar of ointment. "You'll have to rub this stuff all over you, and leave it on for forty-eight hours. Then you can wash it off and come back here. Anything else wrong with you?" I hesitated for a moment. "Yes," I said, "my eyesight isn't too good. I'm told it's a result of malnutrition. Is there an eye specialist in this hospital?" The Indian gave me a look which plainly signified that he disbelieved me. I felt a little pulse of anger beat suddenly in my throat. "I don't see anything wrong with your eyes," he remarked carelessly, "but if you're so keen to see an eye specialist, I suppose it can be arranged." "When?" I demanded abruptly. "Oh, we'll let you know later." "When?" I repeated obstinately. The Indian's eyes flashed with a sudden gleam of anger. "You fellows are all the same," he cried, "you've only just been released, and you want to be cured in a day. You come here, covered with scabies, complaining that your eyes aren't right and expect us to work wonders. You should be thankful enough to be alive at all." With difficulty I kept my temper under control. "I am thankful to be alive," I replied as evenly as I could, "and I hope you are too. Now, when do I see the specialist?" The Indian seated himself heavily at the table and scribbled something down on a piece of paper. "I'll give this to the M.O. whenever he comes in," he growled, "will that please you?" "Perfectly," I said, "now—that pot of ointment." In silence he handed me the jar and watched as I smeared the stuff over my face and chest. "I'll do your back," he volunteered, with an ill grace. The task completed, I knotted a towel about my middle and padded back to the ward.

The room was empty, and I seated myself thoughtfully on the edge of my bed. My interview with the Indian had shaken me much more seriously than I had imagined. The fellow had been insolent, it was true, but insolence was no stranger to me. I thought, after four years of captivity, that I had become inured to insolence, even from my fellow-prisoners. Two men had maligned me in a broken-down hut in Chungkai once. One of them had even struck me with a boot. The Indian had not struck me at all. Yet his words had seared like a burning iron. "You fellows are all the same." He thought we were impatient, because we wanted to shake the dust of Rangoon from our heels. But it was surely cruel to accuse a man of impatience when he had so patiently suffered indignities and hardships such as the world had known only in the Middle Ages? Like the others, I had steeled myself to expect inevitable delays before I finally returned to England. There were thousands of us to be sent home, and we were in no state to undertake a long, tiring journey. Yet, in this war-scarred Indian hospital, I felt that I had somehow drifted into a sluggish backwater from which I simply could not regain an outlet to the main stream. That slip of a girl at the airport had called us wolves, but the Indian orderly had regarded me as if I were a leper. For the first time since my release, I felt that I was a social outcast, a pariah, unwanted and reviled. It was a bitter, soul-destroying thought. It made a man feel so infinitely worthless.

In the hospital they had mingled us with sick men from Slim's victorious 14th Army. The other occupants of my ward were all veterans of Kohima and Imphal. These were brave lads who had fought a good fight, who bore their scars nobly—but they were not the stripes of the bamboo cane or the barbed-wire whip. These men had never known the agony of captivity, the weary years of waiting to return to a world where a new order had displaced the old. They spoke to us glibly of events whose mention drew from us little more than a vacant stare. We had no idea what S.E.A.C. stood for; we had never heard the word "python" applied to anything else than that lithe, crushing monster which lurked in the deepest jungle. This new language of abbreviations bewildered us. We were awkward and nervous in conversation. We, who were the throw-backs to an earlier age, did not trust ourselves in this strangely unstable post-war society. For a time those men of the Burma campaigns tried to bring us up to date, but the task was far beyond their limited knowledge and experience. Their patience exhausted, they again sought the surer company of men who had not been captives. The more unfeeling of them winked at one another and tapped their heads significantly as we passed them by; or they might look away from us and whisper "dulalley". They never saw our eyes, pleading so desperately for forbearance and under-standing. The fault was not of their making, nor was it of ours. It lay squarely on the shoulders of those who had so rashly, so uncomprehendingly brought us together. The free man and the released prisoner should never have been expected to meet on common ground, for, at that time, no common ground was possible. Often we were implored to 'come down to earth' and look at things like normal human beings. Surely there was no need to treat us thus? After four bitter years of prison life, we were no misty-eyed visionaries; our task was not to come down to earth, but to crawl painfully back to it, up out of the hideous, cloying morass into which we had sunk, and in which so many of us had perished. Desperately, inch by inch, we had pulled ourselves back to the edge of firm ground, but our feet were still caught fast in the green, devouring slime.

I had been only four days in hospital when I heard that Lord Louis himself was coming to see us. We who had been prisoners had still only scant knowledge of the exploits of this great personage, but the name of Lady Mountbatten was already familiar to most of us. She it was who had travelled thousands of miles, bringing comfort and a new hope to prisoners in many Japanese camps. She had been seen in Northern Siam, she had appeared, like a modern Nightingale, amongst the hollow-eyed, heavy-hearted captives in Singapore. She was tireless in her duty, generous in her understanding. The roughest men had come to bless her name.

As I stood with others on the cool avenue which ran past our hospital, I could not but think back to a far-off day in 1942, when, on the dusty, sun-baked Changi Road, I had waited thus for the arrival of an all-conquering, oriental Caesar, who had vowed to bring the British soldier lower than any coolie in the Far East. Fuku and his victorious army of the Rising Sun had now been driven as chaff before a strong wind. The despised British soldier had risen again, and in the end his cause had triumphed, but it had been a weary drawn-out struggle.

Lord Louis was late. He had promised to be with us at three o'clock, and now it was nearly five minutes past the hour. We would allow him another ten minutes for good measure and then return to our wards. Fuku also had been late, but then, of course, the Japanese always liked to keep their captives waiting.

Far along the distant highway I heard a cheer which gradually swelled to a full-throated roar as a brown staff-car wheeled swiftly along our avenue. The press of men in front of me was so great that I could see only the car's roof, gleaming in the bright sunshine. Eagerly I wriggled forward through a mass of legs and arms and suddenly emerged in the front row. As I straightened up I found myself gazing into the face of a man who bore such a resemblance to our King that I knew instinctively that our distinguished visitor had arrived.

The cheering broke out afresh, and I found myself shouting

with the rest. The throng surged forward, and brigadiers suddenly found themselves elbowed unceremoniously to the rear. I glanced along the front row on both sides of the avenue. They were all thin, haggard men, striving bravely to force their sagging shoulders back and stand once more to attention. The prisoners had come to the forefront at last. It was fit and proper that they should be there. Lord Louis had not come to see brigadiers but the tattered remnants of a vanished army. We were gathered before him, arrayed in the dignity of our suffering.

He was smiling—a friendly, cheerful smile which gave a man the feeling that he mattered tremendously. "Has anybody got a chair or a box?" he shouted, "I want to make a speech." There was a spontaneous burst of laughter, and a chair appeared mysteriously from somewhere in the crowd. Lord Louis stepped upon it and raised his hand. There was instant silence, and all men waited expectantly for him to speak.

"Before I begin, I should like to ask you a question. Does anybody know where my wife is?" The audience tittered, and a deep voice sounded from the rear. "In Singapore, sir." "Thanks," said Lord Louis with a broad grin, "she moves about so much these days that I didn't know myself." His face suddenly became solemn. "I have really come here this afternoon to bid you all a most hearty welcome back from captivity. I know the hard time you've had under the Japanese, and how many of you haven't come back. We're here to help you get well and home again as soon as possible, for your folks will be anxious to see you, I have no doubt." He paused for a moment, and I quickly looked round the faces of the men who stood by me in the front row. There was a light in those lustreless eyes which I had not seen there for years. Lord Louis, with his simple, earnest words, had brought tears to the eyes of many, and had struck a warm, responsive chord in the very souls of his hearers. I found myself thinking of my homeward journey with a new interest and a reawakened enthusiasm. Here was a man who understood our sufferings, who did not regard us as a burden, but as personal friends whom it was his desire and intention to assist to the very utmost. If we were to be restored to our families, he would see to it, quickly, conscientiously, efficiently. "Of course you must understand," he continued, with an apologetic gesture of his hand, "that a lot of you just aren't fit to go home yet. You need a lot of building up, but we can do that all right, never fear. The main difficulty in our way at present is to find a sufficient number of ships to transport you away from Rangoon. We lost a great many in the war, but the ships will be here, very shortly." A great cheer went up from the crowd. "What about the Japs, sir?" came a voice from the ranks. Lord Louis grinned again. "That little matter is being taken care of, you can rest assured," he said. "There are still quite a few of the enemy lurking in Burma, but we've sent an army to rout them out. These lads will soon have the situation well in hand, and I can guarantee that those who treated you as they have done for over three years are going to be sufficiently punished for their misdeeds." As he stepped down again and re-entered his car he waved to us all. We cheered until we were hoarse. Lord Louis Mountbatten's visit had been a tonic of which we had stood most sorely in need. As the car moved off men followed it, laughing and shouting excitedly. I turned back to the hospital, feeling that I had found the main stream once more, and that a new life was opening up before me, full of fresh hope and renewed opportunity. For over three years I had waited for this new life, and now it was within my grasp. The waiting had not been in vain after all.

It was evening, and the M.O. was making his final round of the wards for the day. He was a tall, thin man, going slightly grey at the temples. He sat on the edge of my bed and looked at me with tired eyes. "And how are you getting along?" He asked the same question of every man he visited. His gaze travelled quickly over my bony frame. I huddled myself more closely together, for I felt ashamed somehow of my skeleton-like arms and legs. In the jungle, all men had been like me, and I had passed unnoticed by them. Here, in this ward of comparatively plump strangers, I stood out in complete and shocking contrast. My scabies had, for the most part, disappeared, but the tan was beginning to wear off my skin, and I was keenly aware of my unusual whiteness. As I sat at my meals in the mess-hall, other men turned and stared at me curiously. Some even declared in an undertone that my release had come too late, and that I would be distinctly fortunate if I ever saw England again. It was not easy to disregard such things, and I knew that my recovery to health would be an exceedingly slow business in that uncongenial atmosphere. If only I could get away from Rangoon, I thought, I should feel much better. But where was there to go? I could not hope to go home until Mountbatten's transports had arrived. To stay on indefinitely in this gloomy, sluggish backwater was equally impossible. I simply must try to jog things up a bit.

"I don't feel too bad, sir," The M.O. continued to regard me sceptically. Then he turned to the Indian orderly with whom I had already crossed swords in the inspection room several days before. "What's his record?" The Indian pored over a flimsy case-sheet. "Malaria, tropical ulcers, beri-beri—all the usual things," he said, in rather a disinterested voice. I recalled giving those details on my arrival in the hospital. "Anything else?" the M.O. queried. "Yes, sir," I interrupted quickly, "these things don't really matter very much. They're over and done with. But my eyesight is still affected. I mentioned it to the orderly before. I should like to see an eye specialist." I saw the Indian flush for a moment and I knew he had failed to give the doctor the note he had written. The M.O. fingered his chin thoughtfully. "Are you still having bouts of fever?" I shook my head emphatically. "Not a trace since they flew me out," I replied. "All right then," he said, "I'll put you down to see the eye specialist tomorrow morning. You'll have to get transport to get you there. The eye ward is in a different hospital." He turned to the orderly. "See that's done," he said curtly, and moved on to the next bed.

I unrolled my mosquito-net and crawled between the cool sheets. There was a strange feeling of security inside a lowered mosquito-net. It gave one a sense of privacy which was otherwise lacking in that large, busy hospital. I began to think of home. How long would it be before I was fit to travel? A week? A fortnight? A month? Would I sail direct from Rangoon, or would there be a further period of recuperation in India? This so-called 'python' system whereby a man was passed from hospital to hospital on his homeward journey could be most frustrating. It meant intolerable delays, muddles and disappointments. Yet it was done with a purpose, doubtless. It did give a man a chance to build himself up a little before returning to his family. In my present state I simply could not show myself to my parents. They would be horrified and sick. The very thought of meeting them again disturbed me. I would have really so little to say, for I had been out of touch so long. They would look older and so would I. I lay and racked my brains trying to think of how I should greet them. There would also be the hosts of well-wishers crowding round, eager to hear my story. That would be too much. I couldn't face it.

Of course I didn't need to, if I didn't want to. I could stay on in Rangoon until I had recovered, and then turn back East to Malaya and the jungle. I could be pretty sure of a job in a rubber plantation, for I had learned the ways of rubber trees. It would be quite peaceful back on the Mergui Road now, if one were fit and well. I could stay on in the jungle for another year or so, perhaps, and by that time I might have regained some of my lost confidence, and would be quite ready to meet the world on equal terms.

I stirred restlessly. These were terrible thoughts. To return to that foul jungle which had well-nigh killed me? Back to the swamps and fever? Back to the memories? No, I must steel myself and go home. My parents would never begin to understand. My friends would be dumbfounded, and would think me mad. I could not honourably forsake them by refusing to go home. It would be a complete and abject admission of failure, of inability to readjust myself to the ways of society. Shaw and Nunn would surely have wished me to go on. They would not have had such doubts. Nunn had always been so sure, even in his last hours, that I would get back alive. I must not let him down.

The eye specialist saw me at eleven-thirty the following morning. He was a genial, sympathetic man who knew his job. His examination lasted nearly half an hour. He put me through every available test, and shone bright lights into my eyes until they watered violently. I studied wall-charts, and tried several pairs of spectacles. But it was no use. The punched-out vision had not righted itself. I knew already what the expert's verdict would be.

The specialist shook his head sadly. "You've been through a lot, and I dare say you've had more than one shock before. I won't beat about the bush, then. As far as I can find out, the central focus has gone from both your eyes—for good, I'm afraid. The nerve had just withered and died, but your lateral vision is still O.K." He placed a kindly hand on my shoulder. "I shouldn't worry unduly about it, if I were you. You'll just get used to it as the years go by, and nobody would ever notice there was anything wrong." I smiled back at him, a trifle grimly. "I suspected this," I replied, "in fact, I have almost known it since it began away back in 1942—but I always thought that they might be all right with decent treatment." The specialist shook his head slowly. "We will try everything we can, you can rest assured of that. But, privately, I think the treatment might have come too late. I'm sorry." "Oh, I don't know," I said as cheerfully as I could, "it might have been worse. I might never have come back at all." "Good lad," said the specialist, shaking me by the hand, "that's the sensible way to look at it. Good-bye and good luck." I left his consulting room, and went out into the long corridor.

Near me, at the top of the broad staircase, stood a high-backed wooden form. I moved over and seated myself upon it. The news that my eyesight disability was likely to be permanent had shaken me, although I had been half prepared for something of the kind. I had been hoping so much against hope that my vision might be restored to normal before I reached England again, but that was apparently not to be. It was going to make things even harder. I should be passing my most intimate friends in the street and not seeing them. They would not like that, but I should just have to explain the trouble to them. I should have to explain it to everyone.

A tall orderly came along the corridor towards me, bearing a tray upon which stood a bowl of soup and a plate of thin-looking milk pudding. As he came abreast of me, I hailed him. "What's the time, chum?" I asked, "I haven't got a watch." The orderly glanced at his wristlet-watch. "Quarter past twelve. Had any dinner?" I shook my head. "I don't belong to this hospital." I replied, "I only came here this morning to see the eye specialist," "Which hospital do you belong to then?" I looked at him for a moment in puzzled amazement. "Do you know," I said slowly, "I can't remember." The orderly stared at me hard and then, depositing his tray on the floor, sat down beside me. "You can't remember? Try hard, chum. Was it a British hospital?" "Well, there was a British M.O." I said, sinking my head in my hands in a frantic effort to remember, "there was a beast of an Indian orderly there too—but that's all I can recall." "There are hospitals all over Rangoon," muttered the orderly, "you might have come from any one of them. Do you not remember what street it was in?" I shook my aching head. "I was only once out of the place," I said, "and that was only down to the avenue to see Mountbatten." "Wait a minute," said the orderly hurriedly, "I'll see the eye specialist. He'll have your name and hospital likely." He disappeared into the consulting room. I sat on the form with a cold sweat standing out on my brow. What was happening to me in heaven's name? Was I losing my memory? I hastily repeated my name and address. No, that was all right. I could still remember these details quite distinctly. Why not, then, the name of the hospital from whence I had come that very morning? The orderly returned quickly. "We've found your hospital all right," he said, "it's an Indian hospital, not a British one. I'll have to try to get some transport arranged right away to take you back. It's quite a distance from here." He picked up his tray again, but, with a sudden impulse, I laid a hand on his arm. I had taken a decision which I could not explain, but I knew within me that it was a right one. "Look, chum," I said earnestly, gazing into his honest face, "I don't want to go back there—ever. I hate the place. They think I'm dulalley back there, and I can't stand it, because I know I'm not. Could I not stay on here in this place?" The orderly eyed me in amazement. "Stay here? Good God, no! You'll have to go back where you came from." "Well," I replied determinedly, "I'm not going, and that's all there is to it." I thought of those rows of faces round the mess-tables, those pitying glances, those hardly-muffled, cruel remarks. I could not face them again.

The orderly shook his arm free of my grasp and hurried along the corridor, disappearing through a distant door. Presently he returned empty-handed, accompanied by an older man, whom I at once took to be a doctor. The two men came up to me. "There's the man, sir," said the orderly, and the older man came forward. "Sit down a moment, lad," he said in a gruff but kindly voice, "and tell me what's wrong." Here was a man I could trust. I turned to face him. "I came here this morning from one of the unhappiest hospitals in the whole of Rangoon," I said, "I am a released Japanese prisoner-of-war from Siam, and they treated me there as if I were some sort of outcast. If I don't get away from that place, I'll go clean off my head." The doctor turned and dismissed the gaping orderly. "I think I am beginning to understand," he said slowly, his brows furrowed in thought. I grasped his hand. "Do you?" I exclaimed excitedly. "Do you understand? It's been absolutely ghastly back there. They treat a man as if he were a guinea-pig. I couldn't stand it much longer. I came here to see the eye specialist this morning, and then, suddenly, I couldn't remember where I had come from —but I know now." The doctor eyed me keenly. "Do you remember if you saw the eye specialist?" I nodded my head. "Definitely," I replied, "he told me my eyes would never get better." "Was I the eye specialist you saw?" asked the doctor suddenly. I stared at him for a moment, and then smiled. "No, sir," I said, "I haven't lost my bearings to that extent. You weren't the man." "Good," said the doctor, and a look of relief passed quickly over his face. "Look, if I ring through to the other hospital, and tell them you're staying here with us, and get them to send on any kit you have, will you promise to stay here and not run away?" "Certainly," I replied, "but all the kit I have back there is hospital kit—spare shirt, toothbrush, pyjamas, and so on." "Oh, yes," said the doctor, "I was forgetting that you had been a P.O.W. Well, we won't need to send for it after all. Come through to this ward and have some dinner."

I rose mechanically and followed him into a large, sunlit ward, where men lay in neat white beds, chatting quietly together, scanning magazines, or doing jigsaw puzzles. They looked well fed and at ease in their surroundings. In silence I chose a vacant bed near the door, and stretched myself upon it. I felt very weary. I closed my eyes. When I opened them again, the doctor had gone.

I soon began to pick up in my new surroundings. The whole atmosphere was so vastly different from what it had been in the last hospital. We no longer had our meals in a general mess-hall, but in the ward itself. I was not any more subjected to the curious stares of other men, for several of my companions in the ward were also released prisoners-of-war. None had been with me on the Mergui Road, but three had been at Kanchana Buri, and two others at Nakawn Patom. One had known Bill Shaw, and another said he could remember Nunn on the railway. Thus we had common experiences and shared a host of memories. Every day I felt myself getting stronger. I could now move up and down stairs without panting like a tired horse, and my sleep was much more restful. My weight had begun to rise very slowly. With careful diet, the doctor said, I should be almost back to normal in a couple of months. He thought it would take me roughly that length of time to get back to England. Once he asked me if I were really looking forward to going home, and I assured him that I was. He looked at me searchingly for a moment, and I wondered whether he possibly suspected that I was by no means so decided on the subject as I appeared. The odd lack of confidence in myself and in my future, which I had experienced in the last hospital, had not been entirely overcome, although I had fought resolutely against it. It came in spasms, as suddenly as a black cloud will appear in a bright summer sky. For a time my little horizon would be darkened, and I could not enter into conversation with other men. Then the cloud would pass over, and a new hope would spring up. I could not bring myself to open my heart, even to the doctor, lest he considered me selfish and ungrateful. He stood without the veil.

There were eight beds in the ward, but only seven were occupied. The eighth stood directly opposite mine, across the passage. Since my arrival it had been empty, and we had come to use it as a sort of general dumping-ground for newspapers, magazines and jigsaw puzzles. On the seventh morning, the orderly cleared the vacant bed of its accumulated debris, and we all waited expectantly for the newcomer to arrive. It was always interesting to see fresh faces.

The doctor had just completed his morning tour of inspection when the orderly entered the ward, carrying in his arms a clean set of hospital attire, towel and shaving-gear. He deposited the bundle at the foot of the vacant bed. We all glanced towards the door. There was silence in the sunlit room.

Suddenly the door opened, and a stranger entered, clad in white shirt and khaki shorts. For a moment he stood, as if uncertain of his welcome, and then, seeing the vacant bed, he moved quickly across to it. I noticed that he went barefooted, and his skin was deeply tanned. I raised myself up to a sitting position. The stranger glanced over quickly, and then padded over to where I lay. "Welcome to the menagerie," I said with a smile, and held out my hand. The stranger shook hands and grinned back at me in a friendly sort of way. The other men in the ward, not wishing to appear unduly interested, had picked up their magazines, and begun chatting together in low tones. But they also were waiting for the stranger to speak.

"Thanks," said the latest arrival, in a deep voice, "how long have you jokers been here?" His face and limbs were very lean, but he looked fitter than any of us. He was a wiry man, not quite so tall as I, but broader in the shoulder. He looked to be in his late thirties. I smiled as I heard him call us jokers. "About a fortnight, most of us," I replied, "but I've only been here a week. You're an Australian, aren't you?" "Yeah, sure." His voice had that long, easy drawl which I remembered so well from Changi and Nong Pladuk days. "You're a pommey, aren't you?" "I'm a Scotsman, all the way from Aberdeen," I replied with a smile. "You're a long way from home, then," remarked the Aussie, producing from his shirt pocket a tin of tobacco and a packet of cigarette-papers. "How about a roll? D'ya smoke?" I thanked him and rolled myself a cigarette. My fingers were clumsy, for I had been out of practice since coming to Rangoon. I watched him as he deftly prepared his own cigarette. These Australians certainly knew the art of rolling a neat, even cigarette. He struck a match for me, and his hand was steady as a rock.

"Sit down here on the bed and tell me about yourself." I patted the white coverlet. "First of all, what's the name?" "Donald," he replied, inhaling deeply, "but most folks call me Don for short." I started involuntarily. "That's my name too." I remarked, "funny coincidence isn't it? The only other Donald I know is an Englishman, Donald Joyce." I stared hard at the Australian's face, and suddenly fancied I caught a fleeting resemblance to a very famous personage whose photograph I had often seen in magazines before the war. He had been an Australian too. He also had been called Donald. I sat up in bed excitedly, laying a hand on the stranger's arm. "Your second name isn't Bradman, is it, by any chance?" I exclaimed. At this the man flung back his head and laughed loudly. "No, I'm afraid not. My second name's Fell—and I don't play cricket—not like Bradman anyway. Donald Horsley Fell is the name, Petty-Officer, Australian Navy." "You're very like Bradman," I persisted. "So they tell me," said Fell, "but I've never met the fella. Were you in the Army?" I nodded my head. "I was a Japanese P.O.W.," I replied, "were you?" Fell shook his head. "No, I was spared that," he remarked quietly, "but I've met quite a lot of you jokers. Had you any Aussies with you?" "Yes," I said, "I knew a lot of your chaps very well. We had them with us in Singapore, and up-country, on the railway." "Were you on that job, then?" asked Fell. "Yes—at the beginning." He glanced at my thin body. "I just wondered how you got yourself so washed up. Now I know." He returned to his bed and set about arranging his kit. I lay back, watching him idly through a cloud of cigarette smoke.

I had found before that I got on pretty well with most Australians, and I liked this newcomer instinctively. His face was frank and his manner open and friendly. When he smiled, his whole countenance seemed to crease, and his eyes became two thin, twinkling slits. He would be able to laugh at his misfortunes, this son of the open windswept prairies, and come up fighting, every time. A good man to have on your side on any occasion, I judged. He wouldn't let his team down.

During the rest of that day, Fell kept strictly to his own little corner of the ward. After lunch I tossed across a cigarette, and he raised his hand in thanks. But he did not come over again to speak to me. It seemed to me almost as if he had felt he had said too much at the beginning, and was now waiting for me to make the next move. I decided to let him alone until after our evening meal. Aimless conversation could become very tiring unless one felt up to it, and perhaps this newcomer was not so fit as he looked after all. I turned over and fell asleep.

I awoke to the noisy clatter of mess-tins and the cheerful voice of the orderly as he brought in the food. I felt hot, sticky and rather cross, for I hated to eat before having a quick shower. Asking my neighbour in the next bed to draw my rations for me, I got up and knotted my towel round my waist. Then I padded off to the bathroom, which was next door.

I found Fell in the next cubicle, lathering himself busily. He stood with his back to me and turned on the hot shower. As the water washed the soap-flakes from his shoulders, I saw they were dotted with those little brown freckles which every Australian seemed to possess. A cloud of steam began to arise in the cubicle, and as I passed, I hesitated for a moment. The temptation was too great. I leant over his shoulder and turned the cold shower full on. For a delicious, expectant moment nothing happened, and then suddenly with a yell he leapt from the cubicle as if he had been bitten by a scorpion. I stood back, roaring with laughter. The broad-shouldered Aussie gave a grunt and seized his dripping face-flannel. I ducked too late, and the next moment I felt my arms pinioned by my sides in a vice-like grip, and I was frog-marched under the stream of cold water. "And that serves you right," said Fell with a merry laugh, as I gasped and spluttered violently. The incident broke the ice completely. That evening after supper, I sat on his bed and helped him to put together a gigantic jigsaw puzzle. It was one of those irritating things with hundreds of apparently unidentifiable pieces, some green, some blue, some white, but finally the picture was complete. It had taken us till bed-time, and we had hardly spoken a word, but we were at ease in each other's company. "Some day," said Fell, lying back wearily, "I'll figure out a whale of a puzzle, cut it out in plywood, and send it on to you. It'll have over a thousand pieces." "What will the picture be—another of the *Queen Mary*?" I asked, laughing. "No, it'll be a large-scale map of Australia," he retorted with a grin, "and there'll be no names on it. That'll flummox you, won't it?" "I don't know," I replied, getting to my feet, "Australia's got an easy coastline. Ever seen the West Coast of Scotland?" "Oh, go to bed," he growled, "good night and pleasant dreams." The two Donalds got along very well together.

It was just after lunch the following day when Fell crossed quietly to my bedside. The silence of the ward was broken only by the heavy breathing of men who, having eaten their fill, were lazily preparing themselves for the afternoon siesta. Outside, the noonday sun shone brilliantly. From my bed I watched its rays shimmering on distant roofs and nearby tree-tops. The whole world seemed to be lying hushed and asleep around me. Only a fly buzzed angrily against the window-pane. "Don't tell me you're going to sleep again." Fell spoke almost reproachfully as he seated himself on the edge of my bed. "I was about to suggest that we take a walk downstairs to the front veranda, where it's cooler. You can sit there and watch the world go by. How about it?" "Spirit willing, flesh weak," I replied with a smile, "frankly, I can't be bothered." Fell looked at me with a twinkle in his eye. "I'll help you. First of all——" and without warning, he pulled the bedclothes from off my prostrate form. I turned over on my back with a drowsy grunt, but the next instant the wiry Australian had rolled me out on the floor. "Come on," he said, "that's an order." "O.K.," I said with a mock salute, "where are my pants?" I struggled dreamily into my white shirt and regulation hospital blues, and slid my feet into plimsolls. Together we moved out into the cool, airy corridor, down the broad staircase leading to the main entrance hall. The big outer glass doors swung open noiselessly, and we sank into two comfortable deck-chairs on the shady veranda. We were quite alone.

"Smoke?" Fell held out his tobacco-tin towards me. "Thanks," I replied, "I've left mine upstairs." I carefully rolled myself a cigarette and passed the tin back. Fell watched me intently. "Trouble with you pommeys is you always must cram too much baccy in, and then you can't smoke the flaming thing. Oh, I forgot—you're an Aberdonian!" I looked at him pityingly. "Where I come from," I said, with mock severity, "that's fighting talk." "No offence meant," said Fell, grinning broadly, "but put the whole lot back in the tin, and I'll roll you one." I let him go ahead. He was much better at the job than I anyway. We lit up and lay back in our chairs, gazing out at the green lawn which looked deliciously cool in the bright sunshine.

I felt stronger than I had done for months. The rest and good food were having the desired effect on me. When clothed thus, I was at ease with the world, for no man could see the thinness of my limbs. I was not particularly in love with the bright blue trousers and scarlet tie, but they were infinitely less revealing than a loin-cloth.

"What d'ya reckon on doing when you get home, Don?" The question startled me, and, for a moment, I did not reply. Home. That word again. The little black cloud on the clear horizon. Why did it disturb me so? I looked up slowly and met Fell's keen gaze. Did he also suspect the truth—that I was afraid to face that long journey, and the nerve-racking welcome which lay at the end of it? I must be wary in what I said. "Oh, I don't know," I replied as carelessly as I could, "I was training to be a school-teacher before the war, but things have changed a bit now, and I'm not so sure. A lot will depend on my eyes, I should imagine. What are you going to do when you get back to Aussie?" Fell laughed. "Oh, I had figgered on staying on in the Service—if they'll have me." "You're lucky," I said, gazing out on the lawn, "you know where you're going." There was a sudden creak as the Australian swung his chair nearer to mine. He laid a kindly hand on my knee. "Don," he said in a low, earnest voice, "why are you so scared to go back?"

A cool breeze blew through the veranda, and I closed my eyes, not trusting myself to speak for a moment. So Fell knew after all. Somehow or other he had managed to pierce the veil, although I thought it to be impenetrable. Could I trust myself wholly to this man? I opened my eyes again, and turned my chair slightly towards him.

"How do you think I'm scared?" I was parrying blindly, and my defences were down. "I don't think—I know," he replied quietly. "Every time I've mentioned going home, you've sheered off the subject like a red-hot iron. What's biting you, laddie?" The voice was so patient, so full of encouragement and understanding. "Well," I said, with a rush, "you've never been a prisoner-of-war, and I thought you'd never understand." "I understand," he said, "go on." "For over three long years I've sweated my heart out, first on the railway, then on the Mergui Road, and I've tried to keep my mind off the work I was doing, looking always to the future. Like other men, I longed desperately for the end of the war to come, so that I could hurry home and take up the broken threads again. Day after day I prayed for release, but nothing happened, and then, at last, the war did end—but the end had come too late—for me anyway. I had lost everything I possessed, I had lost my friends, my hope, my nerve. I couldn't be sure of anything any more, and my whole mind had been smitten dumb with suffering. When I was released and flown over here to Rangoon, I kidded myself that my mind, as well as my body had escaped from that rough, barbarous life— but it hadn't. I was still back at the old 'ichni, ni, nessay-o', although everybody did their best to persuade me that was over and done with. My mind had been geared up to that kind of existence, and it just wouldn't slow down. It's hard to explain, somehow, but I felt unclean—defiled almost. Every time anyone mentioned going home, I thought of the long journey, the flags waving at the quayside, the rows of smiling, welcoming faces— and I felt I just couldn't bear it. I should have all sorts of questions flung at me about the Japanese, about the work we had done, about the men I had known—and those were subjects which were fresh and raw in my very soul. Mountbatten's visit did a power of good though. When he spoke about the boats hurrying to Rangoon to get us away, I felt a new surge of hope, and a pang of real honest-to-goodness nostalgia. Then he went away, and

I was back in that God-forsaken hospital, where men stared and whispered together. When I came here to see the eye specialist, I felt that wild horses couldn't drag me back, and I was so determined about staying on here that they let me have my way. But now, when my body is getting strong again, my mind is slipping and slithering, like a man on a muddy road. Now I have almost decided I just can't make it back to England—not for a year or two, anyway." I fell silent, my eyes fixed on the cool, green lawn before me. I had told my story. I had laid bare my most intimate feelings. How would this man judge me? Would he understand?

Fell had been looking out on the lawn too. Then he slowly turned his head towards me. I glanced up. His face was very serious, but his eyes were smiling. "And what were you intending to do—for this year or two, I mean. Stay on in Rangoon?" "Oh no," I cried quickly, "not that. For God's sake, not that." "What then?" "I had thought of trying to get a jungle job— back in Malaya or Siam. I know the ways of the jungle better than most men, and could maybe land a plantation job." Fell shot forward in his chair so quickly that I thought for a moment that he was going to strike me. "A jungle job?" he repeated hoarsely, "did you say a jungle job? Good God, man, d'ya know what you're saying? D'ya want to kill yourself? That would sure be the quickest way of doing it. In less than a week you'd be down with malaria, and then it would be curtains for you. You were talking just now about Mountbatten's boats, weren't you? Well, it's up to you to get yourself fit enough to step aboard one of them. Take it from me, son, you're going West, not East. You're going to take your courage in both hands and face those waving flags and cheering crowds, just like as if it was your due. It is, you know, for you jokers have no call to be ashamed of yourselves. From what I've ever heard, you gave the Japs hell in Singapore, and it wasn't your fault you landed up as prisoners. You can hold your head up to any man when you get home, even if you were shackled for over three years, for all you've got to do is show him those marks of your suffering that won't wash out, and he'll know what you've been through—for him, maybe. I figger what you need right now is for somebody to give you a push forward. For all you know, there's maybe a nice, big hospital-ship lying in the river right now, just hanging on for you to make up your mind. Why don't you go down there now, this afternoon, and see for yourself? It won't wait all your life, you know." I hesitated. "Come on, Don," said Fell, getting to his feet, "let's go and have a look-see. We won't be missed here for an hour or so. Everybody's asleep." "What about hospital regulations?" I stammered, "we aren't allowed out in the town." Fell grasped my arm. "You're going home, remember? Are you going to let little things like regulations stand in your way? Are you afraid?" I looked at his tense, earnest face, and suddenly made my decision. "No," I said quietly, "I'm not afraid. Let's go now."

Together, clad in our hospital uniforms, we strode down the short avenue which led out to the main thoroughfare. There was no one there to question us or turn us back. We were free men, bent on a mission of vital importance.

Fell was apparently no stranger to Rangoon, for he moved forward quickly and surely, and I kept pace silently beside him. I was quite amazed at my own strength. My legs were a little weak, and the unaccustomed brightness of the sun's glare made me blink, but my head was clear and I breathed easily and deeply. At first we kept to the broad, tree-lined highway, but soon we were threading our way through an intricate maze of narrow back-streets, thronged with jostling natives and brown-skinned children. Here and there a passer-by would turn and stare after us curiously, and once a ragged pedlar shouted at us in a language which I could not understand. We paid no heed, but continued on our way. Fell did not speak, but kept his gaze fixed steadily ahead. Sometimes we became separated in the moving crowd, but he waited patiently for me to rejoin him.

Crossing a railway line, we came at length to a long, narrow road, almost deserted. For a brief moment I stood still, for I had caught the unmistakable smell of the sea just ahead. It brought back so many memories that smell—memories of home, of Singapore, of Prachuabkherikun. "The harbour?" I asked. Fell shook his head. "Not quite," he said, "but near enough, I reckon." We walked on to the end of the road, and again I pulled up, gazing out over a broad expanse of sunlit water. Fell touched my arm and pointed down-stream.

I stared incredulously, my mouth half-open. My hopes, my dreams, they had all come gloriously true. I had never really thought that we should find the pot of gold at the rainbow's end, believing that our long walk would finish only in bitter disappointment. We should find an empty river, or, at best, dotted with native craft, and would have to turn and make our weary way back to the hospital. But our journey had not been in vain.

In the centre of the stream, like a great white swan, lay my hospital-ship. She was not too far out for me to see the red crosses painted on her sides. From one of her funnels a lazy column of smoke curled upwards like a prayer. Forgetting Fell for a moment, I ran excitedly forward, over the road and down a short jetty to the very edge of the water. I stretched out my arms towards the white ship as if in supplication. There were tears in my eyes, and I could not trust myself to speak. I could only gaze and gaze at this gleaming vessel, the chosen means of my deliverance, the proud symbol of mercy and unbounded hope. I turned to Fell, who had now joined me, and grasped his hand. "You were right after all," I whispered, "and I was wrong. Did you know she was here?" He shook his head slowly. "I knew she would be here," he replied, in a low voice, "if we both wanted her so much."

And then, as I stood on the jetty, I suddenly made another startling decision. Whatever the consequences, for good or evil, I felt I must get out to the ship, for, to turn my back on her, would mean, somehow, a denial of my most firm purpose. I would not return to the hospital at all. If need be, I would steal a native boat and make my way out there alone across that narrow stretch of water. Once on board, I would be safe. They would not put me ashore again. I turned to Fell. He was smiling at me in a kindly way. "You want to go out there," he said, as if it were the most natural thing in the world to do. "Well, there's a native who'll lend us his boat, I'm certain." He turned and walked towards a tall Burmese fisherman who sat in the sun a little way along the river-bank. I watched impatiently as the two men conversed. Fell seemed to have a good grasp of the language, for, in a few moments the fisherman stood up and came towards the jetty. A small native boat lay drawn up on the muddy shore and the fisherman held it steady as Fell as I got in. "Are you coming too?" I asked the Australian. "I'm going to row you out," he replied abruptly, and set the two heavy oars in the wooden rowlocks. I sat in the stern, and suddenly we were afloat. "How much did you pay the man for the boat?" I asked, as he bent his back and pulled out into the main stream. "Nothing at all," he said, "I told him I had need of it."

The current was fairly swift, but Fell was an expert oarsman. As we approached, the white ship seemed to loom up to the very heavens. "We'll take her from the stern," he said quietly. "Can you read the name?" I strained my eyes but could not make it out. "*Dorsetshire*," said Fell, "that sounds homely, doesn't it?" I smiled across at him and he smiled back. "We'll cut round to her starboard side," he said, "there's sure to be a ladder there."

A long stanchioned ladder, with a wooden landing-platform, hung down from the ship's side to within a few feet of the water. Softly we came alongside. Fell quickly shipped his oars and grasped the edge of the platform, steadying the boat. Then he turned and looked upwards. Two sailors in sparkling white uniforms were standing guard at the top of the steps. They looked at us curiously but did not speak. "Can you make it, Don?" asked Fell. "I'll hold the boat steady." "What about you?" I said. "Aren't you coming too?" He shook his head and laughed. "Oh no, you've forgotten I'm an Aussie, and I'm going South, not West." I held out my hand. "Well, it's good-bye then," I said quietly. "And God speed on your journey home. Thanks for everything you've done for me." Fell gripped my hand. "Safe journey to you too," he said, "you're on the right road now." I began to scramble up the steps towards the ship. Half-way up I turned and looked down. Fell was still standing in the boat, looking up at me. I raised my hand in salute and he waved back, encouragingly.

"'Ullo, mate, where the dickens do you think you're going?" I looked at the tall sailor who barred my passage. He eyed me carefully up and down, and summoned his other guard. "'Ere a mo', Charley, here's a bloke wiv blues on, trying to bust aboard." The guard strolled over interestedly. I faced the two men calmly. "I'm going home to England," I said as firmly as I could, "and I'm not leaving this ship." I grasped the rope rail of the ladder, as if defying them to move me. "Oh, aren't you then?" said the first guard, with a grim smile, "we'll see about that. 'Ere, Charley, give us a hand wiv this fellow." The two men approached me determinedly. I glanced down. Fell was still there in the boat. Would I go down that ladder again, beaten at the last hurdle? I strengthened my grip on the rope. I would not go back.

"What's going on here?" An officer came along the deck towards us. The guards stood instantly to attention. He heard their story and then turned to me. "Come aboard if you want to," he said, with a faint smile. "You can walk round the deck and have a look at the ship, but you've got no papers with you, so we can't let you stay here." I loosened my limpet-like grip on the rope and stepped forward past the two guards. "Thank you, sir," I said, "I should like to look round, if I may—but I'm not going back." I began to move forward along the trim, shining deck, and saw the officer give a curt nod to the two guards at the top of the ladder. They resumed their position, watching me intently. It was almost as if they were expecting me to make trouble at any moment. The officer fell into step beside me, and we went slowly forrard.

I had never been aboard a hospital-ship before, and marvelled at her spick-and-span appearance. Everything which could be humanly made to shine was sparkling in the sunlight, and the paintword was dazzling in its whiteness. I paused near the port rail and looked over. Just below me I could see the top of one of the red crosses. The officer leant over the rail, his elbow against mine. He was studying me intently, I knew, but I did not turn my head. To this man, my conduct during the past few minutes must have appeared unusual in the extreme, and I felt, somehow, that I owed him a full explanation. It would not be easy to make him understand. I swung round suddenly to face him.

"The guards only gave you the bare details, sir," I said, "I should like to tell you more." "Go on," said the officer quietly. "Well, you may have noticed that I came over here in a rowing-boat with another man?" The officer nodded. "I had been watching you through glasses since ever you began to make for the ship. Who is this other man?" "An Australian Petty-Officer I met in hospital," I replied, "we are in the same ward." "Which hospital?" asked the officer. I mentioned the name and how I had come to be there. Of my conversation with Fell on the veranda, however, I said nothing. Then I told him about our journey through the town and about the borrowed boat. The officer raised his eyebrows in surprise. "You must have been pretty desperate to get home if you took all that bother," he said. "Did you think you were going to be left in Rangoon?" I nodded my head. "But that's ridiculous. You're a released P.O.W. and you'll go home, just as soon as you're fit to travel, but you can't go breaking your way aboard a hospital-ship, you know. You've got to wait your turn, just like all the other men." We resumed our walk round the stern of the vessel, and again approached the top of the ladder. The two guards were waiting there expectantly. "You'll have to go back now," said the officer, "we can't keep you here until you've got the necessary papers. There's a tender going ashore now, and it will take you and your friend back. Your boat can be taken in tow. You *will* go without any fuss, won't you?" I moved quickly across to the ship's rail, grasping it firmly with both hands. "I'm afraid not," I said fiercely, "I've come aboard and I'm going to stay aboard." The two guards, at a signal from the officer, silently closed in on me. One laid his hand on my shoulder, firmly but not roughly, while the other put his arm round my waist and began to drag me backwards. I clenched my teeth and hung on desperately. "Come on, chum," whispered Charley in my ear, "we're not going to hurt you. Let go, will you." I shook my head. "I'm not going back," I shouted, "and I'm not going to let go." "All right," said Charley in a matter-of-fact sort of way, "have it your own way, but you're coming off that rail." He bent forward quickly, grasping the little fingers of both my hands and jerked them upwards. I had not sufficient strength to resist, and in a trice the two men had me free from the rail. "Put him on the tender," said the officer. I struggled furiously to break free, but I was no match for the two guards. Half-carrying, half-leading me they eventually brought me down to the wooden platform at the foot of the ladder. It was by no means an easy operation, but they accomplished it smoothly. Realising that further resistance was impossible, I ceased my struggles and dropped quietly aboard the waiting tender. Fell stretched out his arm towards me and guided me to a seat beside him. For a moment we floated idly on the stream and then the tender's engines burst into life and we shot quickly away from the ship, towing the empty rowing-boat behind us. I glanced upwards. The guards were back at their position at the top of the ladder, and the officer was leaning over the rail watching our departure. I could not see his face clearly, but he seemed to be smiling. "No go," I said ruefully, turning to Fell, "I'm afraid we'll just have to let her go without me." "Don't worry, you've had a darn good try, and there'll be other ships." I closed my eyes. My struggle with the guards had exhausted me utterly. I did not look up again until we had reached the jetty. The sun still shone brightly, but for me the world had lost its sparkle and the skies were grey and cold.

On the main road above the landing-stage stood a jeep. Mechanically I stepped out of the tender and walked towards the dusty little vehicle. Fell came along beside me. It had never once occurred to me, during the whole of that afternoon, that the hospital authorities would have received quick warning of our departure, long before we had reached the riverside, and that they would naturally be waiting to bring us back. I had ceased to wonder about anything any more. Silently we boarded the jeep and the driver, without addressing a word to us, let in his clutch with a jerk. In less then ten minutes we were back at the hospital. Our little escapade was over. We gave our names to an orderly in the reception hall, and re-entered our ward just as the evening meal was being brought round, and the other men were awakening from their afternoon sleep. The sun still shone brilliantly, and the fly was still buzzing angrily up and down the window-pane.

Next morning I awoke, tired and aching in every limb. I felt

certain that I was about to go down once more with malaria.
When the doctor came round at ten o'clock, I decided I would tell
him, but he addressed me first. "Corporal Smith," he said,
examining a sheaf of papers in his hand, "you will report with
your kit downstairs in the main entrance-hall at ten-thirty today.
You're going home." I stared at him vacantly, my mouth half-
open. "Going home?" I repeated, and my heart seemed to
have risen into my throat. "Yes," said the doctor, "you're a
good deal better, and we think you're fit enough to travel. I
wish you the best of luck, and a safe return to England." What
ship will I be going on?" My voice was hardly above a whisper.
The doctor looked at me with a smile. "The *Dorsetshire*," he
said. "She's lying in the river now."

As a man in a dream, I began to get my kit together. I did
not hear the good wishes of the other men. I had forgotten all
about my malaria. I had forgotten about everything. Fell
came across to my bedside and grasped my hand. He was also
deeply moved. "Good-bye," he whispered, "and don't look
back now—ever." "Good-bye, Don," I whispered back, "and
give my regards to Aussie." With my kit in a bundle under my
arm, I walked out of the ward, down the broad, cool staircase, to
the entrance-hall. An orderly quickly checked my bundle and
directed me to a waiting ambulance. I clambered aboard with a
dozen or so other men. The doors were closed and we moved
off.

The journey was a short one. The doors were opened and
once more I saw the jetty sloping down to the water's edge. In
silence I boarded the waiting tender. Once more the engines
burst into life and we were off.

On the wooden platform, two sailors were waiting to help us
up the steep ladder. They were not the same men whom I had
seen the previous afternoon. Slowly I mounted to the top and
went aboard the trim white ship. I moved over to the rail and
looked down. The last man had just been unloaded from the
tender and she was once more moving off, back to the shore.
As I watched, I seemed to see another vessel draw up at the
platform, with only two men aboard, clad in hospital blues. A
white-coated orderly touched my arm. "Come along, chum,"

he said in a kindly voice, "let's go below and find you a berth."
Without a word I turned and followed him. I had come aboard
the *Dorsetshire* for the second time, but no one would put me off
again. Life was so funny somehow—and yet, so eternally
complicated.

We sailed with the afternoon tide. I had wanted to stand on
deck to bid Rangoon farewell, but instead I lay in my berth,
dizzy and sick, smitten by one of the most violent attacks of
malaria which I had ever experienced.

I had thought, on leaving the Mergui Road, that I had suffered
the worst that tropical fever could do to me. On my arrival at
Rangoon, I had been asked how often I had had malaria, and I had
found it somewhat hard to explain that, just before my release, I
had gone down with fever so frequently that individual attacks
could no longer be counted. I had not been conscious, during
those last few dreadful days of my captivity, of the end of one
attack and the beginning of another. I had not often been conscious of the difference between night and day, but I could not
tell that to the Indian orderly at the hospital. He would not
understand. His task was to note down exact figures. So I
gave fifteen as a rough estimate, and left it at that. The orderly
was satisfied. In due course, I should receive a complete new
revolutionary treatment which would rid me for ever of all remnants of fever. With nine small yellow tablets, the orderly said,
I should be cured. But I would not get these until I was fit
enough to stand their effect.

Undoubtedly, my excursion with Fell had not helped matters.
The hot afternoon sun had brought the dormant fever to a head,
and now, aboard the *Dorsetshire*, the attack had burst out upon
me with a suddenness and severity which had taken everybody,
including myself, entirely by surprise. I had gone an ashen grey
just after lunch, and the orderly had sent post-haste for a doctor.
By the time he arrived, they had managed to get me berthed
down, but I had become delirious, and my mind was far away
from the ship and my immediate surroundings. They did what
they could, but little could be done at that stage in the illness.
It was up to myself alone to find my way back.

Throughout that night the fever raged like an angry fire. For a few moments at a time I would realise that there were solemn-faced men standing by me, ready to help, but unable to do a thing for me, except to bathe my burning limbs. For the rest of the time I was sunk in a world of bright lights and dark shadows, where the faces of the dead and the living mingled inextricably together. Once I screamed as I fancied I saw a great rock bearing down on my head from a white cliff-face. In the very nick of time two men pulled me clear, and when I turned towards them, I saw that they bore the faces of Nunn and Fell. I writhed in agony as a tall, murderous Korean struck me on the face with his fist, and then I was once more walking beside the buffalo on the Mergui Road. Shegara also was beside me on the shaft, striving to push the beast away with his outstretched arm. There was a continual, high-pitched humming in my head, as if it contained a giant dynamo, and several times I heard voices calling me by name. Some were raised in anger, others quietly beseeching. The hours slipped by. Towards morning I fell into a deep, dreamless unconsciousness.

When I awoke, it was high noon. The fever had run its course and I was dimly aware that I was a good deal better. Through half-closed eyes I looked up at the white roof of the little cabin. It shimmered with sparkling lights, as the sun was reflected by the water outside. I could feel the ship roll ever so slightly. I opened my eyes and tried to move my head.

"Don't move," said a quiet voice at my shoulder, and an orderly bent over my pillow. "Do you feel any better?" Slowly I nodded my head. The movement was agony. "Water," I croaked, "I'm thirsty." A small beaker was put to my lips and I began to drink greedily. The orderly gently drew it away. "Not too much at a time," he said, "try to get a bit more sleep." Thankfully I closed my eyes again. I could feel the bedclothes around me, wringing wet. I must have had a tremendous bout. When next I awoke, it was evening.

My recovery was a slow business, but by the afternoon of the third day I was able to get out on deck with my legs wobbling below me at every step. My head was clear again, and the cool air revived me greatly. I sat under a shady awning and gazed out on the lazy rolling ocean. The ship was steaming forward on a leisurely course, and, glancing in the direction of the sun, I suddenly realised that we were heading north-west. I hailed a passing orderly. "Feeling better, mate?" he inquired cheerfully, "Gave us all quite a turn, you did. Thought you were a goner." "I almost was," I said, "but the thought that you're going home is good medicine. Why are we going north-west? I thought we should have been heading south." The orderly glanced out to sea for a moment. "We're heading for Calcutta," he said, "you're not well enough to go straight home yet. You're being sent to India for a spell to recuperate. How about a spot of char?" "Thanks," I replied, leaning back in the deck-chair, "I'd love it." He moved off along the deck.

So I was going to Calcutta. I felt rather disappointed, for I liked the *Dorsetshire* and had been hoping to see more of her on the homeward journey, but that was just how this mysterious python system worked. I was, after all, somewhat ahead of schedule. Had things remained as they were before I met Fell, I should still have been lying, undecided and restless, in a Rangoon hospital. Calcutta was a definite step in the right direction.

We berthed the following morning, and speedily disembarked. On the quay a kilted band of Gurkha pipers marched up and down, and I stood in silence listening to the wild skirl of the bagpipes. It was strange how that Highland music pulled at my very heart. I could not hear it without thinking of the bens and glens of home, of the purple, heather-clad slopes and the misty sheilings. So many exiles must have stood thus, yearning to return to the land which had given them birth. The dark-skinned, turbaned pipers played as to the manner born, their kilts and sporrans swinging proudly as they went. When was the last time I had heard the pipes? My thoughts went back to a moonlit night in January, three years before, while I stood with Nunn on the Bukit Timah Road, and watched a tired, vanquished army pass me by. But the pipes had not been vanquished. They had thrown defiance at the advancing hordes, just as they had done in so many grim, forgotten battles, just as they would always do when the need was sorest. They were indomitable. They were the spirit of a nation.

We went to a small hospital on the outskirts of the city, where British nurses moved noiselessly to and fro, and a cool fountain played in the middle of a lush, green lawn. During my four-days' stay, I sat for hours in the cloistered shade of the little patio, skimming through the pages of old magazines, filling in the yawning gaps which three years had created, finding once more my bearings and a growing confidence in myself. The world went by unheeded, but I was slowly catching up with it again. In the hospital I found a young doctor who had been with me in my earlier University days. I recognised him at once, but he did not know me until I mentioned my name. I did not realise that I had so greatly changed.

On the fifth day I left Calcutta, laden with the comforts which a generous Red Cross had showered upon me. We went by train, but I knew no one in the party. We travelled north-west into the pine-clad uplands of Southern Bihar, where the air was cooler and the countryside green and peaceful. By early afternoon we had reached the little town of Ranchi, where we halted and got out. We were assembled on the broad platform, and directed to waiting lorries. A crowd of dusty children followed us, crying for backsheesh. The lorries moved off through a flat wooded countryside, along a smooth road, bordered by gnarled, overhanging trees. Within half an hour we had drawn into a great, sprawling hospital camp of low, white-washed wards and dazzling concrete paths.

Jessie Macleod was a daughter of the Western Isles. When the call had come, she had left her native Skye to train as a hospital nurse, and the tide of war had caught her up and borne her across the seas relentlessly. She had never really liked India. It was a hot, dusty land, where myriads of flies swarmed unheeded, and a poor man existed in conditions of such indescribable squalor and misery that her warm Highland heart rebelled at such suffering. Everywhere she went it seemed to be the same. In Bombay a host of hollow-eyed beggars had come after her, tugging at the very hem of her garments; in Hyderabad, a blind woman, smitten with a hideous cancer on her cheek, had implored her sympathy; in a dark Calcutta back-street, she had stumbled across a dead child.

Early in September, 1945, she was transferred to the staff of the convalescent hospital at Namkun. In this great, sprawling rest centre, set in the uphills of Southern Bihar, life was altogether more pleasant. The air was much fresher and cooler than in Calcutta, and her daily round of duties less exacting. Every week she had a free afternoon, when she would set out with her picnic-basket for the Hondra Falls. She had discovered a broad pool, just below the roaring cataract, where it was deep enough for swimming, and she had come to look on that little place as her very own—a forgotten corner of a foreign land, where she could be alone with the river, the pine-trees and her thoughts of home. In the evening, as the shadows were lengthening along the Ranchi road, she would return to her quarters in the camp, with the sun still in her cheeks and a new warmth in her heart.

Jessie had a smile for everyone. As she trotted briskly from ward to ward, men would raise themselves on their elbows in bed to wish her good morning. The face of the dhobi would break into a cheerful grin as she passed him by, and he would let his twisted bundle of laundry slip back unheeded into the long water-trough. The derzi too, sitting cross-legged with his busy needle and thread, would watch expectantly for her passing. Then his brown-skinned children would run out excitedly to grasp her hand.

For the men of Ward 8, Jessie was an eternal source of courage and inspiration. Besides caring for their every need, she had time to pause and speak to them in her soft, lilting, Highland voice, as she went from bed to bed, pouring out nasty medicine or tucking in straggling arms and legs. She did not talk much about the war, for that was now over and done with. Rather did she probe into the future, dwelling on the simple, homely things which she knew would be of the greatest interest. For the most part, her children of Ward 8 were fit enough to look after themselves very well, but they would be quick to invent the flimsiest excuse to seek her company, if only for a few moments. There would be a long letter from home, maybe, with photographs of the wife and kids, and Jessie had to be told all about it; or a short tragic note would lie crumpled on the white sheet till Jessie could read it over again, softening its unhappy message. Young Peter Grierson was her special charge. For weeks past, the lad had lain in the narrow confines of an iron lung, hanging on grimly to a life which seemed empty and useless. It was so hard to be paralysed when all the world lay at one's feet, just waiting to be conquered. Jessie tended him with a devotion and faith which were unshakable. Inch by inch they were winning the battle together. Every day he would be removed from the lung for a few moments to breathe naturally. In a year, the doctors said, he would be able to walk again. For Jessie it was a personal triumph, but she only smiled, and said Peter was the pluckiest lad she had ever nursed. Jessie was always like that.

Of course there were constant changes in Ward 8. Every fortnight men would be sent on to other wards, or, if they were fit enough, put on a home draft. They never forgot to come and say good-bye to the slim, shy Highland girl to whom they owed so much. Sometimes she received a gift, thrust abruptly into her hands by some rough, tongue-tied veteran of the Burma battle-lines. She would watch her children go, and then turn quietly to prepare a place for the next arrivals.

Towards the end of September, a party of sick reached Namkun from a Calcutta transit camp. Most of them were able to walk without much difficulty, but many looked drawn and tired, and several were painfully thin. Jessie watched them curiously as they were directed to their various wards. There might be Scotsmen on the party—a man from Skye, even. Only one vacant bed remained in Ward 8. Which of these men would be placed in her keeping?

The group had dispersed, but one man still stood as if uncertain where to turn in the puzzling maze of paths and buildings. Jessie went out immediately to help him. He was a tall, gaunt individual, clutching tightly in his hand a bundle of Red Cross comforts. As she drew near him, he turned his head aside quickly, unwilling, apparently, to meet her gaze, and waited for her to pass on the narrow path.

"Can I help you?" The gaunt man stared at her for a moment, and then replied in a low, quiet voice, "I'm afraid I'm lost. Where is Ward 8, please?" Jessie smiled to herself. So this lost sheep was coming to her after all! "This way," she said briskly, and made to take his arm. But he stood back, as if afraid of her touch. "I'll follow you," he said, and Jessie let her hand drop by her side. With a slight shrug, she turned on her heel and led the way back to the ward.

During her stay in India, she had handled many difficult cases, but there was an aloofness about this stranger which she could not understand. At heart, she herself was shy, but her work had taught her confidence. This man was reserved to the point of rudeness. He had scarcely let his eyes rest on her, ignoring her outstretched arm completely. The Burma boys were not usually so awkward, nor so forgetful of their manners.

On entering the ward, the stranger had stopped beside the iron lung, gazing down intently on the face of the sleeping Grierson. Then he moved round to the back of the machine, and stood watching the bellows as they heaved gently up and down. "How does it work?" He asked the question so suddenly that Jessie started in spite of herself. "By electricity. Now, if you're quite satisfied . . ." "What happens if the power fails?" interrupted the thin man, without raising his eyes from the bellows. Jessie leant forward quickly. This newcomer was asking too many questions. "Never mind about that just now. Come along and I'll show you your bed." "Yes, but what would happen if the power DID fail," persisted the thin man. "The chap would die, wouldn't he?" This was exasperating, and from a distant bed came the sound of a muffled laugh. "The power has never failed yet," said Jessie fiercely, "but, if it did, there's a steel bar hanging there which fits into that socket in the lung . . ." "And you pump the bellows by hand? That's all I wanted to know." The thin man turned obediently, and followed her along the ward.

It was not until the M.O. had completed his tour of inspection that evening that Jessie discovered for the first time that her new patient had been a prisoner-of-war in Japanese hands. He seemed to get along fairly easily with the other men, and had been accepted by them without question, but towards her he had continued to maintain a determined reticence. Only once during the afternoon had she caught his eyes upon her, and that was when she had gone to ease the pillow below young Grierson's head, but he had not spoken, and when she smiled he had turned his face away.

The M.O. asked her to go round with him that night. He was a newcomer to Ward 8, a young man freshly arrived from England, and he seemed anxious to get to know his patients well. Before entering the ward, he glanced through the men's case-sheets, questioning her closely about Grierson's condition. She merely mentioned that a new patient had moved in that afternoon from Calcutta, and the M.O. said he would see him last.

In the ward every man sat to attention on the edge of his bed, awaiting his turn expectantly. Only the rhythmic beat of the iron lung broke the silence. The new doctor was evidently con-scientious and thorough, and had a cheerful word for each man as he passed him by. He was deeply interested in Grierson, staying on for several minutes by the lung, chatting with the sick lad. Then he came to the last bed.

"You've only come today, I understand?" He glanced keenly at the thin man, taking in every detail of the sunken cheeks, the bony arms, the lean legs. "Your case-sheet doesn't seem to have arrived yet from Calcutta, so you'll have to tell me a little about yourself. Were you in the 14th Army too?" The whole ward had stopped to listen. The thin man shook his head slowly. "No, sir. My name is Smith. I was in the British 18th Division in Singapore—15th Field Security Section. I am an ex-prisoner-of-war of the Japanese." The young doctor surveyed his patient with a new interest. It was his first en-counter with one of these released prisoners. Before leaving England he had heard tales of their unusual behaviour, of their frequent strange moods, of their apparent disinterest in their surroundings and in their fellow-men. It was said that many of them ate their meals voraciously, like wild animals, that they pre-ferred to squat on their hunkers than to sit in a chair, that they often lapsed into a tongue which was part English, part Japanese. Some had been reported, on their immediate release, to be quite mad, others merely peculiar. From this man's physical condition alone it was evident that he had suffered greatly during his captivity. Had his mind suffered also? The human brain was such a delicate mechanism, so easily and irreparably disturbed by unforeseen rigours or conflicting circumstances. He would have to proceed carefully in his questioning.

"I see. What illnesses have you had?" For a moment the thin man hesitated and then gave a faint smile. "I think I've just about had them all," he said, in his low, quiet voice. "Stomatitis, tropical ulcers, beri-beri and malaria. I haven't had dysentery, though. I was lucky there. And I haven't had cholera either." "You were lucky again," said the doctor, producing his stethoscope, "just stand up for a minute and let me examine you." Jessie watched the thin man closely as he rose to his feet, but he did not look at her. The examination took longer than usual. At last he reseated himself on the bed and crossed his legs, as the doctor tapped his knees with a small, rubber-tipped hammer. "No reflexes," murmured the doctor, and Jessie took a quick note. "Haven't had any for three years," said the thin man, addressing nobody in particular. The man in the next bed chuckled. The doctor fingered his chin thoughtfully. This patient appeared to have had such a variety of illnesses that he had ceased to take much interest in his physical condition. His mind did not seem to have been affected—and yet, could one be sure? There was such a flimsy wall separating the two worlds. Better make arrangements to have him see the camp psychiatrist. He nodded briefly to Jessie, and together they left the ward. The thin man turned and winked to the man in the next bed. "The guy's puzzled," he remarked with a grin and a nod in the direction of the departing doctor. "You shouldn't have had so much wrong with you," retorted the other, and lit a cigarette.

That evening there was an open-air film-show in camp. Jessie stood alone in the gathering darkness on the very fringe of the large noisy audience. She had seen the film months before, and was not particularly interested. Near her sat several of her ward patients. They seemed to be enjoying the show immensely, and in the reflected light of the screen she scanned their faces. Tomlinson, Savidge, Wilson, Matthews, Bradley. Smith was not there. Perhaps he did not care for film-shows. He certainly was a strange, anti-social type. She turned to go back to her quarters. She would scribble off a quick letter home before bed-time.

Suddenly, as if a giant hand had flung over a great lever, the entire camp was plunged into complete darkness. From the audience came an angry, impatient growl, for the film had just reached the best part. For a moment Jessie stood quite still, waiting for her eyes to accustom themselves to the inky blackness of an Indian night. A man blundered into her, but did not apologise. From all quarters came a chorus of hoots, whistles and derisive catcalls. Still nothing happened. Then, all at once, an icy finger of stark panic laid hold on Jessie's heart. She remembered Grierson.

At a crazy gallop she started back in the direction of Ward 8. Men stood in disgruntled groups in the paths and corridors, but she pushed through them wildly. Before her tormented mind rose a terrible picture of a gallant lad, fighting grimly, desperately, to loosen the sudden strangling pressure on his lungs. If only she could have been there beside him, she could have fitted that steel bar into its socket in a moment and brought him relief. Who could ever have guessed that the power would fail? Oh, why, in heaven's name, had she to be off duty that night of all nights! Oh, Grierson, Grierson, hold on, lad, it won't be for long! As she burst into the ward, sobbing for breath, the lights came on again with a brilliance which momentarily blinded her.

She rushed towards the lung. Grierson lay asleep, breathing easily and naturally. The bellows moved up and down with their normal beat. As she stood, almost sick with relief, she saw she was not alone beside the lung. Smith was just with-drawing the steel bar carefully from its socket. There was com-plete silence as he replaced it on its hook. Then the sudden realisation of what this man had done came over Jessie like a surging wave. She gave a great glad cry and laid a hand on his arm. "Oh man, oh man," she said warmly, "you've saved his life! I was nearly beside myself with worry. Thank God you were here!" The thin man shook his head. "The ward orderly was the one who saved him," he said in his low quiet voice. "He beat me to it by a short head. He showed me how to keep the bellows at their proper beat, and then went off for the M.O. He'll be along any minute now." He gave her a quick, nervous smile and turned abruptly away, leaving her standing by the lung alone. She did not follow him.

At ten-thirty the following morning, as the ward M.O. had advised, I went to see the camp psychiatrist. I found him seated at his desk in a rather untidy little office, writing busily on sheets of flimsy paper. He was a weedy-looking young officer. As I entered he glanced up quickly and motioned me to a vacant chair. Then he returned to his writing.

I must confess that I found the general atmosphere somewhat disappointing. I had confidently expected to find myself in the presence of some mysterious necromancer who would unravel the workings of my mind with the same dexterous ease as a skilled mechanic dismantles the engine of a motor-car. Instead, I might have been seated in any Army orderly-room, waiting for some disinterested clerk to provide me with a forty-eight hour pass. There were no magic wands, no cryptic charts, no limpid crystals. Only a white mug, half-full of tea, was perched precariously on the very edge of the desk. I felt I had been rather misled.

"Good morning." The young officer smiled at me across the table. "You're from Ward 8, aren't you?" I nodded my head. "Ex-prisoner-of-war too?" He had pulled a blank sheet of paper towards him, and was now grasping his pencil firmly. "Now tell me, what's your name, home address and Army number? Don't hurry over it. There's plenty of time." This solicitude was most unusual. I felt myself wishing that Nunn could have been present also. This kind of situation would have appealed to him. Briefly I gave the required information about myself, and the officer made a series of rapid notes. He seemed satisfied that, so far, my mental powers appeared normal. I leant back in my chair, awaiting his next question curiously.

"I understand that, during your period of captivity, you suffered from many illnesses, but what, in your opinion, is your main trouble—now?" He had leant his elbows on the table, his chin cupped in his hands, and was gazing at me with the same intentness as one might view a rare species of wild animal, long since believed extinct. I thought rapidly. It was a long time since I had indulged in leg-pulling, and I was not quite sure if my young interrogator would take altogether kindly to it. I decided I had better wait a little longer. "Well," I replied with deliberate hesitation, "I should say my main trouble now was a sort of social maladjustment, if you understand what I mean. You know, it's a bit hard to find your bearings again after all these years." The young man nodded sympathetically and I felt relieved that I had given him an honest answer. He evidently took his duties most seriously. Again he scribbled on the sheet, while I waited in silence for him to resume the conversation.

Had he proceeded throughout the interview along the same more or less reasonable lines on which he had begun, I am sure he would not have considered my visit such a waste of time. Turning quickly to a cupboard just behind him, however, he produced, like some music-hall conjuror, a box of wooden blocks, each bearing a letter of the alphabet. This he upended on the desk and pushed the pile towards me. "Now," he said coaxingly, as one might address a child, "make a word!"

I smiled a trifle grimly to myself. So he was playing a little game with me after all, was he? This was too much. He was apparently crediting me with a mental age of roughly four. He would have no one to blame but himself if his childish experiment went slightly awry. With studied concentration I pored over the gaily-coloured blocks. For a second I hesitated, feeling the officer's eyes upon me. Then I composed the word 'DOG' and sat back quickly with the shy smile of a happy toddler. "Good," said the officer, again busy with his pencil and paper. I pushed the pile of blocks across towards him. "Now you make a word," I said encouragingly.

He blinked at me in amazement, and I actually thought for an instant that he was going to humour me. Then he swept the blocks back into their box and put them away again in the cupboard. I sat back in my chair cheerfully, hoping for more games.

"How far back can you remember?" It was a rather astonishing question. Should I answer truthfully, or invent a psychiatric tale of arresting interest? I decided that I would take a fairly safe middle path. "I can recall falling off a tree when I was four," I replied brightly, "is that far enough back?" The young officer nodded. His face was a study of earnest concentration. I had not the heart to disappoint him by describing my supremely happy childhood. "I can recall living in a big house with many windows," I said, "and there was someone living there whom I feared greatly." "A stranger?" suggested the young officer with a gleam of interest in his eye. "No, my father," I replied shortly, making a mental note to apologise to my good-natured Dad for dragging him into it. "Ah!" cried the officer, writing furiously, "and what happened then?" "I had to go to the University," I said in an aggrieved voice, "and take all sorts of difficult examinations." "So you ran away and joined the Army?" The young officer was becoming thoroughly excited. I judged it high time to bring this pantomime to an end. "No, I didn't," I said slowly, so that every word should go home, "I sat all my examinations, and came through with an Honours Degree in Modern Languages. In addition, as a subsidiary class, I took Comparative Psychology. I found it very interesting—all about Pavlov's dogs, sentiments and emotions, mental processes and—Psychiatrists."

I had no need to go any further. The officer held out his hand. "I'm sorry," he said simply, "I did not realise . . ." "That's all right," I replied quickly, "I shouldn't have led you up the garden path like that." We shook hands. "I didn't run away and join the Army either," I said, rising to my feet, "I was conscripted." He smiled broadly.

I felt much better as I returned to my ward. I had proved my case.

My interview with the psychiatrist had acted on me like a tonic, bringing a sense of confidence in myself which I had not known since my release from captivity. In that untidy little office the spell had been broken completely. I had regained my old assurance in the company of my fellow-men, and they were quick to realise that a marked and steady improvement was taking place in my condition. I was eating well and daily putting on weight. Although no noticeable change for the better had occurred in the state of my eyesight since coming to Namkun, I had become accustomed to the disability, accepting it without protest. If it were to be my lot to go, weak-sighted, through life, then it was not for me to complain, but rather to rejoice that Fate had left me otherwise unscathed. I had almost forgotten about my earlier doubts and fears at the prospect of going home, so eager was I to leave India.

Almost forgotten—but not quite. There was still one tiny cloud on the horizon, which all my new-found confidence could not dispel. I was still acutely nervous and ill at ease in the company of that Highland nurse, Jessie Macleod. Since my arrival in Ward 8, she had tended me so carefully that I should have felt no embarrassment in her presence. Yet, every time she approached my bed, I had to turn my head away. It was just the same with all the other nurses in the camp. With men I had learned, after little more than a month of freedom, to converse easily and naturally once again, but with a girl like Jessie I could not begin to feel assured. I had forgotten the little extra politenesses commonly accorded to ladies, and had sought to hide myself behind a barrier of aloofness, from whence I might not be dislodged.

Towards the middle of October, Jessie, with her inborn forthrightness and perseverance, broke down the barrier and led me out into a fresher, brighter day. Since the night when the camp lights had failed, she had invited me regularly every week to accompany her alone, either to Ranchi or on one of her excursions to the Hondra Falls. Every week I had steadfastly, almost stubbornly refused her invitation. I had visited Ranchi and the Hondra Falls already on several occasions, and always in the company of other men. I told Jessie I was not particularly keen to go again. I told her I had letters to write. I told her anything which would save me from the nervous strain of being with her alone for a whole afternoon. I stuck to my resolve, and Jessie stuck equally tenaciously to her invitation, although I deserved to be completely ignored for my persisting boorishness. Then, all

at once, one memorable morning, in I changed my mind. I
found a mysterious new courage. I asked Jessie diffidently
if I might go with her on her next free day, and, like the
great-hearted lass that she was, she said she would be delighted
to have my company. The first barrier had fallen.

For Jessie that visit to Ranchi must have been something of a
humorous experience, for she had a companion whose nervous
silence was matched only by his crass forgetfulness of the finer
points of chivalry. She gave no sign of displeasure, however,
when I allowed her to scramble on and off the camp wagon unaided—not even when the Punjabi driver gallantly filled the
breach by extending a willing arm in her direction. I scowled at
the fellow and felt uncomfortable, but he only grinned back at me
with a twinkle in his black eyes.

We strolled together through the dusty little Indian town,
stopping frequently in front of native shops, examining the
multifarious array of embroidered traycloths, heel-less sandals,
bright carpets and shining brass-ware. Excited shopkeepers
surrounded us on the roadway, offering their goods at prices
which even I recognised to be extortionate. Jessie was attracted
by a small brass ornament which I could have bought her for a
trifling matter of a few rupees, but somehow I could not summon up sufficient courage to present her with the gift. By normal standards I was rich, for I had drawn a fair amount of back-
pay on my arrival at Namkun, but instead of pleasing the girl,
I strode on along the white, unpaved road and waited for her to
catch up.

It was Jessie who suggested that we go in search of a cup of
tea. Of course I should never have thought of it. She said she
knew of a nearby café where we could be sure of a nicely-served,
appetising meal. In silence she led the way along a pleasant
avenue of trees until we reached the place. It was she who
ordered tea for two. I simply sat back, waiting, like some
faithful Pekinese, to be fed.

I found I was hungrier than I thought, and fell to without
delay. I accepted a cup of tea with a brief nod of thanks, and
proceeded to help myself to sugar and cream, without thinking
once to serve my companion first. She had to ask me, in fact, to

pass the sugar. It was fortunate that she preferred tea without cream, otherwise she would have had to ask for that also. The little scones were delicious, and it was only after I had eaten two that I realised that Jessie had not even eaten one. "Here," I said, pointing to the plate, "eat up. These are good." "Yes," said Jessie with a faint smile, "I see you're enjoying them." Then I suddenly remembered the beginnings of my manners and pushed the plate towards her.

By the time we had finished the meal, I had found myself once more. My table-manners had been shockingly uncouth. This pleasant girl must think me impossible. I leant across the table with a sudden impulse. "Jessie," I said humbly, "I'm terribly sorry I was so rude. It's been years since I took a girl out to tea, and I've been feeling desperately nervous all afternoon." Jessie regarded me, merry-eyed, across the table. "I knew no man could be quite so rude as you, and mean it," she said with a warm, understanding smile, "I was just waiting to see if you'd apologise. Now that you have it makes all the difference in the world. It shows that you knew the right thing to do all along, but that you were too shy to do it. When you get home, you'll never feel really nervous in a girl's company any more, will you?" "No," I said, shaking my head slowly, "this afternoon you broke down a big barrier and set me free—for the last time. I shall always be grateful to you for that." "Nonsense!" she replied briskly, picking up her gloves and handbag. "You did the most of the breaking down yourself. It wasn't easy, and I admire your grit. Some men would have funked it. I just helped you along a little bit—but that's my job. I'm a nurse, you see. Now, if you're quite ready, we'll go out into the town again, and see a bit more of it before we go back." She rose to her feet. "I'll take the bill," I said with a broad smile. "You see—I'm still remembering." "Clever boy!" murmured Jessie, and walked out into the sunshine. I followed her out in a little while, my head held high. I had won the last battle. It had been a signal victory.

I sailed from Bombay for England on the *Llandovery Castle* on 4th November. The train journey across India from Ranchi had lasted several days, but the python had begun to move more rapidly than even I had dared to hope, and there were no last-minute delays nor disappointments. As the great liner drew steadily away from the busy wharf, I took a last, long look at India. I might not see this land again in my lifetime; I might never again set foot in Malaya and Siam. It was a wonderful thought to be going home, but those bitter-sweet memories of what had once been came crowding round me, as if unwilling to let me go. Four years had rolled by like a great sea, bearing their swirling wrack of suffering and unhappiness, but in their wake had come courage, and experience, and a new hope. With every day that dawned, those years would be buried deeper in my heart, as they would be buried in the hearts of other men who had survived them, but they would not wither, nor would they die, for they held within themselves the imperishable quintessence of a life eternal. I had given them much of what I held most dear, but I had received a great plenty in return. I was content. As I leant on the ship's rail, gazing down at the sunlit waters, a gull soared past and was gone into the limitless blue of skies ahead. It would go before me, the harbinger of glad tidings. I would take the gull's way, and spread white wings for home.

We were the thirty-fifth ship to arrive in Southampton with repatriated prisoners-of-war. Had I but known, there was no need for anxious fears anent our homecoming. There were no bands, no waving flags, no surging, tumultuous crowds to greet us. Only a handful of well-wishers stood by the quayside. As the last ropes were made fast, and members of our company set foot once more on English soil, I saw an old, grey-haired man stiffen painfully to attention and remove his rough cloth cap. I saw a young girl fumble in her handbag and produce a handkerchief to wipe away a tear. It was enough. These had still remembered us.

In their gracious majesty, our King and Queen had not forgotten. We were proud indeed to receive their message of welcome, proud to have served them, and their peoples, in our own small way, through the free and fettered years. They wrote on behalf of a thanksgiving nation, which had known, as they themselves had known, the dark rigours of war and the sharp stab of personal loss.

"The Queen and I," the message ran, "bid you a very warm welcome home.

"Through all the great trials and sufferings which you have undergone at the hands of the Japanese, you and your comrades have been constantly in our thoughts. We know from the accounts we have already received how heavy those sufferings have been. We know also that these have been endured by you with the highest courage.

"We mourn with you the deaths of so many of your gallant comrades.

"With all our hearts, we hope that your return from captivity will bring you and your families a full measure of happiness, which you may long enjoy together."

The message bore the signature: GEORGE R.I.

I came back to my own folk in the dark gloaming of a December evening. There were no tears, only a great thankfulness. As the train swept round the Bay, I saw once more the tall white lighthouse, pointing ever upwards to the stars. Its beam flashed out in welcome. I was safe.